Name ____________________ Skill: Sums to 10

# Try These Facts!

Score ____ / 50

Write the answers.

| | | | | | | |
|---|---|---|---|---|---|---|
| A. | 5 + 2 | 1 + 6 | 0 + 6 | 4 + 6 | 9 + 1 | 1 + 4 |
| B. | 6 + 3 | 2 + 5 | 1 + 1 | 3 + 4 | 7 + 2 | 4 + 3 |
| C. | 1 + 3 | 3 + 5 | 6 + 2 | 3 + 1 | 1 + 8 | 5 + 4 |
| D. | 0 + 7 | 3 + 7 | 1 + 9 | 2 + 6 | 2 + 2 | 8 + 0 |
| E. | 3 + 0 | 4 + 4 | 2 + 3 | 0 + 8 | 8 + 1 | 2 + 8 |
| F. | 1 + 5 | 7 + 3 | 0 + 0 | 8 + 2 | 5 + 3 | 4 + 2 |
| G. | 3 + 2 | 4 + 1 | 4 + 5 | 2 + 1 | 2 + 7 | 1 + 7 |
| H. | 2 + 4 | 0 + 1 | 6 + 4 | 0 + 5 | | |
| I. | 5 + 5 | 1 + 2 | 3 + 6 | 3 + 3 | | |

Name ____________________ Skill: Sums to 12

# Addition Facts-s-s-s

Score ____ / 50

Write the answers.

| | | | | | | |
|---|---|---|---|---|---|---|
| A. | 8 + 1 | 5 + 5 | 8 + 0 | 1 + 9 | 6 + 1 | 3 + 5 |
| B. | 3 + 9 | 2 + 7 | 6 + 2 | 7 + 3 | 5 + 0 | 7 + 0 |
| C. | 8 + 2 | 5 + 6 | 9 + 2 | 0 + 9 | 7 + 2 | 2 + 5 |
| D. | 4 + 2 | 3 + 6 | 6 + 3 | 5 + 3 | 4 + 5 | 3 + 8 |
| E. | 3 + 7 | 4 + 4 | 7 + 1 | 9 + 1 | 5 + 4 | 1 + 8 |
| F. | 7 + 4 | 8 + 4 | 6 + 5 | 5 + 2 | 4 + 6 | 2 + 4 |
| G. | 6 + 6 | 2 + 6 | 9 + 3 | 7 + 5 | 2 + 8 | 4 + 8 |
| H. | 6 + 0 | 8 + 3 | 5 + 7 | 4 + 7 | | |
| I. | 3 + 4 | 6 + 4 | 4 + 3 | 2 + 9 | | |

Name ________________________________________ Skill: Sums to 18

# Think and Write

Score ____ / 50

Write the answers.

| | | | | | | |
|---|---|---|---|---|---|---|
| A. | 6<br>+ 6 | 9<br>+ 2 | 6<br>+ 4 | 7<br>+ 7 | 2<br>+ 7 | 3<br>+ 8 |
| B. | 3<br>+ 9 | 7<br>+ 6 | 4<br>+ 6 | 6<br>+ 9 | 4<br>+ 4 | 9<br>+ 9 |
| C. | 9<br>+ 5 | 3<br>+ 5 | 8<br>+ 2 | 8<br>+ 5 | 9<br>+ 3 | 6<br>+ 3 |
| D. | 4<br>+ 5 | 9<br>+ 1 | 6<br>+ 8 | 4<br>+ 9 | 6<br>+ 7 | 9<br>+ 4 |
| E. | 8<br>+ 6 | 6<br>+ 5 | 7<br>+ 8 | 9<br>+ 6 | 8<br>+ 3 | 7<br>+ 4 |
| F. | 3<br>+ 7 | 8<br>+ 4 | 5<br>+ 7 | 3<br>+ 6 | 7<br>+ 5 | 5<br>+ 6 |
| G. | 9<br>+ 7 | 4<br>+ 7 | 1<br>+ 9 | 8<br>+ 7 | 2<br>+ 9 | 5<br>+ 8 |
| H. | 2<br>+ 8 | 7<br>+ 9 | 4<br>+ 8 | 7<br>+ 3 | | |
| I. | 8<br>+ 9 | 8<br>+ 8 | 5<br>+ 9 | 9<br>+ 8 | | |

# Lost Spaceship

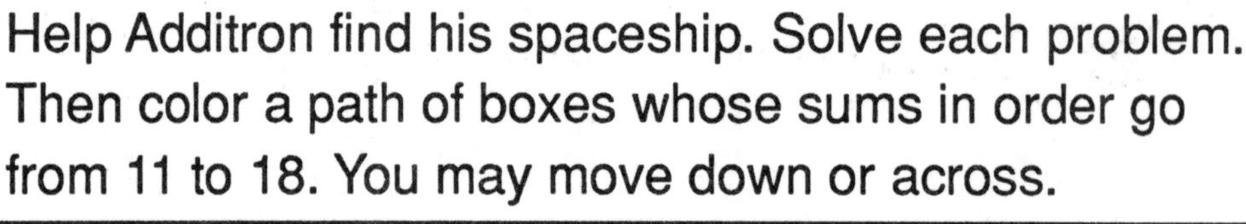

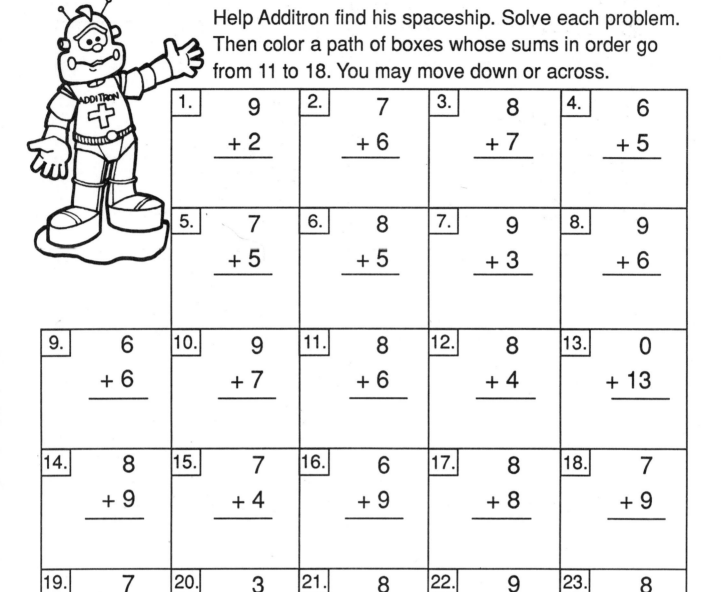

Help Additron find his spaceship. Solve each problem. Then color a path of boxes whose sums in order go from 11 to 18. You may move down or across.

| | | | | |
|---|---|---|---|---|
| | 1. 9 + 2 | 2. 7 + 6 | 3. 8 + 7 | 4. 6 + 5 |
| | 5. 7 + 5 | 6. 8 + 5 | 7. 9 + 3 | 8. 9 + 6 |
| 9. 6 + 6 | 10. 9 + 7 | 11. 8 + 6 | 12. 8 + 4 | 13. 0 + 13 |
| 14. 8 + 9 | 15. 7 + 4 | 16. 6 + 9 | 17. 8 + 8 | 18. 7 + 9 |
| 19. 7 + 7 | 20. 3 + 8 | 21. 8 + 3 | 22. 9 + 8 | 23. 8 + 4 |
| 24. 9 + 5 | 25. 6 + 7 | 26. 9 + 4 | 27. 9 + 9 | |

**Try This!** Write the addition facts that are "doubles" (1+1=2, 2+2=4, 3+3=6). Continue through 9+9.

Name Score /20

# Twenty Team

Sums to 18

| | |
|---|---|
| 6 + 4 = ____ | 7 + 8 = ____ |
| 8 + 8 = ____ | 1 + 1 = ____ |
| 4 + 2 = ____ | 5 + 9 = ____ |
| 4 + 3 = ____ | 6 + 4 = ____ |
| 8 + 9 = ____ | 5 + 4 = ____ |
| 6 + 7 = ____ | 0 + 0 = ____ |
| 4 + 7 = ____ | 3 + 1 = ____ |
| 1 + 0 = ____ | 5 + 6 = ____ |
| 6 + 3 = ____ | 7 + 3 = ____ |
| 2 + 1 = ____ | 3 + 3 = ____ |







Name Score /20

# Twenty Team

Sums to 18

| | |
|---|---|
| 4 + 5 = ____ | 5 + 5 = ____ |
| 9 + 2 = ____ | 3 + 5 = ____ |
| 6 + 7 = ____ | 9 + 9 = ____ |
| 2 + 5 = ____ | 2 + 0 = ____ |
| 6 + 3 = ____ | 2 + 2 = ____ |
| 2 + 3 = ____ | 7 + 7 = ____ |
| 8 + 5 = ____ | 5 + 2= ____ |
| 9 + 9 = ____ | 6 + 9 = ____ |
| 1 + 2 = ____ | 7 + 5 = ____ |
| 8 + 2 = ____ | 4 + 1 = ____ |

Name Score /30

# Thirty Thinkers

Sums to 18

| | |
|---|---|
| 8 + 5 = ____ | 7 + 5 = ____ |
| 4 + 9 = ____ | 5 + 0 = ____ |
| 7 + 3 = ____ | 6 + 3 = ____ |
| 5 + 6 = ____ | 8 + 9 = ____ |
| 7 + 1 = ____ | 4 + 2 = ____ |
| 9 + 5 = ____ | 7 + 8 = ____ |
| 7 + 2 = ____ | 2 + 7 = ____ |
| 2 + 5 = ____ | 2 + 4 = ____ |
| 5 + 3 = ____ | 8 + 6 = ____ |
| 5 + 4 = ____ | 4 + 7 = ____ |
| 0 + 8 = ____ | 9 + 7 = ____ |
| 8 + 2 = ____ | 7 + 6 = ____ |
| 3 + 1 = ____ | 8 + 8 = ____ |
| 6 + 2 = ____ | 2 + 9 = ____ |
| 8 + 9 = ____ | 9 + 1 = ____ |



 

Name Score /30

# Thirty Thinkers

Sums to 18

| | |
|---|---|
| 9 + 3 = ____ | 8 + 1 = ____ |
| 2 + 2 = ____ | 5 + 0 = ____ |
| 4 + 9 = ____ | 8 + 6 = ____ |
| 3 + 8 = ____ | 8 + 9 = ____ |
| 6 + 3 = ____ | 4 + 2 = ____ |
| 9 + 9 = ____ | 5 + 3 = ____ |
| 4 + 4 = ____ | 3 + 3 = ____ |
| 3 + 9 = ____ | 2 + 4 = ____ |
| 1 + 1 = ____ | 8 + 6 = ____ |
| 7 + 7 = ____ | 4 + 7 = ____ |
| 2 + 9 = ____ | 9 + 7 = ____ |
| 8 + 3 = ____ | 7 + 6 = ____ |
| 7 + 5 = ____ | 8 + 8 = ____ |
| 6 + 5 = ____ | 2 + 9 = ____ |
| 4 + 9 = ____ | 9 + 1 = ____ |



 

Name Score /40

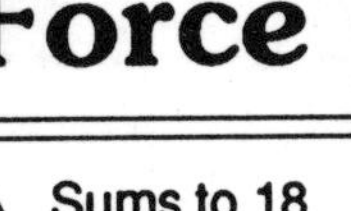

# Forty Force

Sums to 18

| | |
|---|---|
| 9 + 4 = ____ | 9 + 6 = ____ |
| 8 + 8 = ____ | 4 + 9 = ____ |
| 4 + 2 = ____ | 1 + 7 = ____ |
| 4 + 3 = ____ | 8 + 8 = ____ |
| 8 + 9 = ____ | 3 + 6 = ____ |
| 6 + 7 = ____ | 8 + 3 = ____ |
| 4 + 7 = ____ | 7 + 6 = ____ |
| 6 + 6 = ____ | 9 + 2 = ____ |
| 6 + 3 = ____ | 7 + 7 = ____ |
| 6 + 8 = ____ | 8 + 6 = ____ |
| 1 + 4 = ____ | 1 + 8 = ____ |
| 7 + 5 = ____ | 4 + 6 = ____ |
| 6 + 9 = ____ | 7 + 4 = ____ |
| 7 + 9 = ____ | 1 + 9 = ____ |
| 9 + 8 = ____ | 7 + 2 = ____ |
| 2 + 2 = ____ | 4 + 8 = ____ |
| 2 + 0 = ____ | 5 + 5 = ____ |
| 9 + 9 = ____ | 4 + 4 = ____ |
| 3 + 5 = ____ | 2 + 8 = ____ |
| 5 + 5 = ____ | 5 + 7 = ____ |



 FS-32003 Math

Name Score /40

# Forty Force

Sums to 18

| | |
|---|---|
| 4 + 5 = ____ | 3 + 9 = ____ |
| 6 + 2 = ____ | 8 + 2 = ____ |
| 9 + 7 = ____ | 4 + 8 = ____ |
| 5 + 2 = ____ | 1 + 6 = ____ |
| 9 + 3 = ____ | 6 + 2 = ____ |
| 2 + 3 = ____ | 8 + 4 = ____ |
| 8 + 5 = ____ | 9 + 5 = ____ |
| 6 + 6 = ____ | 6 + 4 = ____ |
| 1 + 5 = ____ | 2 + 3 = ____ |
| 9 + 9 = ____ | 5 + 1 = ____ |
| 3 + 3 = ____ | 3 + 7 = ____ |
| 7 + 3 = ____ | 8 + 7 = ____ |
| 5 + 6 = ____ | 5 + 4 = ____ |
| 3 + 1 = ____ | 7 + 2 = ____ |
| 0 + 0 = ____ | 2 + 5 = ____ |
| 8 + 9 = ____ | 5 + 8 = ____ |
| 1 + 0 = ____ | 5 + 9 = ____ |
| 5 + 9 = ____ | 4 + 4 = ____ |
| 1 + 1 = ____ | 2 + 9 = ____ |
| 7 + 8 = ____ | 3 + 8 = ____ |



 FS-32003 Math

Name ______________________________ Skill: Subtracting from 10 or less

# Fishing for Facts!

Score ____ / 50

Write the answers.

| | | | | | | |
|---|---|---|---|---|---|---|
| A. | 9 − 9 | 7 − 5 | 8 − 8 | 9 − 2 | 10 − 7 | 2 − 1 |
| B. | 7 − 4 | 10 − 9 | 7 − 6 | 7 − 3 | 6 − 5 | 4 − 1 |
| C. | 8 − 2 | 10 − 2 | 9 − 8 | 10 − 3 | 9 − 5 | 3 − 2 |
| D. | 8 − 7 | 9 − 1 | 7 − 2 | 8 − 3 | 6 − 4 | 5 − 1 |
| E. | 6 − 3 | 7 − 1 | 4 − 3 | 9 − 0 | 8 − 5 | 9 − 6 |
| F. | 5 − 4 | 9 − 4 | 8 − 1 | 6 − 2 | 10 − 1 | 5 − 5 |
| G. | 10 − 8 | 5 − 3 | 8 − 6 | 10 − 4 | 9 − 3 | 10 − 6 |
| H. | 4 − 2 | 7 − 7 | 9 − 7 | 6 − 1 | | |
| I. | 3 − 1 | 10 − 5 | 5 − 2 | 8 − 4 | | |

Name ______________________ Skill: Subtracting from 12 or less

# Think and Subtract

Score ___ / 50

Write the answers.

| | | | | | | |
|---|---|---|---|---|---|---|
| A. | 3 − 2 | 4 − 1 | 7 − 2 | 5 − 2 | 8 − 1 | 10 − 9 |
| B. | 6 − 4 | 9 − 6 | 10 − 5 | 7 − 6 | 11 − 2 | 6 − 3 |
| C. | 7 − 5 | 11 − 3 | 9 − 8 | 12 − 3 | 10 − 3 | 9 − 4 |
| D. | 10 − 4 | 6 − 5 | 7 − 3 | 8 − 2 | 8 − 6 | 5 − 3 |
| E. | 7 − 4 | 11 − 7 | 8 − 5 | 6 − 2 | 10 − 6 | 8 − 4 |
| F. | 9 − 7 | 12 − 8 | 9 − 3 | 11 − 4 | 8 − 3 | 9 − 2 |
| G. | 11 − 5 | 12 − 6 | 10 − 7 | 9 − 5 | 11 − 9 | 8 − 7 |
| H. | 12 − 7 | 10 − 2 | 11 − 6 | 12 − 4 | | |
| I. | 10 − 8 | 12 − 5 | 12 − 9 | 11 − 8 | | |

Name ______________________________ Skill: Subtracting from 18 or less

# A Flock of Facts!

Score ____
50

Write the answers.

| | | | | | | |
|---|---|---|---|---|---|---|
| A. | 11<br>− 9 | 16<br>− 9 | 12<br>− 7 | 15<br>− 8 | 12<br>− 6 | 9<br>− 4 |
| B. | 14<br>− 8 | 11<br>− 3 | 13<br>− 9 | 11<br>− 4 | 9<br>− 8 | 10<br>− 9 |
| C. | 9<br>− 3 | 14<br>− 6 | 12<br>− 5 | 17<br>− 9 | 14<br>− 7 | 13<br>− 4 |
| D. | 11<br>− 7 | 12<br>− 3 | 17<br>− 8 | 13<br>− 6 | 10<br>− 4 | 15<br>− 6 |
| E. | 13<br>− 5 | 15<br>− 7 | 11<br>− 8 | 10<br>− 6 | 12<br>− 4 | 13<br>− 7 |
| F. | 11<br>− 5 | 18<br>− 9 | 9<br>− 7 | 14<br>− 9 | 9<br>− 6 | 10<br>− 5 |
| G. | 10<br>− 2 | 10<br>− 7 | 12<br>− 8 | 9<br>− 5 | 11<br>− 2 | 12<br>− 9 |
| H. | 15<br>− 9 | 13<br>− 8 | 10<br>− 3 | 16<br>− 8 | | |
| I. | 10<br>− 8 | 16<br>− 7 | 14<br>− 5 | 11<br>− 6 | | |

# Which Tool Kit?

Help Subtractron find the tool kit he needs to repair his ship. The one he needs contains only problems whose answers are less than 7. Find all the differences. Then color the correct tool kit.

**A.**

1) 11 − 7 =
2) 12 − 4 =
3) 13 − 6 =
4) 14 − 8 =
5) 16 − 7 =
6) 14 − 7 =
7) 16 − 8 =
8) 13 − 9 =

**B.**

9) 17 − 8 =
10) 15 − 6 =
11) 11 − 7 =
12) 13 − 5 =
13) 14 − 5 =
14) 12 − 9 =
15) 13 − 8 =
16) 18 − 9 =

**C.**

17) 14 − 6 =
18) 13 − 7 =
19) 15 − 7 =
20) 15 − 8 =
21) 13 − 4 =
22) 12 − 5 =
23) 12 − 3 =
24) 16 − 9 =

**D.**

25) 12 − 7 =
26) 14 − 9 =
27) 12 − 6 =
28) 11 − 6 =
29) 12 − 8 =
30) 15 − 9 =
31) 11 − 8 =
32) 13 − 7 =

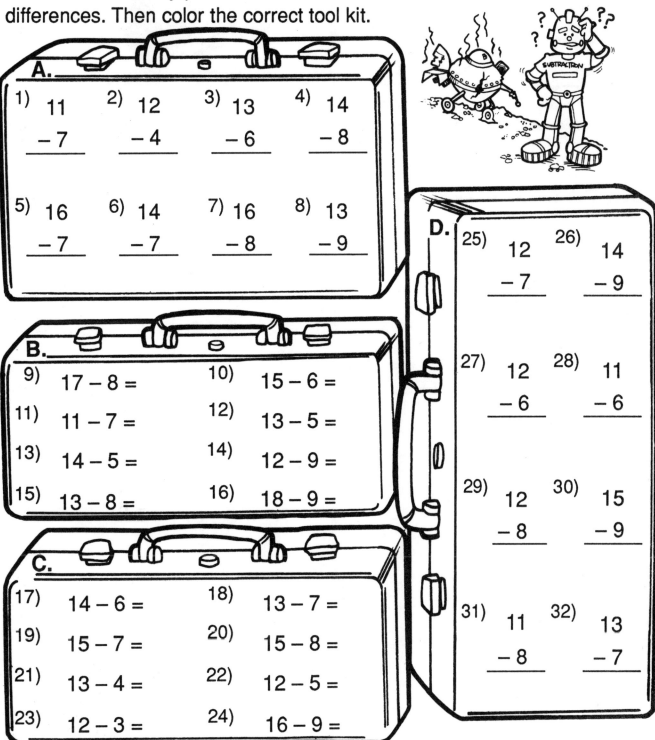

**Try This!** You can check subtraction by adding. For example, if 14–6=8 then 8+6=14. Check your answers for all the problems in tool kit C.

Name Score /20

# Twenty Team

Subtracting from 18 or less

| | |
|---|---|
| 7 − 0 = ____ | 6 − 0 = ____ |
| 12 − 4 = ____ | 10 − 3 = ____ |
| 9 − 4 = ____ | 4 − 2 = ____ |
| 11 − 7 = ____ | 9 − 4 = ____ |
| 9 − 3 = ____ | 10 − 6 = ____ |
| 12 − 3 = ____ | 5 − 2 = ____ |
| 9 − 8 = ____ | 16 − 8 = ____ |
| 7 − 4 = ____ | 12 − 6 = ____ |
| 10 − 2 = ____ | 10 − 9 = ____ |
| 7 − 2 = ____ | 15 − 7 = ____ |



 FS-32003 Math

Name Score /20

# Twenty Team

Subtracting from 18 or less

| | |
|---|---|
| 13 − 4 = ____ | 14 − 6 = ____ |
| 9 − 0 = ____ | 7 − 6 = ____ |
| 17 − 9 = ____ | 11 − 5 = ____ |
| 8 − 6 = ____ | 6 − 3 = ____ |
| 8 − 3 = ____ | 10 − 5 = ____ |
| 12 − 8 = ____ | 3 − 1 = ____ |
| 11 − 8 = ____ | 13 − 6 = ____ |
| 10 − 4 = ____ | 11 − 2 = ____ |
| 3 − 2 = ____ | 8 − 4 = ____ |
| 18 − 9 = ____ | 0 − 0 = ____ |



 FS-32003 Math

Name Score /30

# Thirty Thinkers

Subtracting from 18 or less

| | |
|---|---|
| 5 − 3 = ______ | 6 − 0 = ______ |
| 7 − 4 = ______ | 10 − 3 = ______ |
| 9 − 1 = ______ | 4 − 2 = ______ |
| 5 − 5 = ______ | 9 − 4 = ______ |
| 6 − 5 = ______ | 10 − 6 = ______ |
| 10 − 9 = ______ | 5 − 2 = ______ |
| 6 − 2 = ______ | 16 − 8 = ______ |
| 8 − 3 = ______ | 12 − 6 = ______ |
| 9 − 6 = ______ | 10 − 9 = ______ |
| 10 − 7 = ______ | 15 − 7 = ______ |
| 7 − 0 = ______ | 18 − 9 = ______ |
| 12 − 4 = ______ | 3 − 2 = ______ |
| 6 − 4 = ______ | 10 − 4 = ______ |
| 11 − 7 = ______ | 11 − 8 = ______ |
| 9 − 3 = ______ | 12 − 8 = ______ |







Name Score /30

# Thirty Thinkers

Subtracting from 18 or less

| | |
|---|---|
| 12 − 3 = ______ | 3 − 3 = ______ |
| 9 − 8 = ______ | 8 − 6 = ______ |
| 7 − 4 = ______ | 12 − 5 = ______ |
| 14 − 7 = ______ | 9 − 0 = ______ |
| 7 − 2 = ______ | 13 − 4 = ______ |
| 0 − 0 = ______ | 9 − 5 = ______ |
| 8 − 4 = ______ | 18 − 9 = ______ |
| 11 − 2 = ______ | 11 − 3 = ______ |
| 13 − 6 = ______ | 4 − 2 = ______ |
| 3 − 1 = ______ | 17 − 9 = ______ |
| 10 − 5 = ______ | 8 − 4 = ______ |
| 6 − 3 = ______ | 2 − 1 = ______ |
| 11 − 5 = ______ | 4 − 0 = ______ |
| 7 − 6 = ______ | 7 − 5 = ______ |
| 10 − 2 = ______ | 10 − 8 = ______ |

Name **Score** **/40**

# Forty Force

Subtracting from 18 or less

| | |
|---|---|
| 10 − 7 = ______ | 8 − 1 = ______ |
| 6 − 2 = ______ | 10 − 3 = ______ |
| 5 − 3 = ______ | 4 − 2 = ______ |
| 11 − 3 = ______ | 9 − 4 = ______ |
| 15 − 6 = ______ | 10 − 6 = ______ |
| 12 − 7 = ______ | 5 − 2 = ______ |
| 13 − 8 = ______ | 16 − 8 = ______ |
| 7 − 3 = ______ | 12 − 6 = ______ |
| 12 − 9 = ______ | 13 − 8 = ______ |
| 8 − 5 = ______ | 15 − 7 = ______ |
| 15 − 8 = ______ | 18 − 9 = ______ |
| 14 − 9 = ______ | 3 − 2 = ______ |
| 4 − 3 = ______ | 10 − 4 = ______ |
| 14 − 6 = ______ | 11 − 8 = ______ |
| 16 − 9 = ______ | 12 − 8 = ______ |
| 10 − 1 = ______ | 8 − 3 = ______ |
| 6 − 5 = ______ | 8 − 6 = ______ |
| 8 − 2 = ______ | 12 − 5 = ______ |
| 9 − 7 = ______ | 16 − 9 = ______ |
| 17 − 8 = ______ | 13 − 4 = ______ |





FS-32003 Math

Name **Score** **/40**

# Forty Force

Subtracting from 18 or less

| | |
|---|---|
| 12 − 5 = ______ | 10 − 2 = ______ |
| 7 − 5 = ______ | 7 − 6 = ______ |
| 9 − 6 = ______ | 11 − 5 = ______ |
| 14 − 8 = ______ | 6 − 3 = ______ |
| 9 − 1 = ______ | 10 − 5 = ______ |
| 13 − 5 = ______ | 5 − 1 = ______ |
| 8 − 7 = ______ | 13 − 6 = ______ |
| 10 − 8 = ______ | 11 − 2 = ______ |
| 11 − 6 = ______ | 8 − 4 = ______ |
| 13 − 7 = ______ | 1 − 0 = ______ |
| 9 − 2 = ______ | 7 − 2 = ______ |
| 14 − 5 = ______ | 14 − 7 = ______ |
| 15 − 9 = ______ | 7 − 4 = ______ |
| 13 − 9 = ______ | 9 − 8 = ______ |
| 16 − 7 = ______ | 12 − 3 = ______ |
| 4 − 1 = ______ | 9 − 3 = ______ |
| 11 − 4 = ______ | 11 − 7 = ______ |
| 17 − 8 = ______ | 6 − 4 = ______ |
| 11 − 9 = ______ | 12 − 4 = ______ |
| 9 − 5 = ______ | 3 − 0 = ______ |





FS-32003 Math

# Rock Samples

These robots collected rock samples from the two moons of Mercatroid. Now they must sort them out.

Solve each problem. If the answer is 5 or less, the rock is from the moon Plutoid. Color Plutoid's rocks yellow. If the answer is more than 5, the rock is from Neptoid. Color Neptoid's rocks orange.

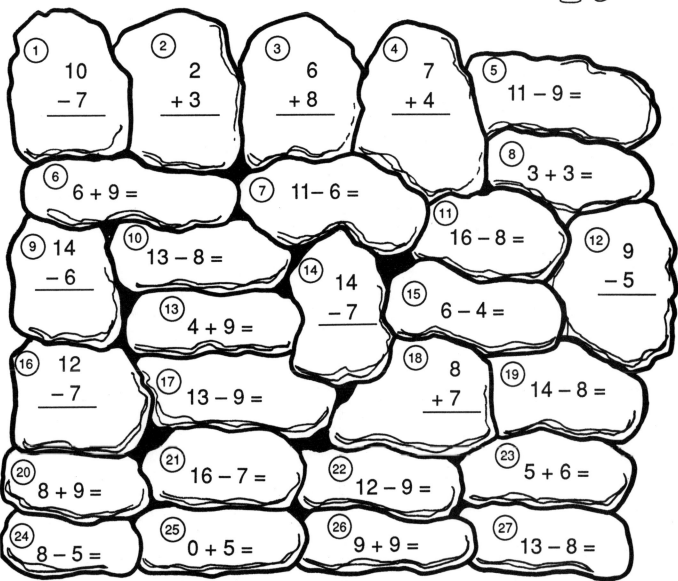


1. $10 - 7 =$
2. $2 + 3 =$
3. $6 + 8 =$
4. $7 + 4 =$
5. $11 - 9 =$
6. $6 + 9 =$
7. $11 - 6 =$
8. $3 + 3 =$
9. $14 - 6 =$
10. $13 - 8 =$
11. $16 - 8 =$
12. $9 - 5 =$
13. $4 + 9 =$
14. $14 - 7 =$
15. $6 - 4 =$
16. $12 - 7 =$
17. $13 - 9 =$
18. $8 + 7 =$
19. $14 - 8 =$
20. $8 + 9 =$
21. $16 - 7 =$
22. $12 - 9 =$
23. $5 + 6 =$
24. $8 - 5 =$
25. $0 + 5 =$
26. $9 + 9 =$
27. $13 - 8 =$

**Try This!** Did the robots collect more rocks from Plutoid or Neptoid?

Name Score /20

# Twenty Team

Sums and differences 0–18

| | |
|---|---|
| 6 − 4 = ____ | 7 + 2 = ____ |
| 2 + 3 = ____ | 8 + 3 = ____ |
| 6 + 5 = ____ | 11 − 5 = ____ |
| 18 − 9 = ____ | 4 + 4 = ____ |
| 8 − 0 = ____ | 7 + 6 = ____ |
| 7 − 5 = ____ | 4 + 2 = ____ |
| 9 + 6 = ____ | 9 − 5 = ____ |
| 4 + 3 = ____ | 3 + 9 = ____ |
| 11 − 3 = ____ | 10 − 5 = ____ |
| 10 − 2 = ____ | 13 − 4 = ____ |







Name Score /20

# Twenty Team

Sums and differences 0–18

| | |
|---|---|
| 7 + 1 = ____ | 15 − 7 = ____ |
| 5 + 9 = ____ | 18 − 9 = ____ |
| 3 + 7 = ____ | 4 + 6 = ____ |
| 13 − 5 = ____ | 12 − 7 = ____ |
| 7 + 7 = ____ | 17 − 8 = ____ |
| 12 − 6 = ____ | 9 + 3 = ____ |
| 1 + 8 = ____ | 0 + 5 = ____ |
| 9 − 6 = ____ | 5 + 8 = ____ |
| 8 + 8 = ____ | 14 − 6 = ____ |
| 15 − 8 = ____ | 16 − 7 = ____ |

Name **Score** **/30**

# ⊕⊖ Thirty Thinkers

Sums and differences 0–18

| | |
|---|---|
| 7 − 2 = ______ | 6 + 9 = ______ |
| 12 − 3 = ______ | 13 − 8 = ______ |
| 5 + 6 = ______ | 8 − 6 = ______ |
| 14 − 8 = ______ | 4 + 7 = ______ |
| 1 + 6 = ______ | 11 − 4 = ______ |
| 5 + 3 = ______ | 5 − 3 = ______ |
| 3 − 2 = ______ | 6 + 2 = ______ |
| 8 − 5 = ______ | 2 + 9 = ______ |
| 11 − 7 = ______ | 9 − 3 = ______ |
| 8 + 2 = ______ | 10 − 4 = ______ |
| 3 + 4 = ______ | 6 + 7 = ______ |
| 6 − 2 = ______ | 15 − 6 = ______ |
| 12 − 5 = ______ | 18 − 9 = ______ |
| 3 + 6 = ______ | 7 + 5 = ______ |
| 8 + 7 = ______ | 8 + 4 = ______ |



 

Name **Score** **/30**

# ⊕⊖ Thirty Thinkers

Sums and differences 0–18

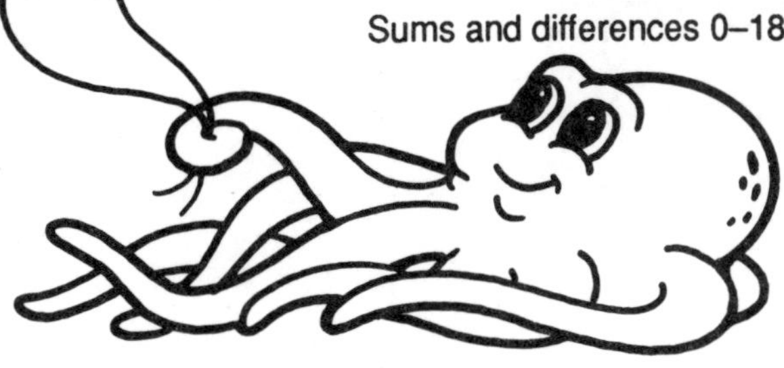

| | |
|---|---|
| 8 + 1 = ______ | 14 − 7 = ______ |
| 6 + 6 = ______ | 15 − 9 = ______ |
| 5 + 4 = ______ | 6 − 3 = ______ |
| 10 − 7 = ______ | 3 + 5 = ______ |
| 11 − 9 = ______ | 2 + 6 = ______ |
| 17 − 8 = ______ | 5 + 2 = ______ |
| 0 + 6 = ______ | 8 + 9 = ______ |
| 4 + 8 = ______ | 9 + 5 = ______ |
| 5 + 7 = ______ | 13 − 7 = ______ |
| 9 + 4 = ______ | 8 − 4 = ______ |
| 6 − 5 = ______ | 17 − 9 = ______ |
| 10 − 8 = ______ | 2 − 2 = ______ |
| 8 + 6 = ______ | 7 + 8 = ______ |
| 13 − 9 = ______ | 4 + 9 = ______ |
| 3 + 2 = ______ | 5 + 5 = ______ |



 

Name Score /40

# Forty Force

Sums and differences 0–18

| | |
|---|---|
| 4 + 7 = ______ | 11 − 6 = ______ |
| 7 + 6 = ______ | 7 + 8 = ______ |
| 4 − 3 = ______ | 13 − 9 = ______ |
| 7 + 9 = ______ | 10 − 7 = ______ |
| 6 + 4 = ______ | 3 + 8 = ______ |
| 8 + 8 = ______ | 14 − 6 = ______ |
| 10 − 6 = ______ | 2 + 7 = ______ |
| 12 − 4 = ______ | 9 + 9 = ______ |
| 9 + 2 = ______ | 14 − 5 = ______ |
| 4 + 1 = ______ | 11 − 8 = ______ |
| 13 − 6 = ______ | 6 + 6 = ______ |
| 5 − 2 = ______ | 4 + 5 = ______ |
| 7 − 4 = ______ | 0 + 9 = ______ |
| 6 + 8 = ______ | 16 − 9 = ______ |
| 11 − 3 = ______ | 1 + 7 = ______ |
| 12 − 7 = ______ | 9 − 8 = ______ |
| 15 − 8 = ______ | 8 + 5 = ______ |
| 1 + 7 = ______ | 1 − 1 = ______ |
| 5 + 5 = ______ | 2 + 8 = ______ |
| 9 + 7 = ______ | 6 + 9 = ______ |







Name Score /40

# Forty Force

Sums and differences 0–18

| | |
|---|---|
| 9 − 4 = ______ | 7 + 3 = ______ |
| 12 − 5 = ______ | 9 − 7 = ______ |
| 3 + 6 = ______ | 12 − 8 = ______ |
| 17 − 8 = ______ | 14 − 9 = ______ |
| 9 + 4 = ______ | 9 + 8 = ______ |
| 14 − 8 = ______ | 3 + 3 = ______ |
| 9 − 9 = ______ | 10 − 9 = ______ |
| 10 − 3 = ______ | 7 − 3 = ______ |
| 12 − 9 = ______ | 4 + 9 = ______ |
| 8 − 7 = ______ | 5 + 8 = ______ |
| 6 + 3 = ______ | 16 − 8 = ______ |
| 5 + 9 = ______ | 11 − 2 = ______ |
| 16 − 7 = ______ | 6 + 5 = ______ |
| 9 − 2 = ______ | 2 + 9 = ______ |
| 10 − 5 = ______ | 7 + 4 = ______ |
| 18 − 9 = ______ | 9 + 6 = ______ |
| 8 + 6 = ______ | 0 + 7 = ______ |
| 2 + 4 = ______ | 15 − 6 = ______ |
| 13 − 4 = ______ | 11 − 9 = ______ |
| 8 − 2 = ______ | 8 − 3 = ______ |

Name ______________________________ Skill: Two-digit addition—no regrouping

# Honeycomb Math

Score ____ / 30

Write the answers.

**Brainwork!** Color all the honeycomb cells with answers in the twenties one color. Color all those with answers in the thirties another color and so on.

Name ____________________ Skill: Adding multiples of 10

# Snail Sums

Score ____ / 40

Write the answers in the shells.

**Brainwork!** Draw your own snail for sums. Write *+ 90* in the center. Trade snails with a friend. Do the addition.

Name ____________________ Skill: Two-digit subtraction—no regrouping

Score ___ / 35

# Taking a Bite

Subtract and write the answers. To find where the worm bit the apple, color the box with the greatest answer.

| | | | | | | |
|---|---|---|---|---|---|---|
| A. | | 24 − 13 | 86 − 52 | 89 − 36 | 77 − 5 | |
| B. | 57 − 22 | 19 − 5 | 68 − 24 | 71 − 50 | 86 − 13 | 50 − 10 |
| C. | 69 − 23 | 88 − 12 | 45 − 13 | 28 − 12 | 94 − 24 | 76 − 73 |
| D. | 52 − 10 | 79 − 61 | 49 − 22 | 70 − 40 | 95 − 4 | 87 − 12 |
| E. | 79 − 70 | 39 − 11 | 36 − 32 | 28 − 2 | 99 − 55 | 98 − 15 |
| F. | | 77 − 45 | 68 − 20 | 49 − 32 | 87 − 30 | |
| G. | | 88 − 72 | 76 − 21 | 99 − 68 | | |

**Brainwork!** Write five of your answers in order from the least to the greatest.

Name ____________________ Skill: Subtracting multiples of 10

# Flower Problems

Score ______ 40

Write the answers in the petals.

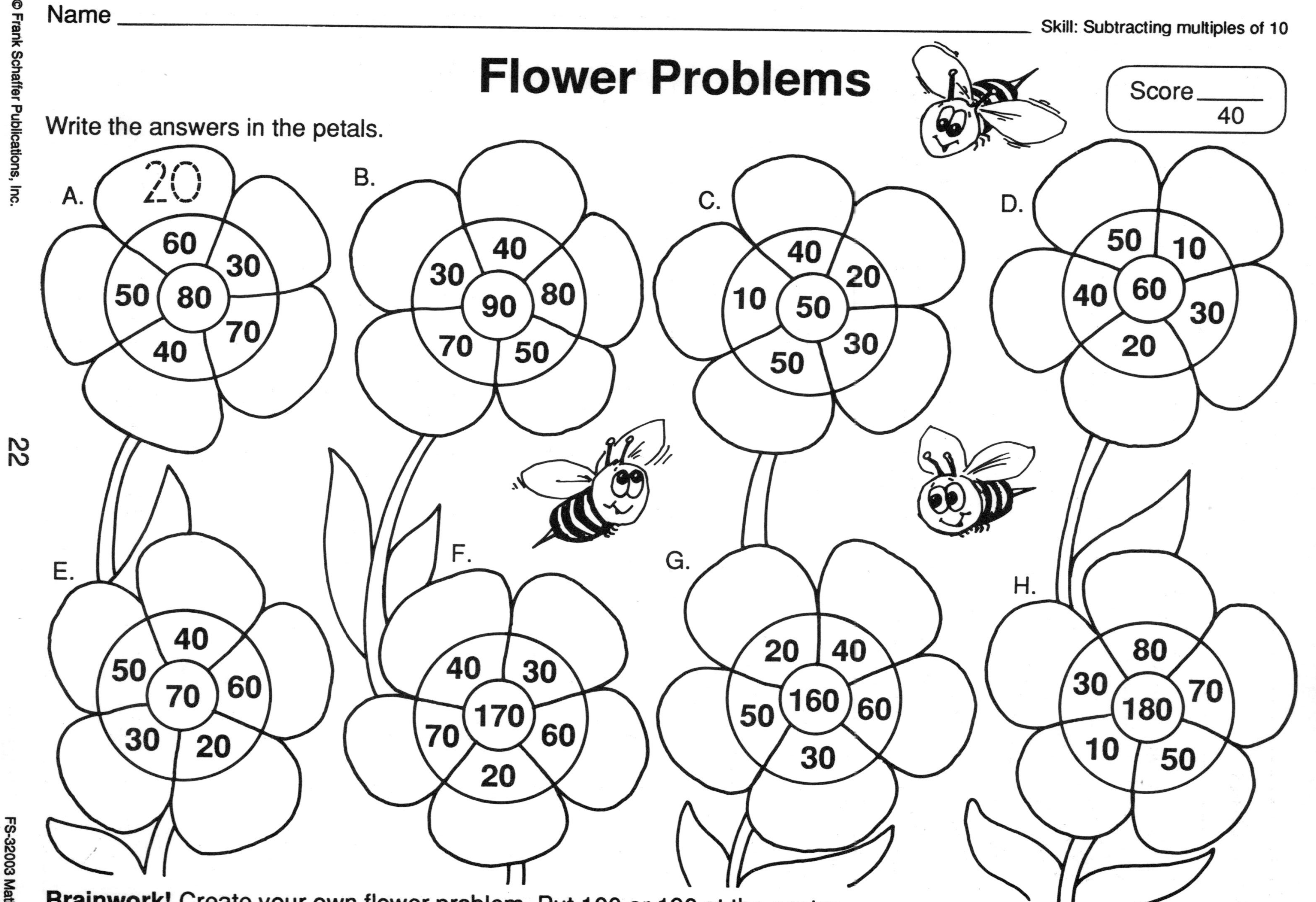


**Brainwork!** Create your own flower problem. Put 100 or 190 at the center.

Name ______________________________ Skill: 2-digit addition—regrouping

**71 — Green** **72 — Blue** **73 — Orange**

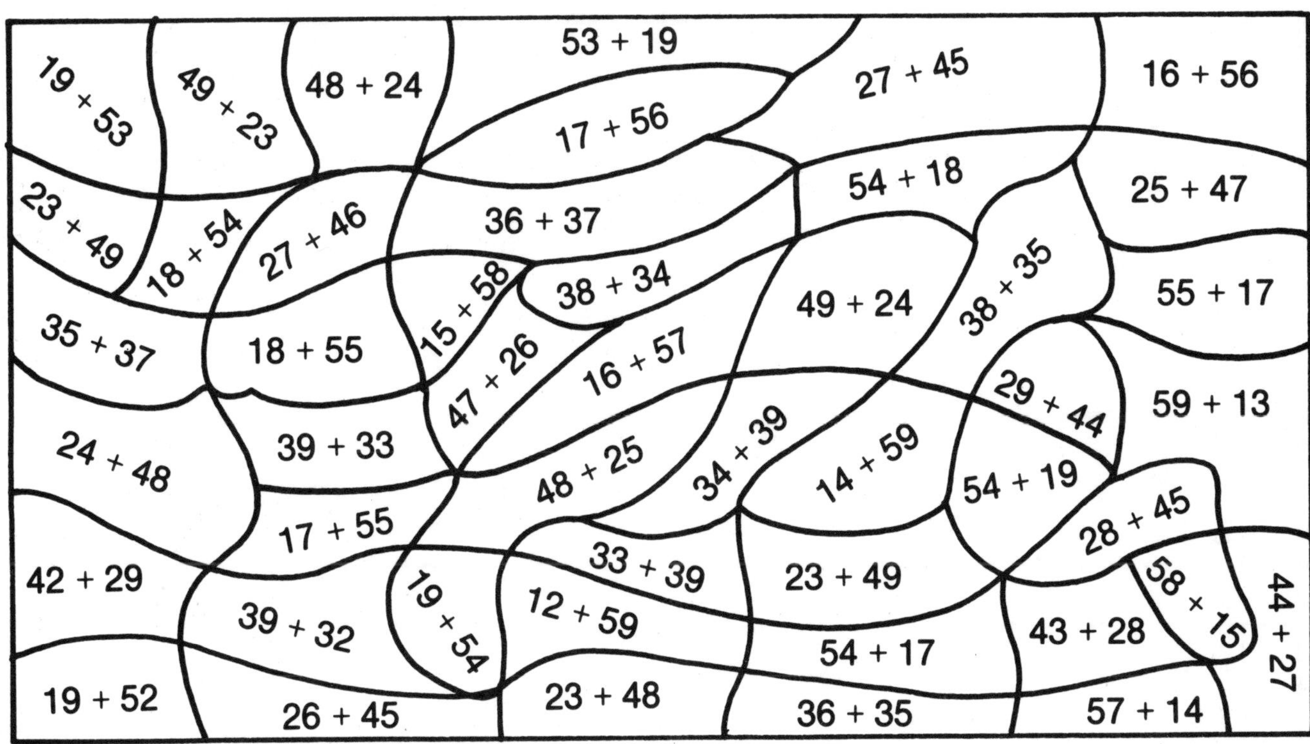


Color all the spaces and boxes.

| 56 + 16 | 58 + 14 | 44 + 29 | 54 + 18 | 45 + 27 | 39 + 32 | 13 + 59 | 37 + 35 |
|---|---|---|---|---|---|---|---|
| 55 + 17 | 24 + 48 | 49 + 23 | 57 + 15 | 54 + 17 | 26 + 45 | 19 + 52 | 48 + 24 |
| 26 + 46 | 44 + 28 | 25 + 48 | 47 + 25 | 49 + 23 | 35 + 36 | 53 + 19 | 49 + 23 |
| 48 + 24 | 34 + 38 | 35 + 38 | 36 + 36 | 33 + 39 | 24 + 47 | 33 + 39 | 43 + 29 |

Name ______________________________ Skill: 2-digit addition—regrouping

**65 — Orange** **83 — Blue** **82 — Yellow** **71 — Green**

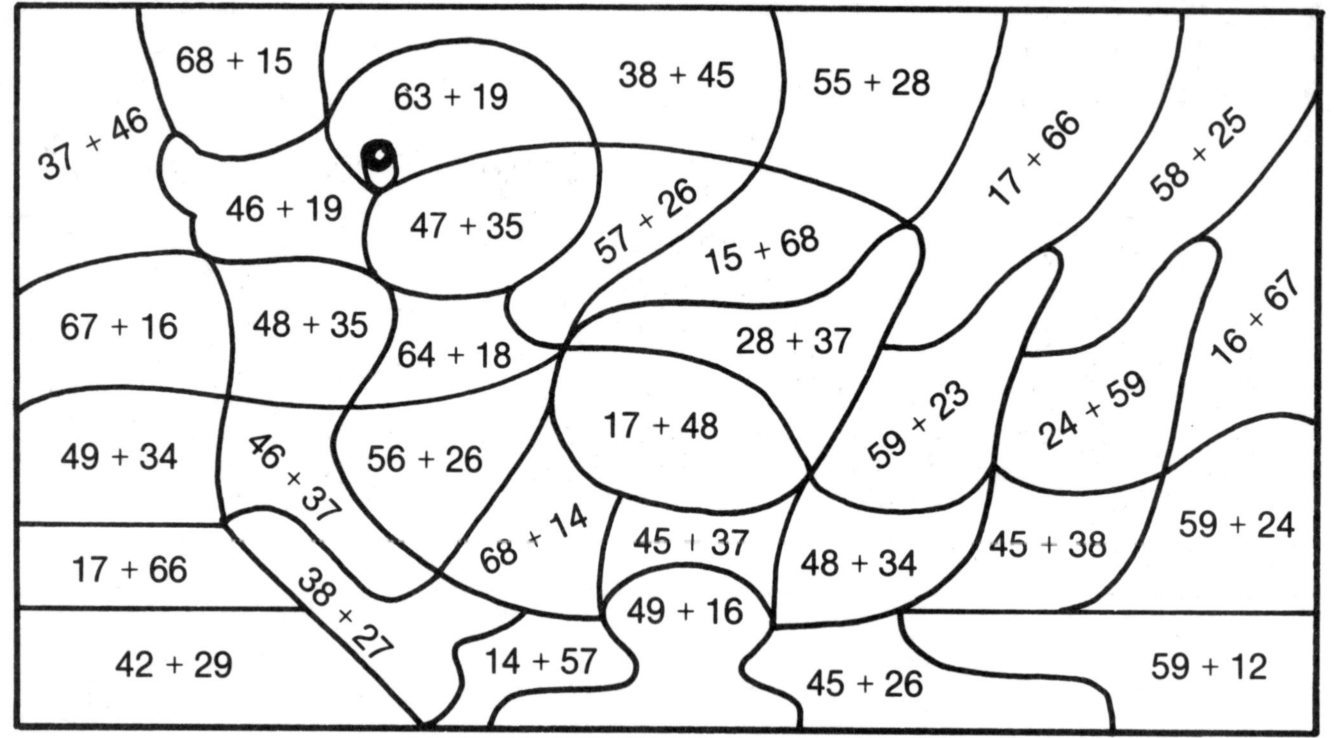


Color all the spaces and boxes.

| 19 + 52 | 29 + 36 | 47 + 35 | 68 + 14 | 44 + 27 | 35 + 36 | 49 + 33 | 45 + 26 |
|---|---|---|---|---|---|---|---|
| 43 + 28 | 18 + 53 | 54 + 28 | 44 + 38 | 23 + 59 | 56 + 26 | 65 + 17 | 23 + 48 |
| 26 + 45 | 37 + 34 | 59 + 23 | 19 + 63 | 47 + 35 | 67 + 15 | 37 + 45 | 25 + 46 |
| 55 + 28 | 19 + 64 | 36 + 47 | 14 + 69 | 57 + 26 | 18 + 65 | 39 + 44 | 54 + 29 |

Name ______________________________________ Skill: 2-digit addition—regrouping

**61** and **83** - **Red**
**71** and **64** - **Yellow**
**82** and **63** - **Orange**

Color all the spaces and boxes.

| 42 + 29 | 55 + 27 | 44 + 27 | 48 + 15 | 26 + 45 | 68 + 15 | 49 + 15 | 35 + 29 |
|---|---|---|---|---|---|---|---|
| 52 + 19 | 16 + 47 | 33 + 38 | 63 + 19 | 29 + 42 | 57 + 14 | 16 + 55 | 43 + 28 |
| 28 + 36 | 47 + 35 | 38 + 25 | 67 + 15 | 48 + 16 | 27 + 34 | 45 + 19 | 45 + 26 |
| 12 + 59 | 54 + 28 | 49 + 15 | 39 + 24 | 47 + 17 | 28 + 55 | 14 + 57 | 18 + 46 |
| 38 + 26 | 35 + 28 | 18 + 46 | 68 + 14 | 39 + 32 | 14 + 47 | 36 + 35 | 25 + 46 |

Name ______________________________ Skill: 2-digit addition—regrouping

**81** and **52** — **Yellow**
**82** and **63** — **Brown**
**83** and **71** — **Red**

Hang in there!

Color all the spaces and boxes.

| | | | | | | | |
|---|---|---|---|---|---|---|---|
| 17 + 66 | 59 + 12 | 48 + 23 | 49 + 32 | 38 + 44 | 64 + 17 | 29 + 42 | 58 + 23 |
| 54 + 17 | 23 + 29 | 56 + 25 | 44 + 37 | 39 + 13 | 43 + 28 | 28 + 55 | 45 + 38 |
| 26 + 57 | 43 + 28 | 59 + 24 | 22 + 59 | 35 + 28 | 36 + 16 | 33 + 38 | 68 + 13 |
| 16 + 65 | 38 + 14 | 55 + 28 | 54 + 27 | 13 + 69 | 33 + 48 | 46 + 25 | 34 + 47 |
| 38 + 45 | 65 + 18 | 29 + 42 | 52 + 29 | 49 + 14 | 14 + 67 | 42 + 29 | 24 + 28 |

Name ____________________ Skill: 2-digit addition—regrouping

**63 — Orange** **84 — Yellow** **73 — Brown** **62 — Blue**

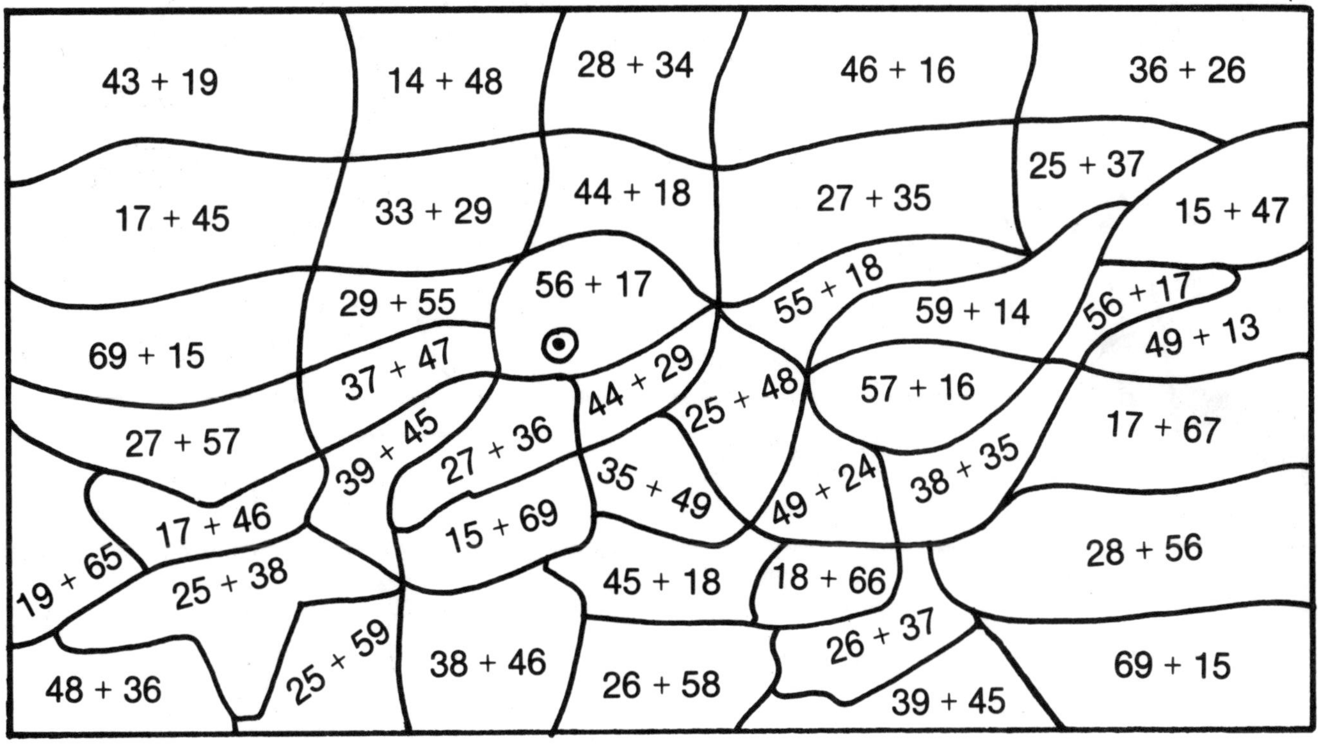

43 + 19
14 + 48
28 + 34
46 + 16
36 + 26
25 + 37
17 + 45
33 + 29
44 + 18
27 + 35
15 + 47
29 + 55
56 + 17
55 + 18
59 + 14
56 + 17
69 + 15
37 + 47
44 + 29
25 + 48
57 + 16
49 + 13
27 + 57
39 + 45
27 + 36
17 + 67
35 + 49
49 + 24
38 + 35
17 + 46
15 + 69
19 + 65
25 + 38
45 + 18
18 + 66
28 + 56
26 + 37
48 + 36
25 + 59
38 + 46
26 + 58
39 + 45
69 + 15

Color all the spaces and boxes.

| | | | | | | | |
|---|---|---|---|---|---|---|---|
| 29 + 34 | 43 + 19 | 68 + 16 | 34 + 28 | 47 + 15 | 29 + 33 | 24 + 49 | 46 + 16 |
| 49 + 14 | 33 + 29 | 36 + 26 | 44 + 18 | 18 + 55 | 39 + 34 | 19 + 54 | 36 + 26 |
| 44 + 19 | 27 + 35 | 47 + 37 | 36 + 26 | 26 + 47 | 45 + 17 | 28 + 45 | 37 + 25 |
| 24 + 39 | 48 + 14 | 45 + 39 | 35 + 27 | 36 + 37 | 14 + 59 | 38 + 35 | 49 + 13 |

Name ______________________ Skill: 2-digit addition—regrouping

**91 — Blue** **82 — Green** **75 — Yellow** **81 — Brown**

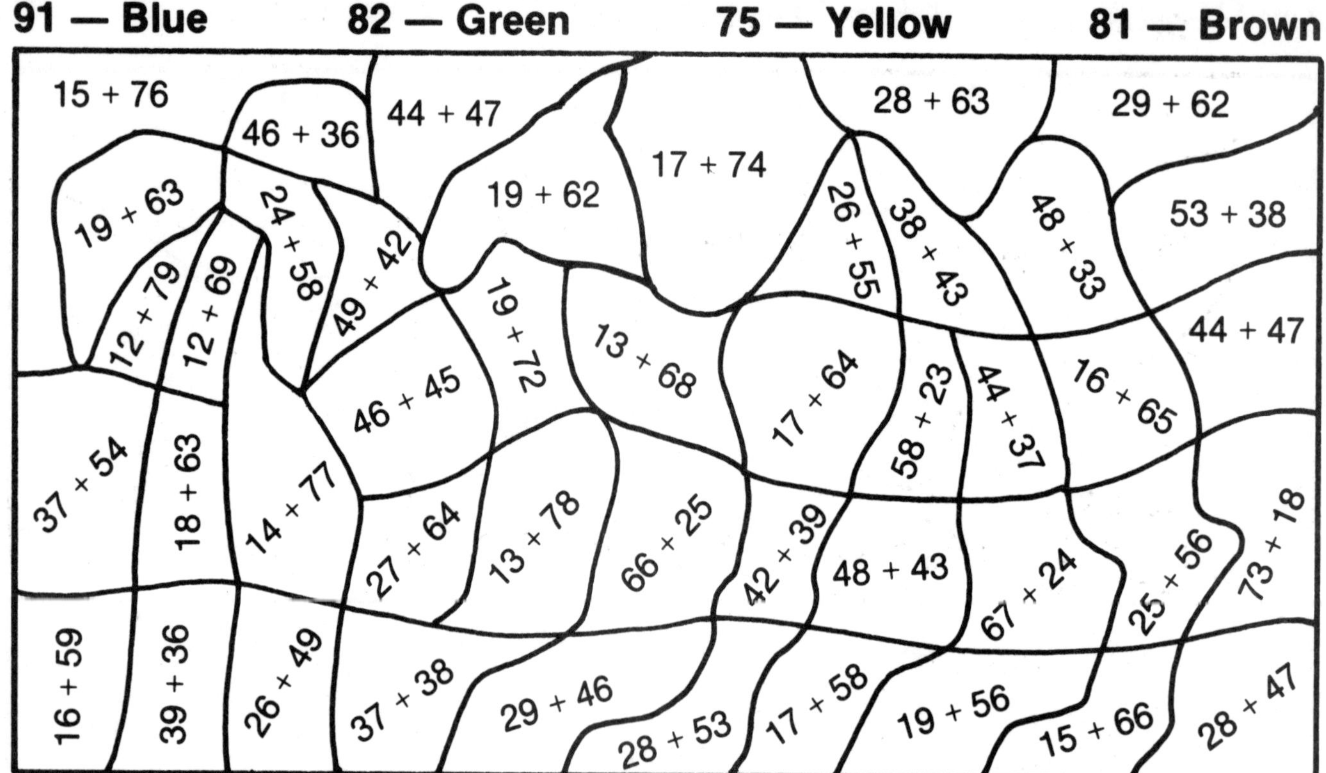


Color all the spaces and boxes.

| | | | | | | | |
|---|---|---|---|---|---|---|---|
| 27 + 54 | 14 + 67 | 46 + 45 | 38 + 37 | 68 + 23 | 72 + 19 | 18 + 64 | 55 + 36 |
| 57 + 24 | 56 + 35 | 75 + 16 | 46 + 45 | 57 + 34 | 16 + 66 | 57 + 25 | 43 + 39 |
| 22 + 59 | 45 + 36 | 78 + 13 | 18 + 57 | 69 + 22 | 18 + 73 | 33 + 49 | 47 + 44 |
| 35 + 46 | 58 + 33 | 65 + 26 | 27 + 48 | 52 + 39 | 76 + 15 | 69 + 13 | 54 + 37 |

Name ______________________________ Skill: 2-digit addition—regrouping

**92 — Blue** **91 — Orange** **93 — Brown**

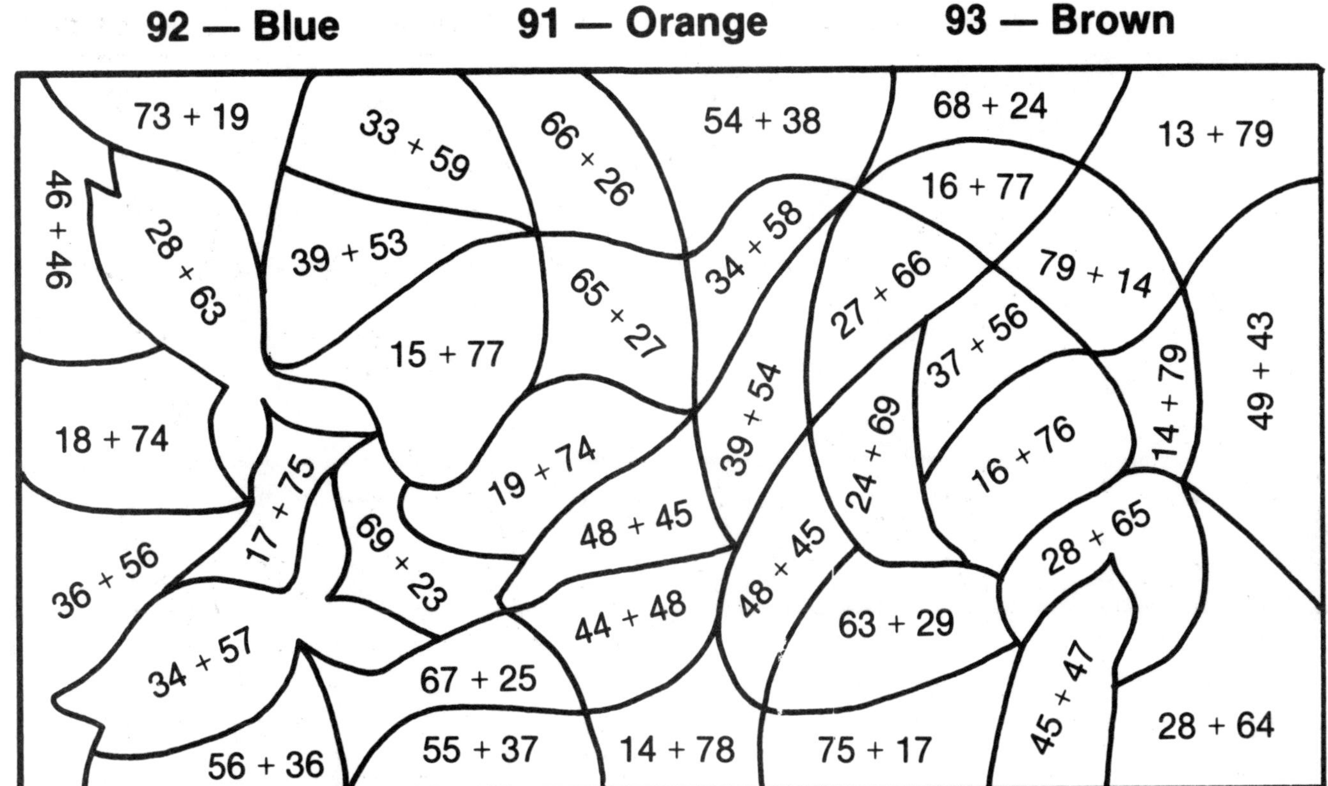


Color all the spaces and boxes.

| | | | | | | | |
|---|---|---|---|---|---|---|---|
| 75 + 18 | 19 + 73 | 37 + 56 | 46 + 46 | 49 + 42 | 34 + 57 | 78 + 13 | 29 + 63 |
| 24 + 69 | 25 + 67 | 27 + 66 | 77 + 15 | 52 + 39 | 56 + 36 | 66 + 25 | 47 + 45 |
| 35 + 58 | 69 + 24 | 54 + 39 | 68 + 24 | 24 + 67 | 68 + 23 | 74 + 17 | 35 + 57 |
| 43 + 49 | 76 + 16 | 53 + 39 | 17 + 75 | 47 + 44 | 18 + 74 | 54 + 38 | 64 + 28 |

Name ______________________________ Skill: 2-digit addition—regrouping

**72** and **65** — **Yellow**
**93** and **74** — **Red**
**81** and **71** — **Brown**

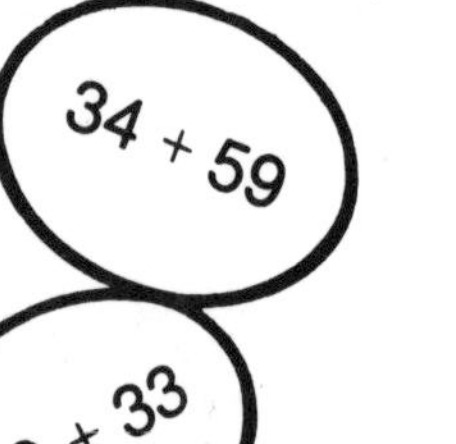


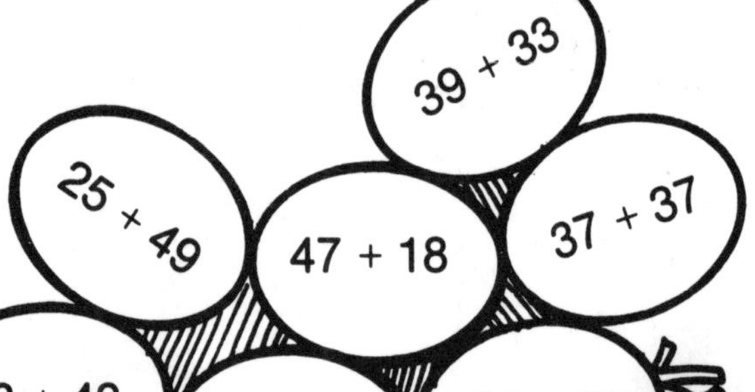

Color all the spaces and boxes.

| | | | | | | | |
|---|---|---|---|---|---|---|---|
| 29 + 42 | 28 + 43 | 25 + 56 | 48 + 33 | 47 + 18 | 38 + 27 | 54 + 18 | 49 + 16 |
| 52 + 19 | 39 + 33 | 38 + 27 | 46 + 26 | 38 + 34 | 33 + 39 | 48 + 17 | 35 + 37 |
| 35 + 36 | 58 + 13 | 64 + 17 | 46 + 25 | 16 + 56 | 39 + 35 | 25 + 49 | 19 + 55 |
| 15 + 57 | 28 + 37 | 56 + 16 | 63 + 18 | 23 + 49 | 14 + 79 | 29 + 43 | 18 + 75 |
| 37 + 44 | 59 + 22 | 43 + 38 | 39 + 32 | 28 + 44 | 25 + 68 | 37 + 37 | 26 + 48 |

Name  Skill: 2-digit addition—regrouping

Color all the spaces and boxes.

**65** and **91** — **Yellow**
**63** and **94** — **Blue**
**64** and **93** — **Brown**

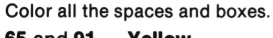

75 + 16

13 + 78 | 49 + 14

24 + 39 | 15 + 48 | 65 + 26

39 + 52 | 45 + 18

15 + 78

37 + 56

29 + 64

48 + 45

62 + 29

| 49 + 15 | 75 + 18 | 47 + 16 | 49 + 14 | 25 + 39 | 34 + 59 | 35 + 28 | 39 + 24 |
|---|---|---|---|---|---|---|---|
| 47 + 16 | 37 + 27 | 16 + 78 | 35 + 29 | 77 + 16 | 55 + 38 | 16 + 48 | 15 + 48 |
| 24 + 39 | 36 + 28 | 68 + 25 | 17 + 47 | 45 + 19 | 59 + 34 | 16 + 48 | 38 + 26 |
| 28 + 35 | 79 + 15 | 45 + 49 | 28 + 65 | 39 + 24 | 49 + 14 | 28 + 36 | 68 + 26 |
| 48 + 17 | 75 + 16 | 38 + 27 | 66 + 27 | 62 + 29 | 53 + 38 | 37 + 56 | 49 + 16 |

Name ______________________________ Skill: 2-digit addition—regrouping

**91 — Blue** **92 — Yellow** **93 — Brown** **94 — Red**

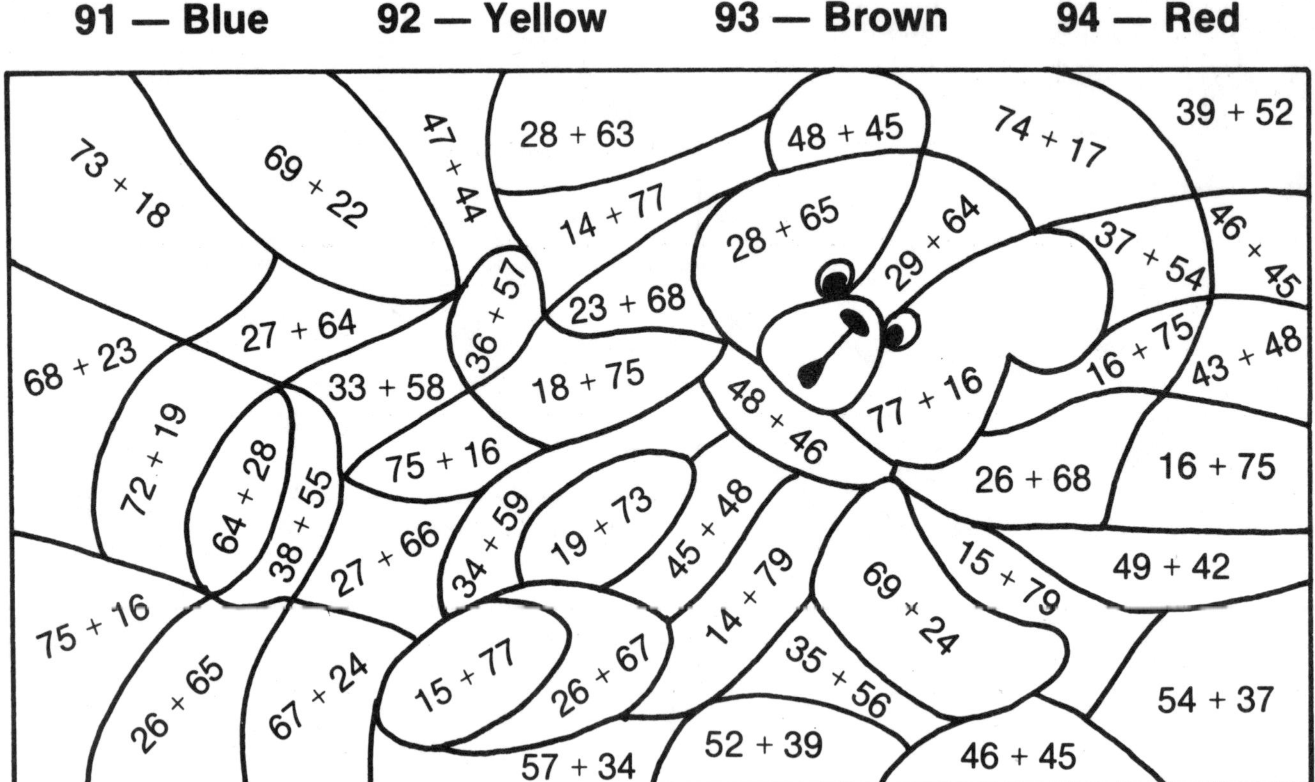


Color all the spaces and boxes.

| 59 + 33 | 46 + 46 | 75 + 17 | 62 + 29 | 19 + 74 | 16 + 75 | 76 + 18 | 72 + 19 |
|---|---|---|---|---|---|---|---|
| 28 + 64 | 16 + 75 | 56 + 36 | 73 + 18 | 68 + 25 | 77 + 14 | 57 + 37 | 64 + 27 |
| 17 + 75 | 34 + 58 | 79 + 13 | 52 + 39 | 66 + 27 | 53 + 38 | 47 + 47 | 56 + 35 |
| 19 + 73 | 17 + 74 | 75 + 17 | 25 + 66 | 59 + 34 | 75 + 16 | 29 + 65 | 78 + 13 |

Name ____________________ Skill: Two-digit addition—regrouping

# Addition Garden Maze

Score ___ / 40

Write the answers. To find the rabbit's path through the garden, begin at START. Color all the boxes with answers that are odd numbers.

| | | | | | |
|---|---|---|---|---|---|
| START → | 24 + 17 | 78 + 7 | 40 + 31 | 16 + 49 | 24 + 25 |
| 72 + 6 | 55 + 43 | 18 + 70 | 15 + 45 | 7 + 57 | 82 + 9 |
| 28 + 48 | 56 + 6 | 7 + 49 | 47 + 42 | 67 + 14 | 60 + 13 |
| 29 + 28 | 36 + 25 | 66 + 7 | 18 + 31 | 88 + 4 | 56 + 24 |
| 24 + 35 | 44 + 26 | 45 + 31 | 22 + 44 | 47 + 13 | 51 + 23 |
| 40 + 39 | 15 + 46 | 37 + 38 | 37 + 32 | 18 + 59 | 36 + 46 |
| 16 + 64 | 21 + 27 | 49 + 5 | 8 + 38 | 47 + 48 | SEEDS |

**Brainwork!** Create another garden row of seven problems for a friend to solve.

Name ______________________________ 

**25 and 14 — Black**
**26 and 15 — Red**
**27 and 16 — Blue**

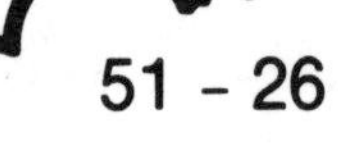


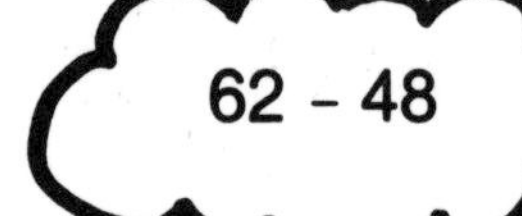


63 - 36

53 - 27

41 - 25

51 - 25

32 - 18

51 - 26

Color all the spaces and boxes.

| | | | | | | | |
|---|---|---|---|---|---|---|---|
| 71 - 55 | 83 - 56 | 91 - 75 | 65 - 49 | 82 - 66 | 64 - 37 | 74 - 58 | 62 - 35 |
| 73 - 46 | 41 - 16 | 41 - 15 | 74 - 59 | 52 - 26 | 80 - 54 | 61 - 46 | 80 - 53 |
| 51 - 35 | 71 - 45 | 82 - 67 | 54 - 28 | 63 - 48 | 83 - 57 | 73 - 47 | 61 - 45 |
| 42 - 15 | 61 - 45 | 50 - 25 | 83 - 67 | 92 - 65 | 75 - 48 | 42 - 28 | 62 - 46 |
| 61 - 34 | 72 - 56 | 84 - 57 | 45 - 29 | 55 - 39 | 53 - 26 | 74 - 58 | 62 - 35 |

 

Name ______________________________ Skill: 2-digit subtraction—regrouping

**25 — Green** **26 — Brown** **27 — Orange**

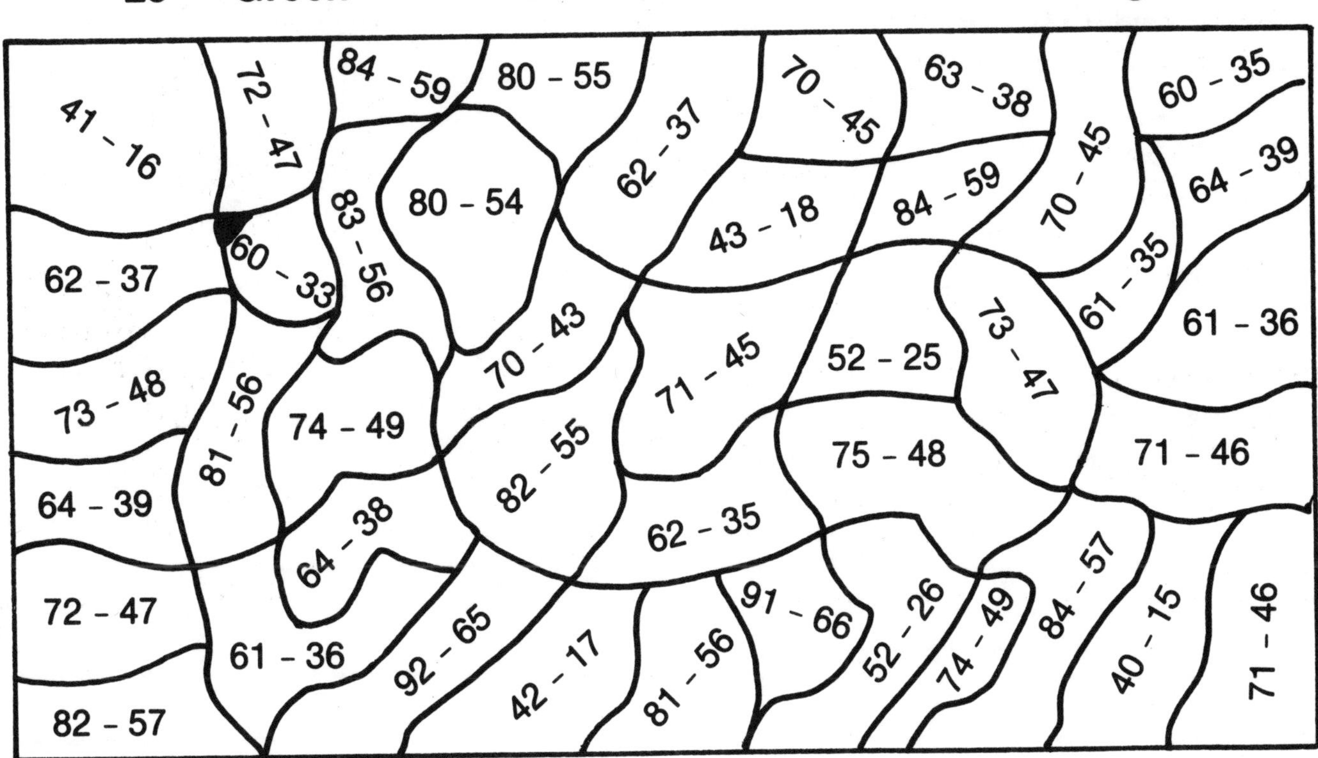


Color all the spaces and boxes.

| 61 − 34 | 80 − 53 | 91 − 64 | 44 − 19 | 52 − 25 | 72 − 45 | 64 − 37 | 64 − 39 |
|---|---|---|---|---|---|---|---|
| 51 − 26 | 71 − 44 | 92 − 66 | 74 − 47 | 81 − 55 | 81 − 54 | 61 − 36 | 71 − 46 |
| 60 − 35 | 93 − 66 | 63 − 36 | 84 − 58 | 90 − 63 | 51 − 24 | 40 − 15 | 83 − 58 |
| 51 − 26 | 63 − 38 | 65 − 38 | 85 − 58 | 73 − 46 | 62 − 37 | 74 − 49 | 53 − 28 |

Name ______________________________ Skill: 2-digit subtraction—regrouping

**13 — Brown** **14 — Blue** **15 — Green**

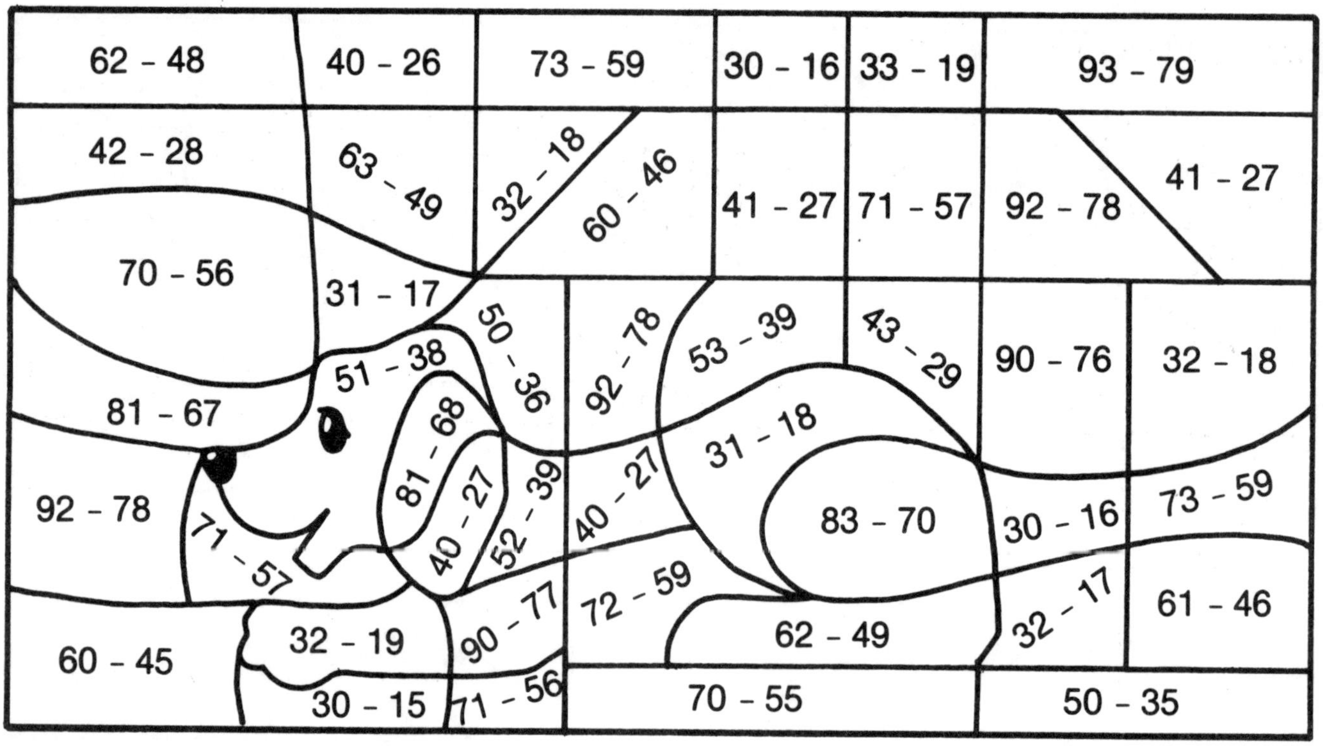

62 - 48 40 - 26 73 - 59 30 - 16 33 - 19 93 - 79

42 - 28 63 - 49 32 - 18 60 - 46 41 - 27 71 - 57 92 - 78 41 - 27

70 - 56 31 - 17 50 - 36 92 - 78 53 - 39 43 - 29 90 - 76 32 - 18

51 - 38 81 - 67 81 - 68 31 - 18

92 - 78 71 - 57 40 - 27 52 - 39 40 - 27 83 - 70 30 - 16 73 - 59

72 - 59 32 - 17 61 - 46

60 - 45 32 - 19 90 - 77 62 - 49

30 - 15 71 - 56 70 - 55 50 - 35

Color all the spaces and boxes.

| | | | | | | | |
|---|---|---|---|---|---|---|---|
| 93 - 79 | 72 - 59 | 61 - 48 | 81 - 67 | 63 - 49 | 62 - 49 | 91 - 77 | 53 - 39 |
| 60 - 46 | 51 - 37 | 82 - 69 | 91 - 78 | 50 - 37 | 70 - 57 | 41 - 27 | 80 - 66 |
| 43 - 29 | 71 - 57 | 31 - 18 | 61 - 47 | 52 - 38 | 81 - 68 | 91 - 77 | 50 - 36 |
| 30 - 15 | 92 - 77 | 74 - 59 | 62 - 47 | 54 - 39 | 60 - 45 | 72 - 57 | 83 - 68 |

Name ______________________ Skill: Two-digit subtraction—regrouping

# Early Risers

Score ____ / 30

Subtract and write the answers.

| | | | | | |
|---|---|---|---|---|---|
| A. 71 − 33 | 50 − 25 | 77 − 8 | 45 − 18 | 74 − 28 | 82 − 37 |
| B. 90 − 47 | 91 − 19 | 93 − 38 | 74 − 57 | 30 − 21 | 71 − 39 |
| C. 67 − 8 | 54 − 48 | 80 − 19 | 52 − 18 | 85 − 38 | 54 − 28 |
| D. 70 − 26 | 78 − 59 | 43 − 7 | 75 − 66 | 54 − 15 | 93 − 9 |
| E. 66 − 19 | 93 − 29 | 93 − 18 | 51 − 39 | 80 − 13 | 97 − 19 |

**Brainwork!** Write a subtraction word problem about a farm.

Name ______________________________ Skill: 2-digit subtraction—regrouping

**24 — Orange** **25 — Brown** **26 — Green**

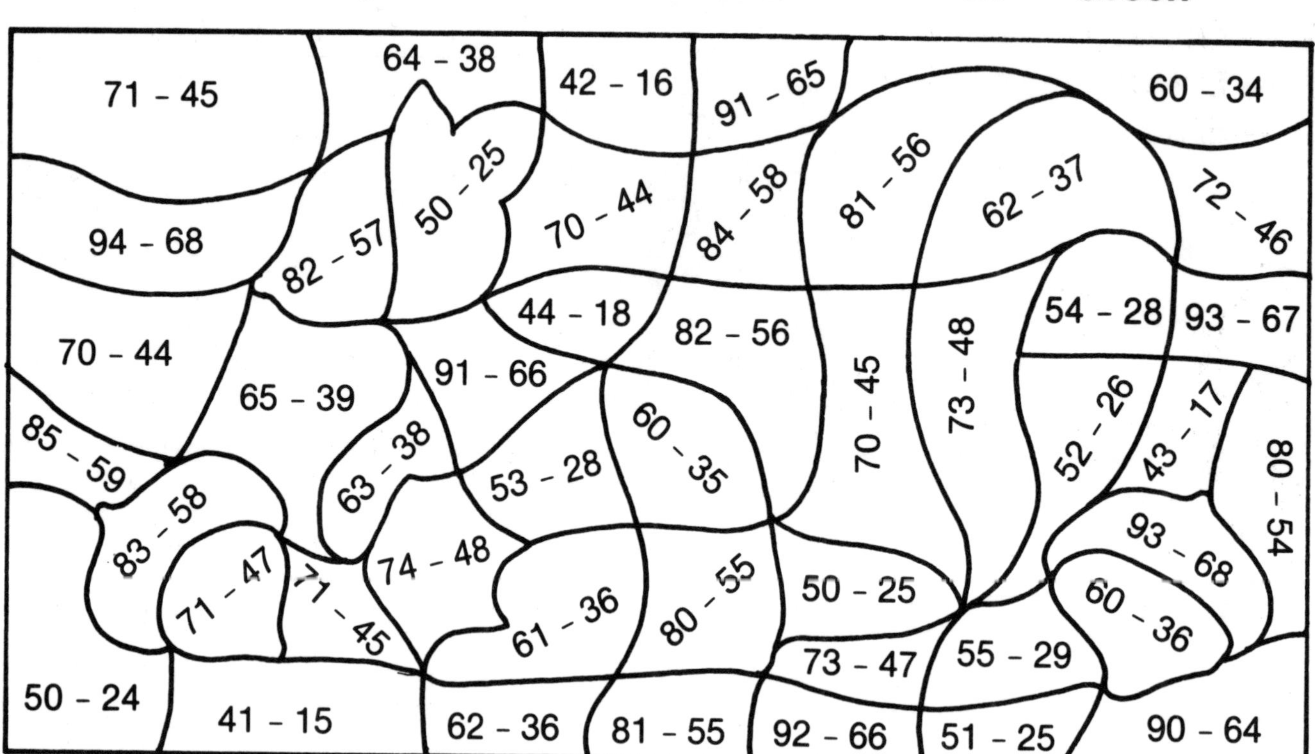


Color all the spaces and boxes.

| 75 − 49 | 63 − 37 | 83 − 59 | 94 − 68 | 85 − 59 | 61 − 35 | 81 − 55 | 60 − 34 |
|---|---|---|---|---|---|---|---|
| 95 − 69 | 51 − 27 | 62 − 38 | 41 − 17 | 83 − 57 | 71 − 46 | 64 − 39 | 92 − 67 |
| 42 − 16 | 54 − 28 | 81 − 57 | 72 − 46 | 45 − 19 | 74 − 49 | 80 − 54 | 52 − 27 |
| 81 − 55 | 73 − 47 | 91 − 67 | 53 − 27 | 40 − 14 | 51 − 26 | 72 − 47 | 54 − 29 |

Name ______________________________ Skill: 2-digit subtraction—regrouping

**34 — Yellow**
**35 — Orange**
**36 — Brown**
**37 — Blue**

52 - 18

61 - 26

53 - 16

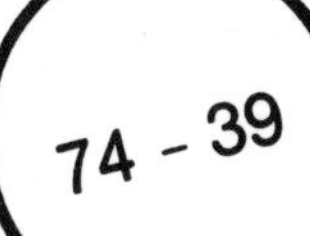


71 - 37

61 - 25

65 - 28

51 - 16

Color all the spaces and boxes.

| 72 − 37 | 66 − 29 | 82 − 45 | 94 − 57 | 54 − 17 | 63 − 27 | 75 − 38 | 56 − 19 |
|---|---|---|---|---|---|---|---|
| 90 − 55 | 74 − 37 | 82 − 48 | 84 − 47 | 64 − 28 | 74 − 38 | 93 − 57 | 66 − 29 |
| 52 − 17 | 93 − 56 | 52 − 15 | 74 − 37 | 95 − 58 | 83 − 47 | 55 − 18 | 63 − 26 |
| 62 − 27 | 95 − 58 | 73 − 39 | 54 − 17 | 76 − 39 | 94 − 58 | 53 − 16 | 86 − 49 |
| 71 − 36 | 50 − 13 | 62 − 28 | 83 − 46 | 64 − 27 | 70 − 34 | 84 − 47 | 65 − 28 |

Name ______________________________ Skill: 2-digit subtraction—regrouping

Color all the spaces and boxes.

**16 — Red**
**17 — Orange**
**18 — Yellow**

| 95 - 79 | 45 - 29 | 70 - 54 | 65 - 49 | 32 - 14 | 94 - 76 | 54 - 36 | 84 - 66 |
|---|---|---|---|---|---|---|---|
| 91 - 75 | 42 - 24 | 71 - 53 | 57 - 39 | 72 - 54 | 91 - 73 | 35 - 17 | 92 - 74 |
| 51 - 35 | 42 - 24 | 82 - 66 | 55 - 39 | 93 - 75 | 60 - 43 | 71 - 54 | 95 - 78 |
| 83 - 67 | 45 - 27 | 54 - 36 | 95 - 79 | 44 - 26 | 62 - 45 | 77 - 59 | 90 - 73 |
| 61 - 45 | 83 - 67 | 41 - 25 | 80 - 64 | 93 - 75 | 74 - 57 | 40 - 23 | 75 - 58 |

Name ______________________ Skill: 2-digit subtraction—regrouping

**17 — Black** **28 — Orange** **18 — Red** **27 — Blue**

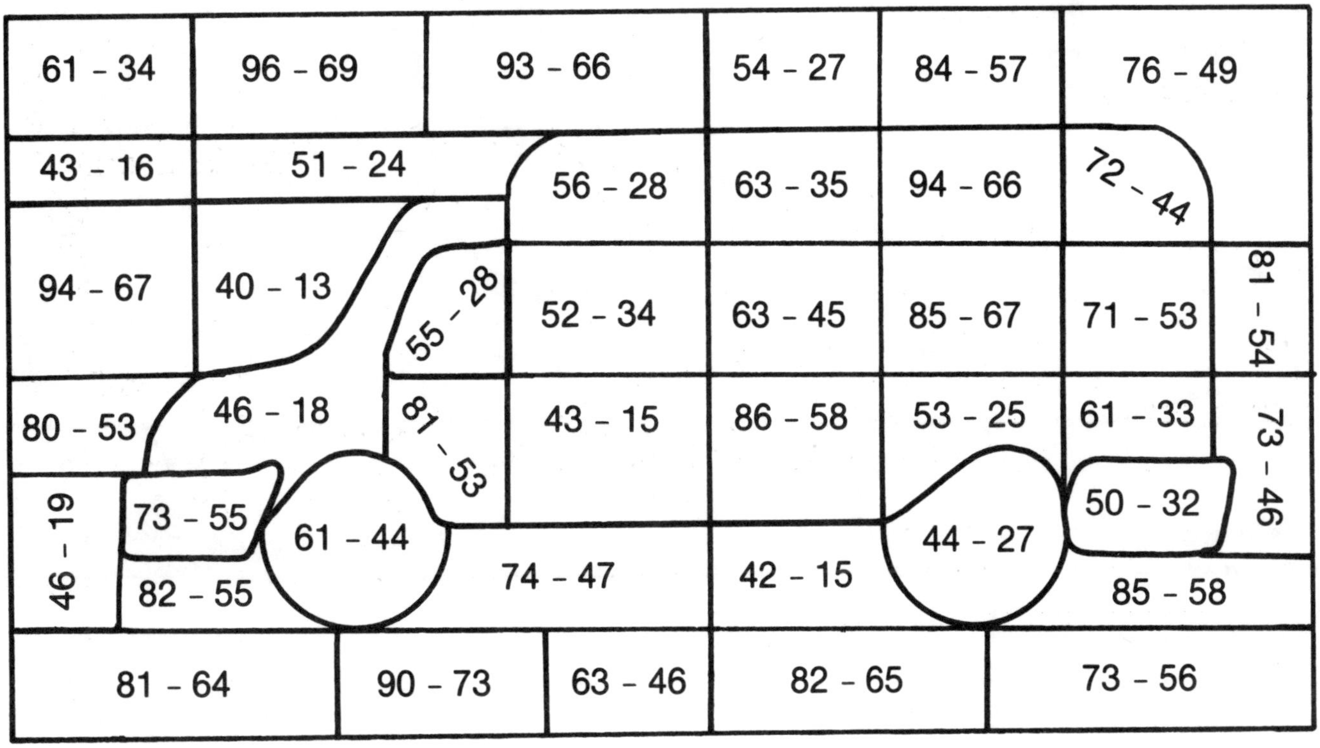

61 - 34 | 96 - 69 | 93 - 66 | 54 - 27 | 84 - 57 | 76 - 49

43 - 16 | 51 - 24 | 56 - 28 | 63 - 35 | 94 - 66 | 72 - 44

94 - 67 | 40 - 13 | 55 - 28 | 52 - 34 | 63 - 45 | 85 - 67 | 71 - 53 | 81 - 54

80 - 53 | 46 - 18 | 81 - 53 | 43 - 15 | 86 - 58 | 53 - 25 | 61 - 33 | 73 - 46

46 - 19 | 73 - 55 | 61 - 44 | 44 - 27 | 50 - 32

82 - 55 | 74 - 47 | 42 - 15 | 85 - 58

81 - 64 | 90 - 73 | 63 - 46 | 82 - 65 | 73 - 56

Color all the spaces and boxes.

| | | | | | | | |
|---|---|---|---|---|---|---|---|
| 84 - 57 | 53 - 26 | 86 - 59 | 71 - 44 | 33 - 16 | 64 - 37 | 84 - 56 | 41 - 14 |
| 46 - 28 | 56 - 38 | 66 - 48 | 95 - 68 | 51 - 24 | 72 - 45 | 76 - 48 | 50 - 23 |
| 85 - 67 | 66 - 39 | 43 - 25 | 91 - 64 | 76 - 59 | 63 - 36 | 92 - 64 | 52 - 25 |
| 93 - 75 | 54 - 36 | 61 - 43 | 90 - 63 | 64 - 47 | 44 - 17 | 45 - 17 | 56 - 29 |

Name ______________________ Skill: 2-digit subtraction—regrouping

Color all the spaces and boxes.

**13** and **27 — Brown**
**14** and **28 — Yellow**
**15** and **29 — Orange**

71 - 58

44 - 17

51 - 23

53 - 38

42 - 29

42 - 28

63 - 48

70 - 43

| | | | | | | | |
|---|---|---|---|---|---|---|---|
| 73 - 59 | 47 - 19 | 61 - 32 | 50 - 36 | 52 - 24 | 41 - 13 | 82 - 68 | 74 - 46 |
| 91 - 63 | 33 - 19 | 82 - 67 | 73 - 45 | 82 - 54 | 71 - 57 | 50 - 22 | 51 - 37 |
| 44 - 29 | 51 - 22 | 43 - 14 | 52 - 38 | 92 - 79 | 84 - 57 | 41 - 28 | 87 - 59 |
| 72 - 43 | 61 - 47 | 73 - 58 | 62 - 34 | 72 - 45 | 96 - 68 | 41 - 14 | 51 - 23 |
| 91 - 62 | 50 - 35 | 84 - 55 | 80 - 66 | 50 - 23 | 31 - 18 | 54 - 27 | 42 - 28 |

Name ______________________________



**34 — Red**
**35 — Blue**
**36 — Brown**
**37 — Green**

Color all the spaces and boxes.

73 - 38

| | | | | | | | |
|---|---|---|---|---|---|---|---|
| 72 - 38 | 80 - 45 | 52 - 17 | 54 - 19 | 84 - 49 | 63 - 28 | 50 - 13 | 70 - 35 |
| 53 - 19 | 90 - 55 | 51 - 16 | 92 - 57 | 50 - 15 | 85 - 48 | 63 - 26 | 96 - 59 |
| 60 - 26 | 82 - 47 | 82 - 46 | 65 - 29 | 62 - 26 | 93 - 58 | 83 - 46 | 61 - 26 |
| 83 - 49 | 71 - 36 | 62 - 26 | 81 - 46 | 73 - 37 | 53 - 18 | 71 - 34 | 62 - 27 |
| 92 - 58 | 83 - 48 | 71 - 35 | 85 - 49 | 84 - 48 | 64 - 29 | 51 - 14 | 74 - 39 |

Name ______________________________ Skill: 2-digit subtraction—regrouping

**16 — Orange** **27 — Blue** **38 — Red**

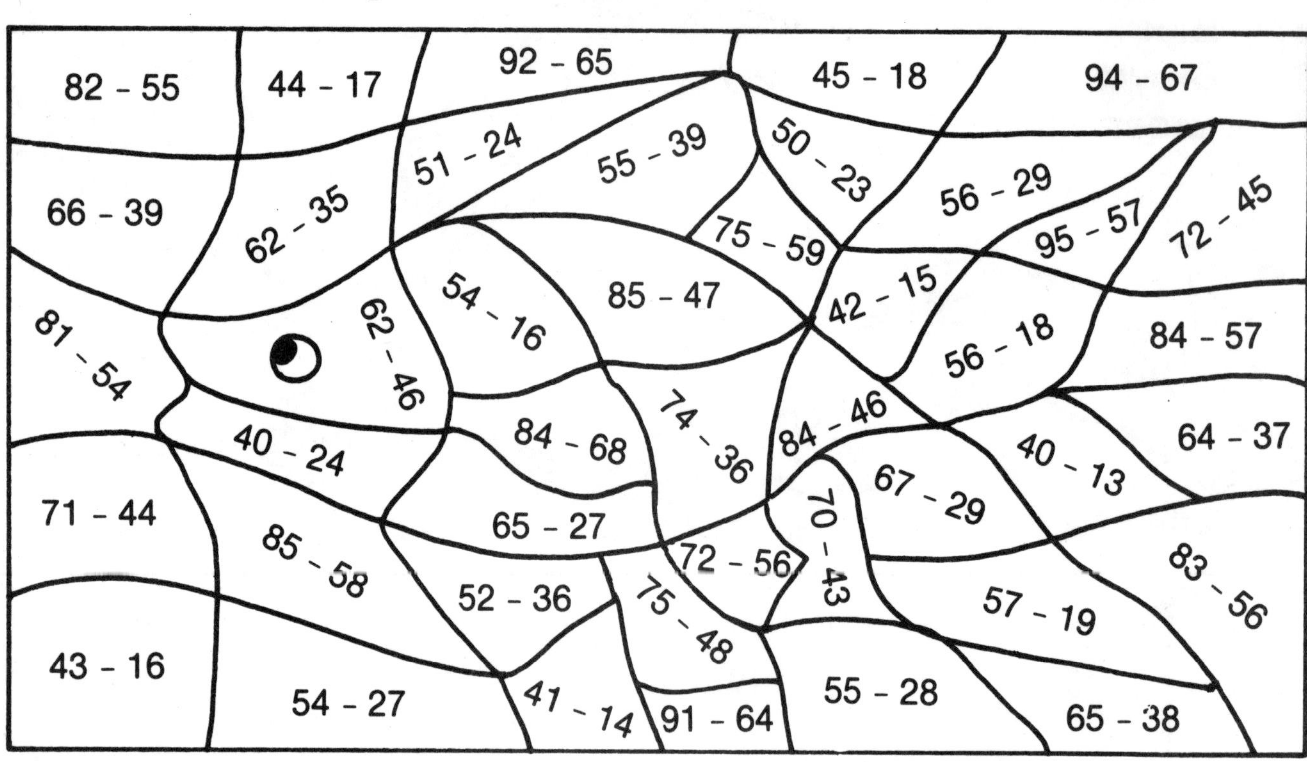


Color all the spaces and boxes.

| | | | | | | | |
|---|---|---|---|---|---|---|---|
| 73<br>- 46 | 64<br>- 26 | 45<br>- 18 | 95<br>- 68 | 32<br>- 16 | 92<br>- 76 | 63<br>- 36 | 93<br>- 66 |
| 96<br>- 69 | 76<br>- 49 | 46<br>- 19 | 90<br>- 63 | 44<br>- 28 | 72<br>- 45 | 86<br>- 59 | 52<br>- 25 |
| 60<br>- 33 | 75<br>- 37 | 83<br>- 56 | 43<br>- 27 | 65<br>- 49 | 53<br>- 37 | 85<br>- 58 | 74<br>- 47 |
| 80<br>- 53 | 86<br>- 48 | 41<br>- 14 | 61<br>- 34 | 90<br>- 74 | 65<br>- 38 | 76<br>- 49 | 53<br>- 26 |

Name ________________________________ Skill: Three-digit addition—no regrouping

# There They Blow!

Score ____ / 35

Add and write the answers.

| | | | | | |
|---|---|---|---|---|---|
| A. | 434<br>+ 234 | 212<br>+ 130 | 117<br>+ 422 | 62<br>+ 204 | 18<br>+ 770 |
| B. | 516<br>+ 80 | 414<br>+ 363 | 541<br>+ 331 | 150<br>+ 40 | 515<br>+ 430 |
| C. | 643<br>+ 253 | 802<br>+ 74 | 625<br>+ 131 | 422<br>+ 222 | 589<br>+ 200 |
| D. | 464<br>+ 511 | 243<br>+ 25 | 571<br>+ 208 | 115<br>+ 522 | 50<br>+ 249 |
| E. | 642<br>+ 231 | 377<br>+ 102 | 555<br>+ 240 | 385<br>+ 12 | 402<br>+ 204 |

F. 924 + 61 = ____

G. 446 + 332 = ____

H. 741 + 208 = ____

I. 333 + 565 = ____

J. 466 + 321 = ____

K. 521 + 54 = ____

L. 805 + 101 = ____

M. 127 + 31 = ____

N. 243 + 243 = ____

O. 307 + 421 = ____

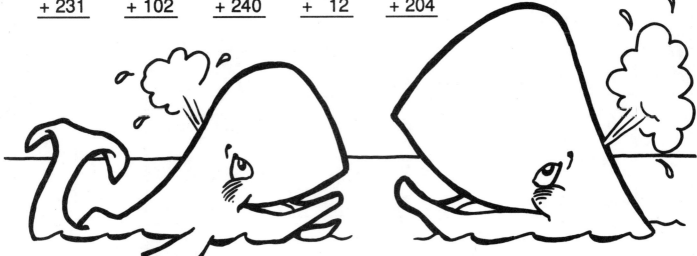

**Brainwork!** Write a word problem for one of the addition problems above.

Name ______________________________ Skill: Adding multiples of 100

# For the Birds

Score ____ / 45

Add.

A.

| 700 | |
|---|---|
| 500 | |
| 200 | |
| 800 | |
| 600 | |
| 900 | |
| 400 | |
| 300 | |

B.

| 700 | |
|---|---|
| 300 | |
| 100 | |
| 900 | |
| 500 | |
| 200 | |
| 400 | |
| 800 | |

C.

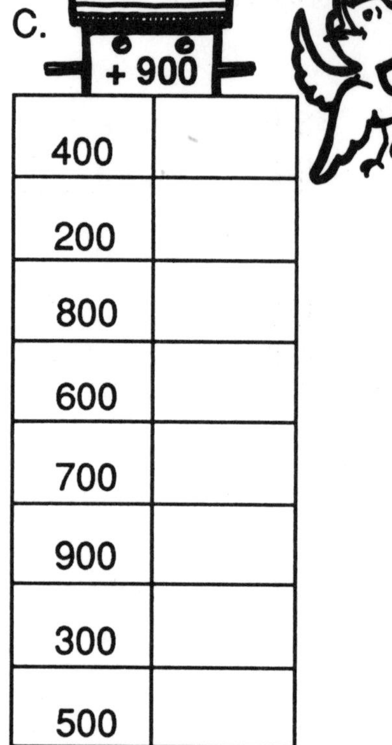


| 400 | |
|---|---|
| 200 | |
| 800 | |
| 600 | |
| 700 | |
| 900 | |
| 300 | |
| 500 | |

D.

| 700 | |
|---|---|
| 500 | |
| 200 | |
| 800 | |
| 600 | |
| 900 | |
| 400 | |

E.

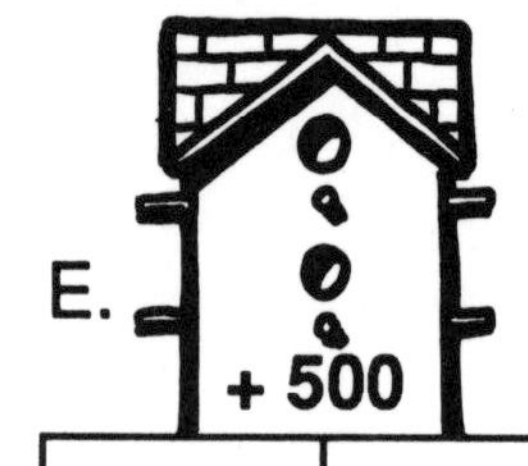


| 700 | |
|---|---|
| 500 | |
| 100 | |
| 900 | |
| 300 | |
| 200 | |
| 400 | |

F.

| 700 | |
|---|---|
| 500 | |
| 200 | |
| 800 | |
| 600 | |
| 900 | |
| 400 | |

**Brainwork!** Draw a *+1000* birdhouse like the ones above. Have a friend write the answers. Check your friend's work.

Name ______________________________ Skill: Adding decimals—no regrouping

# Decimal Dreamer

Score ____ / 40

Write the answers.

A. 0.9 + 0.0 = ____    0.24 + 0.21 = ____

B. 0.3 + 0.2 = ____    0.62 + 0.15 = ____

C. 0.1 + 0.7 = ____    0.30 + 0.29 = ____

D. 0.8 + 0.1 = ____    0.54 + 0.14 = ____

E. 0.2 + 0.4 = ____    0.43 + 0.23 = ____

F. 0.2 + 0.5 = ____    0.31 + 0.61 = ____

G. 0.3 + 0.3 = ____    0.11 + 0.20 = ____

H. 0.6 + 0.2 = ____    0.24 + 0.24 = ____

I. 0.3 + 0.3 = ____    0.35 + 0.22 = ____

J. 0.8 + 0.1 = ____    0.51 + 0.24 = ____

K. 0.2 + 0.5 = ____    0.03 + 0.05 ____

L. 0.9 + 0.0 = ____    0.62 + 0.11 = ____

M. 0.3 + 0.6 = ____    0.95 + 0.02 = ____

N. 0.4 + 0.4 = ____    0.33 + 0.56 = ____

O. 0.2 + 0.3 = ____    0.42 + 0.34 = ____

P. 0.1 + 0.6 = ____    0.14 + 0.13 = ____

Q. 0.6 + 0.1 = ____    0.33 + 0.13 = ____

R. 0.5 + 0.1 = ____    0.17 + 0.11 = ____

S. 0.5 + 0.3 = ____    0.41 + 0.34 = ____

T. 0.4 + 0.1 = ____    0.22 + 0.62 = ____

**Brainwork!** Choose three answers you wrote above. Then write them in order from smallest to largest.

Name ______________________________ Skill: Subtracting multiples of 100

# Tons of Subtraction Fun

Score ____ / 40

Subtract and write the answers.

| | | | | |
|---|---|---|---|---|
| A. | 400<br>– 200 | 800<br>– 700 | 500<br>– 300 | 600<br>– 200 |
| B. | 800<br>– 600 | 900<br>– 700 | 500<br>– 400 | 700<br>– 200 |
| C. | 1,200<br>– 600 | 1,700<br>– 800 | 1,100<br>– 300 | 1,100<br>– 800 |
| D. | 1,500<br>– 800 | 1,200<br>– 800 | 1,600<br>– 800 | 1,400<br>– 800 |
| E. | 1,300<br>– 600 | 1,900<br>– 900 | 1,300<br>– 900 | 1,300<br>– 400 |
| F. | 1,400<br>– 900 | 1,500<br>– 900 | 1,100<br>– 700 | 1,700<br>– 700 |
| G. | 1,700<br>– 900 | 1,400<br>– 400 | 1,600<br>– 700 | 1,200<br>– 400 |

H. 1,100 – 900 = ______

I. 1,300 – 700 = ______

J. 1,100 – 400 = ______

K. 1,800 – 900 = ______

L. 1,200 – 800 = ______

M. 1,100 – 500 = ______

N. 1,400 – 500 = ______

O. 1,200 – 900 = ______

P. 1,500 – 600 = ______

Q. 1,200 – 200 = ______

R. 1,100 – 600 = ______

S. 1,500 – 500 = ______

**Brainwork!** Subtract 200 from this year's date.

Name ______________________________ Skill: Three-digit subtraction—no regrouping

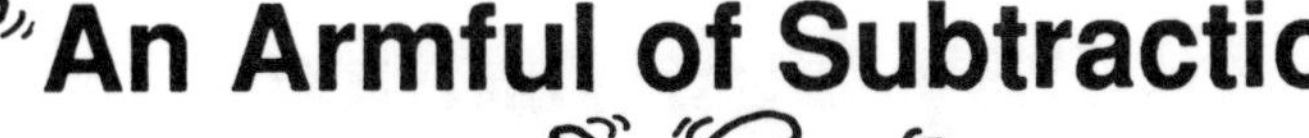

# An Armful of Subtraction

Write the answers.

Score ____ / 35

| | | | | | |
|---|---|---|---|---|---|
| A. | 747 − 231 | 895 − 140 | 668 − 114 | 541 − 320 | 899 − 824 |
| B. | 470 − 150 | 869 − 142 | 346 − 112 | 757 − 231 | 928 − 204 |
| C. | 777 − 521 | 499 − 204 | 998 − 133 | 566 − 223 | 656 − 556 |
| D. | 785 − 552 | 573 − 371 | 579 − 465 | 923 − 612 | 986 − 334 |
| E. | 856 − 715 | 234 − 203 | 784 − 424 | 898 − 676 | 986 − 522 |
| F. | 484 − 142 | 567 − 34 | 268 − 28 | 896 − 514 | 867 − 113 |
| G. | 387 − 301 | 846 − 400 | 879 − 329 | 999 − 128 | 899 − 734 |

**Brainwork!** Choose two of the answers from above. Subtract the smaller number from the larger one.

Name________________________________________ Skill: Subtracting decimals—no regrouping

# Sunny Subtraction

Write the answers.

Score____ 40

A. 0.7 – 0.1 = ______ 0.89 – 0.64 = ______

B. 0.5 – 0.4 = ______ 0.34 – 0.24 = ______

C. 0.7 – 0.5 = ______ 0.97 – 0.75 = ______

D. 0.6 – 0.3 = ______ 0.34 – 0.33 ______

E. 0.5 – 0.2 = ______ 0.69 – 0.42 = ______

F. 0.9 – 0.5 = ______ 0.67 – 0.32 = ______

G. 0.4 – 0.0 = ______ 0.75 – 0.15 = ______

H. 0.9 – 0.7 = ______ 0.46 – 0.26 = ______

I. 0.8 – 0.4 = ______ 0.89 – 0.56 = ______

J. 0.9 – 0.1 = ______ 0.13 – 0.11 = ______

K. 0.6 – 0.3 = ______ 0.79 – 0.40 = ______

L. 0.6 – 0.5 = ______ 0.24 – 0.21 = ______

M. 0.9 – 0.4 = ______ 0.98 – 0.33 = ______

N. 0.6 – 0.2 = ______ 0.56 – 0.42 = ______

O. 0.7 − 0.3 = ______ 0.79 − 0.68 = ______

P. 0.9 − 0.6 = ______ 0.86 − 0.05 = ______

Q. 0.8 − 0.5 = ______ 0.98 − 0.54 = ______

R. 0.5 − 0.2 = ______ 0.89 − 0.21 = ______

S. 0.9 − 0.2 = ______ 0.78 − 0.31 = ______

T. 0.8 − 0.2 = ______ 0.98 − 0.97 = ______

**Brainwork!** Write three decimals that are greater than 0.5.

Name ____________________ Skill: Three-digit addition—regrouping

# Hanging by a Thread

Score ____ / 40

Add and write the answers.

| | | | | | | |
|---|---|---|---|---|---|---|
| A. | 384 + 532 | 291 + 210 | 464 + 65 | 327 + 492 | 193 + 555 | 186 + 761 |
| B. | 212 + 94 | 636 + 171 | 543 + 282 | 238 + 590 | 480 + 463 | 487 + 162 |
| C. | 429 + 80 | 330 + 384 | 688 + 51 | 346 + 393 | 480 + 284 | 487 + 122 |
| D. | 575 + 71 | 370 + 548 | 261 + 97 | 342 + 560 | 156 + 92 | 298 + 520 |
| E. | 175 + 683 | 874 + 94 | 647 + 270 | 253 + 253 | 486 + 141 | 254 + 80 |
| F. | 174 + 333 | 459 + 270 | 796 + 133 | 271 + 555 | 550 + 392 | 437 + 490 |
| G. | 542 + 266 | 358 + 461 | 460 + 460 | 242 + 492 | | |

**Brainwork!** Use the digits *3*, *4*, *5*, *6*, *7*, and *8* to write a three-digit addition problem that needs regrouping. Then solve it.

Name ______________________________ Skill: Three-digit addition—regrouping

# Which Doghouse?

Score ____
40

Write the answers. Then color the path to the doghouse where Spot will hide her bone. Color all the boxes with answers that are even numbers.

| | START → | 836 + 138 | 485 + 306 | 334 + 439 | 185 + 484 |
|---|---|---|---|---|---|
| 247 + 244 | 478 + 751 | 726 + 428 | 576 + 272 | 134 + 392 | 364 + 384 |
| 407 + 548 | 294 + 295 | 665 + 592 | 383 + 354 | 156 + 893 | 328 + 190 |
| 325 + 346 | 108 + 346 | 648 + 748 | 742 + 880 | 115 + 415 | 428 + 628 |
| 961 + 854 | 597 + 221 | 906 + 79 | 527 + 106 | 372 + 331 | 285 + 20 |
| 447 + 448 | 661 + 553 | 544 + 118 | 235 + 247 | 793 + 73 | 603 + 522 |
| 724 + 757 | 369 + 408 | 466 + 561 | 850 + 693 | 377 + 893 | 249 + 116 |

**Brainwork!** Create your own doghouse addition maze. Let a friend solve it.

Name ______________________ 

# Diving for Answers

Score ____ / 35

Write the answers.

| | | | | | | | |
|---|---|---|---|---|---|---|---|
| A. | 284 + 376 | 392 + 548 | 124 + 798 | 377 + 636 | 819 + 395 | 447 + 275 | 256 + 256 |
| B. | 443 + 488 | 155 + 655 | 792 + 488 | 684 + 679 | 185 + 336 | 758 + 84 | 675 + 75 |
| C. | 519 + 388 | 609 + 449 | 477 + 74 | 766 + 766 | 245 + 97 | 248 + 269 | 456 + 277 |
| D. | 504 + 96 | 777 + 567 | 199 + 299 | 143 + 157 | 924 + 76 | 761 + 189 | 498 + 197 |
| E. | 373 + 329 | 123 + 98 | 828 + 676 | 444 + 298 | 586 + 586 | 254 + 947 | 675 + 125 |

**Brainwork!** Circle two answers that have three digits. Add those two numbers together.

Name ______________________________ Skill: Adding money

# Buying a Birdcage

Score ____ / 40

Add and write the answers. Then find the path to Pierre's new birdcage by coloring all the boxes with answers that are odd numbers.

START →

| | | | | | |
|---|---|---|---|---|---|
| | | \$3.25<br>+ 4.26 | \$4.63<br>+ 4.65 | \$3.25<br>+ 3.21 | \$8.27<br>+ .07 |
| \$4.24<br>+ 4.26 | \$ .93<br>+ 4.12 | \$1.36<br>+ 1.37 | \$1.22<br>+ .92 | \$6.82<br>+ .04 | \$ .51<br>+ .45 |
| \$ .97<br>+ 1.41 | \$4.48<br>+ 6.15 | \$5.00<br>+ 6.00 | \$2.36<br>+ 2.16 | \$ .39<br>+ .29 | \$1.04<br>+ 1.04 |
| \$ .72<br>+ .14 | \$ .50<br>+ .21 | \$ .97<br>+ 2.88 | \$6.86<br>+ .03 | \$7.77<br>+ 1.08 | \$ .33<br>+ .51 |
| \$3.58<br>+ .54 | \$2.84<br>+ 1.88 | \$2.41<br>+ 7.51 | \$2.50<br>+ 2.50 | \$5.62<br>+ .61 | \$2.53<br>+ 3.43 |
| \$ .44<br>+ .44 | \$3.34<br>+ 2.24 | \$2.49<br>+ 2.06 | \$2.59<br>+ .48 | \$1.52<br>+ .61 | \$ .81<br>+ 6.45 |
| \$1.90<br>+ 1.90 | \$2.68<br>+ 1.76 | \$2.12<br>+ 6.05 | \$2.76<br>+ .32 | \$5.62<br>+ 4.60 | \$3.33<br>+ 5.55 |

**Brainwork!** Write an addition word problem using money. Solve it.

Name ______________________________ Skill: Four-digit addition

# Adding Larger Numbers

Score ____ 35

| | | | | | |
|---|---|---|---|---|---|
| A. | 2,714 + 3,281 | 4,265 + 5,135 | 6,223 + 290 | 2,227 + 1,462 | 5,540 + 1,628 |
| B. | 4,175 + 377 | 1,097 + 1,983 | 7,142 + 2,355 | 8,426 + 722 | 1,014 + 792 |
| C. | 6,514 + 1,922 | 3,555 + 1,671 | 892 + 3,419 | 5,001 + 4,232 | 1,660 + 2,237 |
| D. | 1,554 + 667 | 8,817 + 1,012 | 5,572 + 918 | 1,090 + 703 | 2,813 + 2,763 |
| E. | 4,272 + 624 | 1,456 + 1,417 | 5,915 + 1,775 | 1,500 + 1,458 | 7,254 + 746 |
| F. | 2,754 + 2,787 | 2,861 + 668 | 7,565 + 1,907 | 4,841 + 1,827 | 5,817 + 2,062 |
| G. | 1,533 + 1,316 | 2,376 + 1,849 | 4,458 + 998 | 8,814 + 1,092 | 3,464 + 3,721 |

**Brainwork!** Add this year's date to next year's date.

Name ______________________________

Skill: Three-digit subtraction—regrouping tens

# Crowing for Corn

Score ____ / 35

Write the answers.

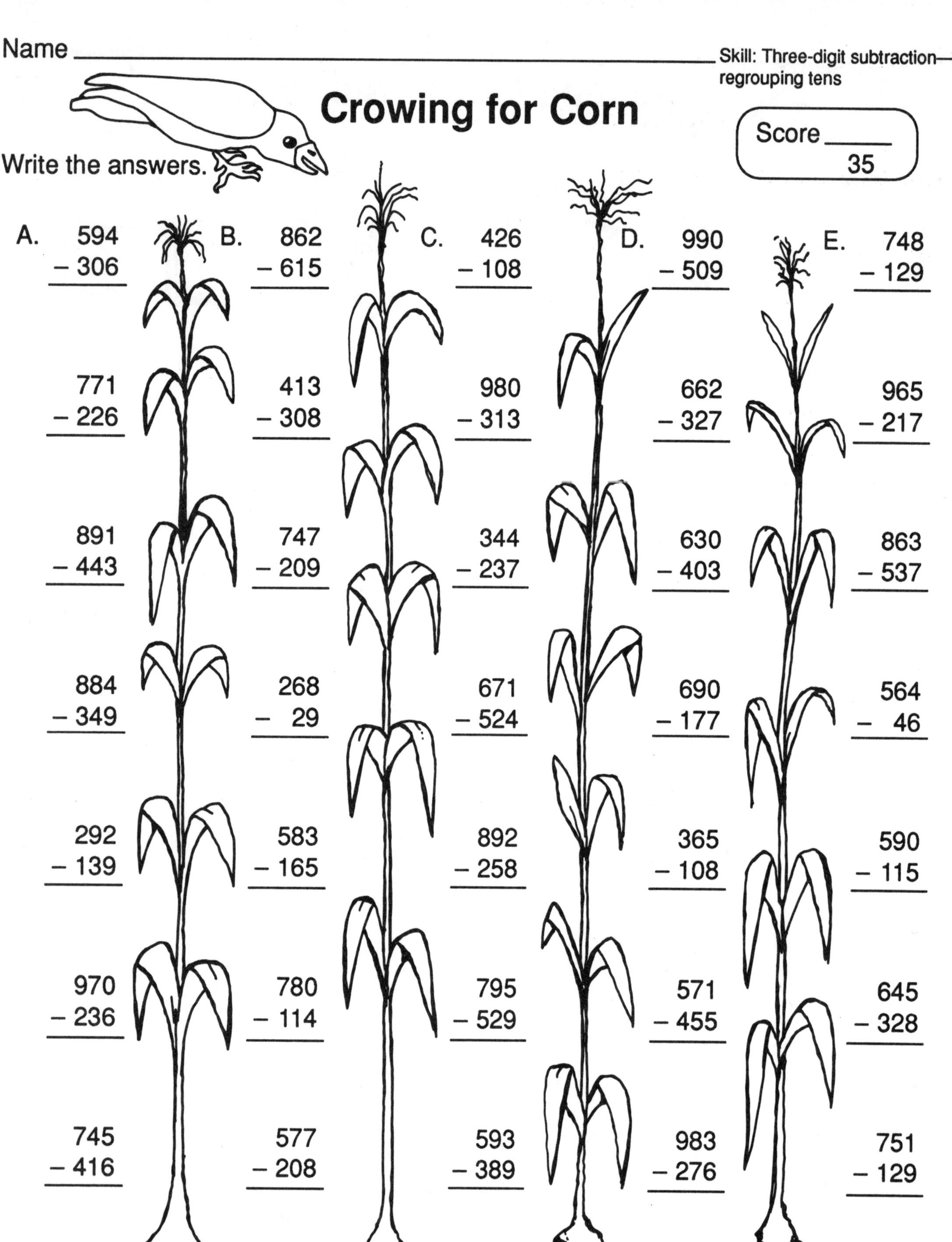

| A. | B. | C. | D. | E. |
|---|---|---|---|---|
| 594 − 306 | 862 − 615 | 426 − 108 | 990 − 509 | 748 − 129 |
| 771 − 226 | 413 − 308 | 980 − 313 | 662 − 327 | 965 − 217 |
| 891 − 443 | 747 − 209 | 344 − 237 | 630 − 403 | 863 − 537 |
| 884 − 349 | 268 − 29 | 671 − 524 | 690 − 177 | 564 − 46 |
| 292 − 139 | 583 − 165 | 892 − 258 | 365 − 108 | 590 − 115 |
| 970 − 236 | 780 − 114 | 795 − 529 | 571 − 455 | 645 − 328 |
| 745 − 416 | 577 − 208 | 593 − 389 | 983 − 276 | 751 − 129 |

**Brainwork!** Circle one of the problems above. Write a word problem to go with it.

Name ____________________ Skill: Three-digit subtraction–with/without regrouping

# Cat and Mouse Maze

Score ____ / 40

Help Mouse run to a hole before Cat wakes up. Subtract and write the answers. Then begin at START and color all the boxes with answers that are even numbers.

START →

| | | | | | |
|---|---|---|---|---|---|
| START | A. 289 − 143 | 856 − 198 | 707 − 158 | 857 − 812 | 709 − 102 |
| B. 645 − 272 | 932 − 285 | 302 − 146 | 682 − 381 | 529 − 120 | 685 − 192 |
| C. 749 − 334 | 456 − 109 | 582 − 498 | 838 − 770 | 511 − 165 | 999 − 283 |
| D. 566 − 233 | 889 − 266 | 631 − 328 | 458 − 291 | 953 − 776 | 804 − 128 |
| E. 880 − 449 | 787 − 184 | 628 − 493 | 489 − 72 | 809 − 139 | 458 − 228 |
| F. 250 − 89 | 179 − 126 | 581 − 126 | 818 − 191 | 832 − 678 | 501 − 178 |
| G. 493 − 256 | 357 − 108 | 701 − 204 | 510 − 99 | 849 − 101 | |

**Brainwork!** Write a word problem to match one of the problems above.

Name ____________________ Skill: Three-digit subtraction— with/without regrouping

# Which Pail?

Score ____
30

Write the answers. Then color the pail with the greatest answer to find which pail the calf kicked over.

| | | | | | | |
|---|---|---|---|---|---|---|
| A. | 901 − 142 | 898 − 423 | 602 − 49 | 604 − 236 | 783 − 610 | 800 − 446 |
| B. | 805 − 447 | 905 − 109 | 500 − 288 | 703 − 177 | 406 − 208 | 202 − 145 |
| C. | 700 − 219 | 402 − 88 | 906 − 597 | 904 − 207 | 600 − 231 | 703 − 114 |
| D. | 400 − 364 | 746 − 601 | 203 − 56 | 900 − 199 | 503 − 408 | 408 − 209 |
| E. | 907 − 718 | 603 − 225 | 802 − 156 | 406 − 139 | 900 − 675 | 805 − 366 |

**Brainwork!** Create a subtraction problem that has an answer greater than the one on the pail you colored.

Name ______________________ Skill: Subtracting money—with/without regrouping

# Money Matters

Score ____ / 40

Write the answers. Remember to write the decimals and the dollar signs.

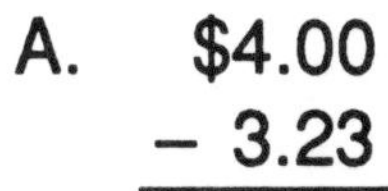

| | | | | | | |
|---|---|---|---|---|---|---|
| A. | \$4.00 − 3.23 | \$4.25 − 2.07 | \$5.43 − 2.72 | \$3.59 − 1.26 | | |
| B. | \$9.50 − 6.20 | \$.95 − .42 | \$7.76 − 1.98 | \$8.00 − 7.06 | \$10.00 − 5.50 | \$6.40 − .39 |
| C. | \$8.88 − 1.27 | \$5.42 − 1.30 | \$.88 − .16 | \$5.00 − 2.25 | \$8.62 − 1.59 | \$9.64 − 2.74 |
| D. | \$.70 − .20 | \$.89 − .43 | \$5.00 − 3.00 | \$2.53 − 1.99 | \$7.86 − 5.95 | \$6.30 − 5.17 |
| E. | \$7.51 − 2.41 | \$1.40 − .70 | \$3.80 − .62 | \$5.17 − 1.66 | \$9.08 − .99 | \$3.12 − .48 |
| F. | \$8.73 − 1.65 | \$.85 − .13 | \$8.25 − 2.64 | \$18.00 − 9.00 | \$7.00 − 2.77 | \$9.44 − 6.66 |
| G. | \$9.68 − 1.92 | \$8.40 − 2.15 | \$8.00 − 5.07 | \$1.10 − .60 | \$8.20 − 3.33 | \$12.00 − 7.00 |

**Brainwork!** Write a subtraction word problem about money. Solve it.

Name ______________________________ Skill: Four-digit subtraction—with/without regrouping

# Coiled for Math

Score ____ / 35

Subtract and write the answers.

| | | | | | |
|---|---|---|---|---|---|
| A. 8,283 − 4,145 | 6,660 − 4,190 | 3,382 − 1,179 | 7,252 − 1,718 | 8,619 − 2,315 | 4,782 − 1,732 |
| B. 3,284 − 2,695 | 6,986 − 3,047 | 1,434 − 126 | 8,188 − 6,589 | 2,318 − 1,094 | 8,964 − 1,151 |
| C. 6,494 − 3,077 | 8,545 − 3,180 | 8,701 − 8,034 | 7,040 − 1,190 | 7,365 − 5,278 | 7,782 − 1,053 |
| D. 8,643 − 2,489 | 5,913 − 2,907 | 4,915 − 2,163 | 8,987 − 2,323 | 8,162 − 2,596 | 3,456 − 1,111 |
| E. 4,303 − 1,884 | 5,421 − 2,187 | 9,682 − 3,335 | 9,481 − 9,003 | 9,949 − 2,336 | 4,652 − 1,572 |
| F. 8,919 − 3,222 | 9,413 − 7,625 | 5,556 − 1,118 | 8,403 − 1,126 | 9,829 − 4,647 | |

**Brainwork!** Choose one of the four-digit numbers above that begin with 7, 8, or 9. Subtract this year's date from it.

Name ____________________ Skill: Column addition

# Underwater Addition

Score ____ / 30

Add and write the answers.

| | | | | | |
|---|---|---|---|---|---|
| A. | 2<br>4<br>+ 6 | 8<br>6<br>+ 4 | 2<br>5<br>+ 2 | 3<br>9<br>+ 6 | 2<br>5<br>+ 6 |
| B. | 3<br>7<br>+ 9 | 9<br>2<br>+ 3 | 8<br>6<br>+ 0 | 1<br>8<br>+ 8 | 8<br>4<br>+ 7 |
| C. | 1<br>8<br>+ 2 | 5<br>5<br>+ 2 | 7<br>4<br>+ 5 | 4<br>5<br>+ 4 | 4<br>4<br>+ 7 |
| D. | 7<br>1<br>+ 4 | 9<br>9<br>+ 2 | 2<br>3<br>+ 8 | 6<br>1<br>+ 7 | 4<br>3<br>+ 6 |
| E. | 5<br>5<br>+ 8 | 3<br>6<br>+ 3 | 4<br>7<br>+ 4 | 0<br>8<br>+ 2 | 5<br>4<br>+ 3 |
| F. | 7<br>0<br>9<br>+ 4 | 4<br>5<br>4<br>+ 6 | 2<br>5<br>1<br>+ 6 | 5<br>0<br>2<br>+ 9 | 7<br>2<br>6<br>+ 3 |

**Brainwork!** Write the ages of five friends in a column. Add the ages.

Name ______________________ Skill: Column addition—two- and three-digit numbers

# Chimp Challenge

Write the answers.

Score ____ / 30

| | | | | | | |
|---|---|---|---|---|---|---|
| A. | 74<br>213<br>+ 112 | 324<br>210<br>+ 707 | 316<br>550<br>+ 22 | 760<br>432<br>+ 24 | 49<br>72<br>+ 116 | 601<br>126<br>+ 50 |
| B. | 217<br>128<br>+ 150 | 208<br>194<br>+ 334 | 112<br>113<br>+ 511 | 202<br>322<br>+ 62 | 201<br>242<br>+ 501 | 660<br>90<br>+ 907 |
| C. | 522<br>127<br>+ 227 | 26<br>448<br>+ 121 | 51<br>153<br>+ 45 | 666<br>121<br>+ 401 | 140<br>220<br>+ 101 | 55<br>346<br>+ 123 |
| D. | 221<br>231<br>+ 262 | 146<br>140<br>+ 190 | 128<br>428<br>+ 481 | 714<br>281<br>+ 102 | 227<br>52<br>+ 311 | 84<br>312<br>+ 302 |
| E. | 22<br>622<br>+ 132 | 837<br>262<br>+ 231 | 242<br>285<br>+ 51 | 454<br>14<br>+ 404 | 102<br>102<br>+ 141 | 346<br>12<br>+ 491 |

**Brainwork!** Write three numbers whose sum is 1,000.

Name ______________________________ Skill: Addition 11-18

Write the number sentence and answer.

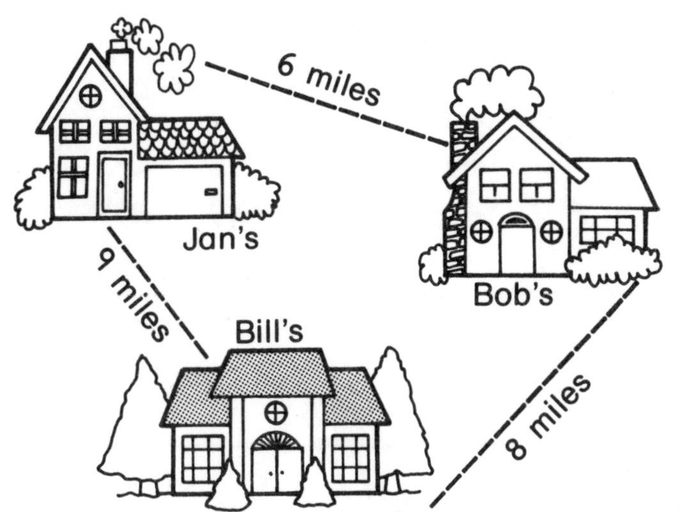


1. Bill rode to Bob's house and then to Jan's. How many miles did he ride in all?

8+6=14

Bill rode 14 miles.

2. Jan went to Bill's house and then to Bob's. How many miles did she ride all together?

______________________________

Jan rode ______ miles.

3. If Bob rides to Jan's house and then to Bill's, how far will he go?

______________________________

Bob would go ______ miles.

4. How many miles will Bill go if he rides to Jan's house and back home again?

______________________________

Bill will go ______ miles.

5. How far is it for Bob to ride to Jan's house, go back home, and then ride to Bill's?

______________________________

It is ______ miles.

Name ______________________ Skill: Subtraction 11-18

Write the number sentence and answer.

1. Tom had 14 balloons. Bill popped 5 of them. How many were left?

14-5=9

Tom had 9 balloons left.

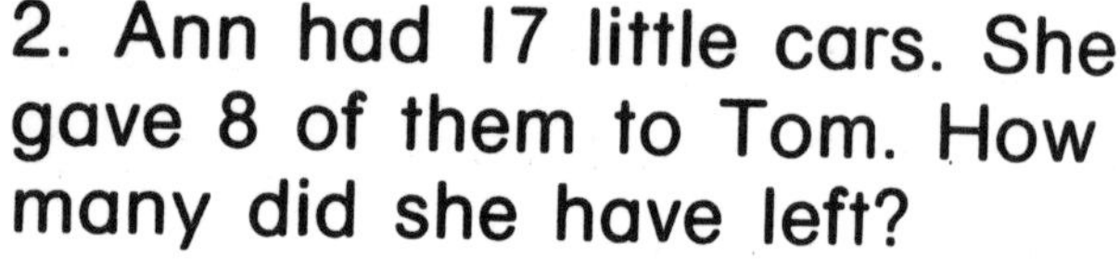

2. Ann had 17 little cars. She gave 8 of them to Tom. How many did she have left?

______________________

Ann had ______ cars left.

3. Mike had 16 play snakes. His mother threw 8 of them away. How many does he have now?

______________________

Mike has ______ snakes now.

4. Nancy had 13 yo-yos. Her brother broke 6 of them. How many does she have?

______________________

Nancy has ______ yo-yos now.

5. John had 11 marbles. He lost 9 of them. How many does he have now?

______________________

John has ______ marbles now.

Name ______________________________ Skill: Addition and Subtraction 11-18

Write the number sentence and answer.

1. Sue bought a donut and a cookie. How much did she spend?

______________________________

Sue spent ______ cents.

2. Bill had 13¢. He bought a cupcake. How much did he have left?

______________________________

Bill had ______ cents left.

3. Linda had 12¢. She bought milk. How much money does she have now?

______________________________

Linda has ______ cents.

4. Jack bought a donut, a cupcake and a cookie. How much did he spend in all?

______________________________

Jack spent ______ cents.

5. Ann had 11¢. She bought a cupcake. How much does she have left?

______________________________

Ann has ______ cents left.

Write the number sentence and answer.

1. Ann is 11 years old. Her sister is 3. How much older is Ann than her sister?

11-3=8

8 years older.

2. John is 16 years old. Bill is 7. How much older is John than Bill?

______________________

_____ years older.

3. Jim is 11 years old. Frank is 9. How much younger is Frank than Jim?

______________________

_____ years younger.

4. If Mike is 14 and Nancy is 9, how much older is Mike than Nancy?

______________________

_____ years older.

5. Jeff, who is 13 years old, has a brother who is 6. How much younger is Jeff's brother?

______________________

_____ years younger.

Name ______________________ Skill: 2 digit addition

Write the number sentence and answer.

| | FIRST HALF | SECOND HALF |
|---|---|---|
| JONES | 14 | 25 |
| BROWN | 23 | 14 |
| SMITH | 12 | 30 |

1. How many points did Brown make in the game?

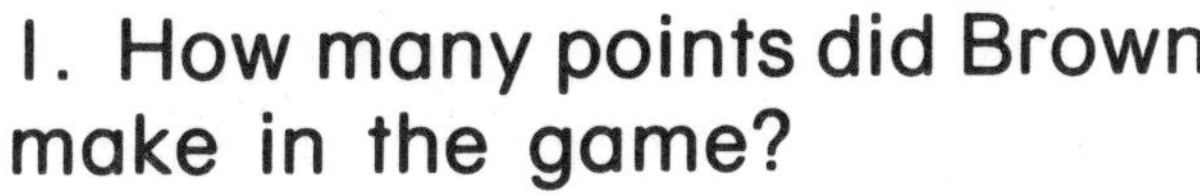

23+14=37

Brown made 37 points.

2. In the first half, how many points did Jones and Smith make in all?

______________________

They made ______ points.

3. How many points did Jones make all together?

______________________

Jones made ______ points.

4. How many points did Smith make in the game?

______________________

Smith made ______ points.

5. In the second half, how many points did Brown and Smith make between them?

______________________

They made ______ points.

Name ______________________________ Skill: 2 digit subtraction

Write the number sentence and answer.

1. Mary had 26 goldfish. The cat ate 12. How many does Mary have now?

26-12=14
______________________________

Mary has __14__ goldfish.

2. John caught 38 lizards. 15 of them got away. How many lizards are left?

______________________________

John has ______ lizards left.

3. Sue had 14 cats. She gave 12 of them to a friend. How many cats does Sue have now?

______________________________

Sue has ______ cats now.

4. Jim had 29 baby hamsters. He gave 14 to a pet shop. How many does he have left?

______________________________

Jim has ______ hamsters left.

5. Bill had 45 rabbits. He sold 25 of them. How many does he have now?

______________________________

Bill has ______ rabbits now.

Name ______________________ Skill: 2 digit regrouping-comparisons

Write the number sentence and answer.

1. How many more miles is it to Back Again than to Forever?

32-24=8

It is 8 more miles.

2. How much farther is it to go to Hurrah than to Goodbye City?

______________________

It is ______ miles farther.

3. **Bill wants to go to Funny Town. John wants to go to Goodbye City. How many less miles is it for John?**

______________________

It is ______ miles more.

4. Ann went to Goodbye City and Nancy went to Forever. How many less miles did Ann travel?

______________________

Ann traveled ______ miles less.

5. How much closer is Back Again than Hurrah?

______________________

It is ______ miles closer.

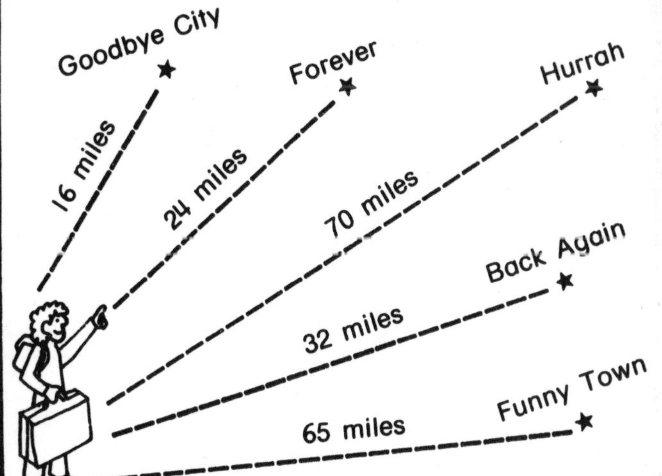

Name ______________________

Skill: 2 digit addition and subtraction-regrouping

Write the number sentence and answer.

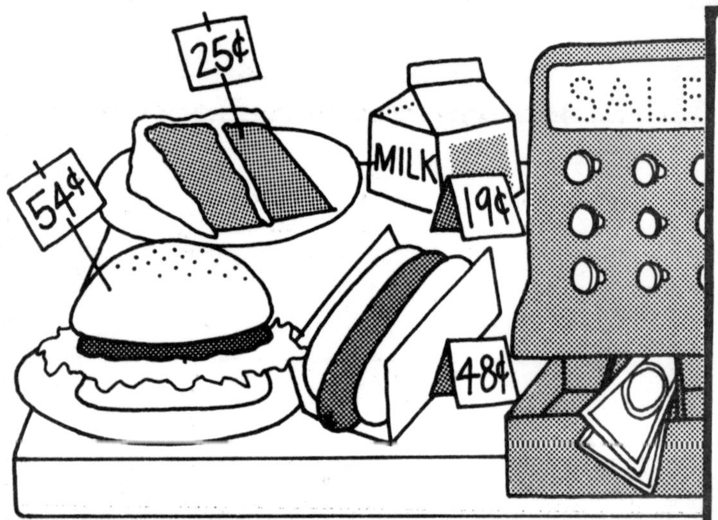


1. Frank bought a hamburger and a glass of milk. How much did he spend?

______________________

Frank spent ______¢.

2. Jan wanted a hot dog and milk. How much money did she need?

______________________

Jan needed ______¢.

3. Bill had 52¢. He bought a piece of cake. How much did he have left?

______________________

Bill had ______¢ left.

4. John had 43¢. He bought a glass of milk. How much money did he have then?

______________________

John had ______¢ then.

5. If Sue buys cake and milk, how much will she pay?

______________________

Sue will pay ______¢.

Name ____________________ Skill: Multiplying by 2

| 2 | 4 | 6 | 8 | 10 |
|---|---|---|---|---|
| orange | black | yellow | green | blue |

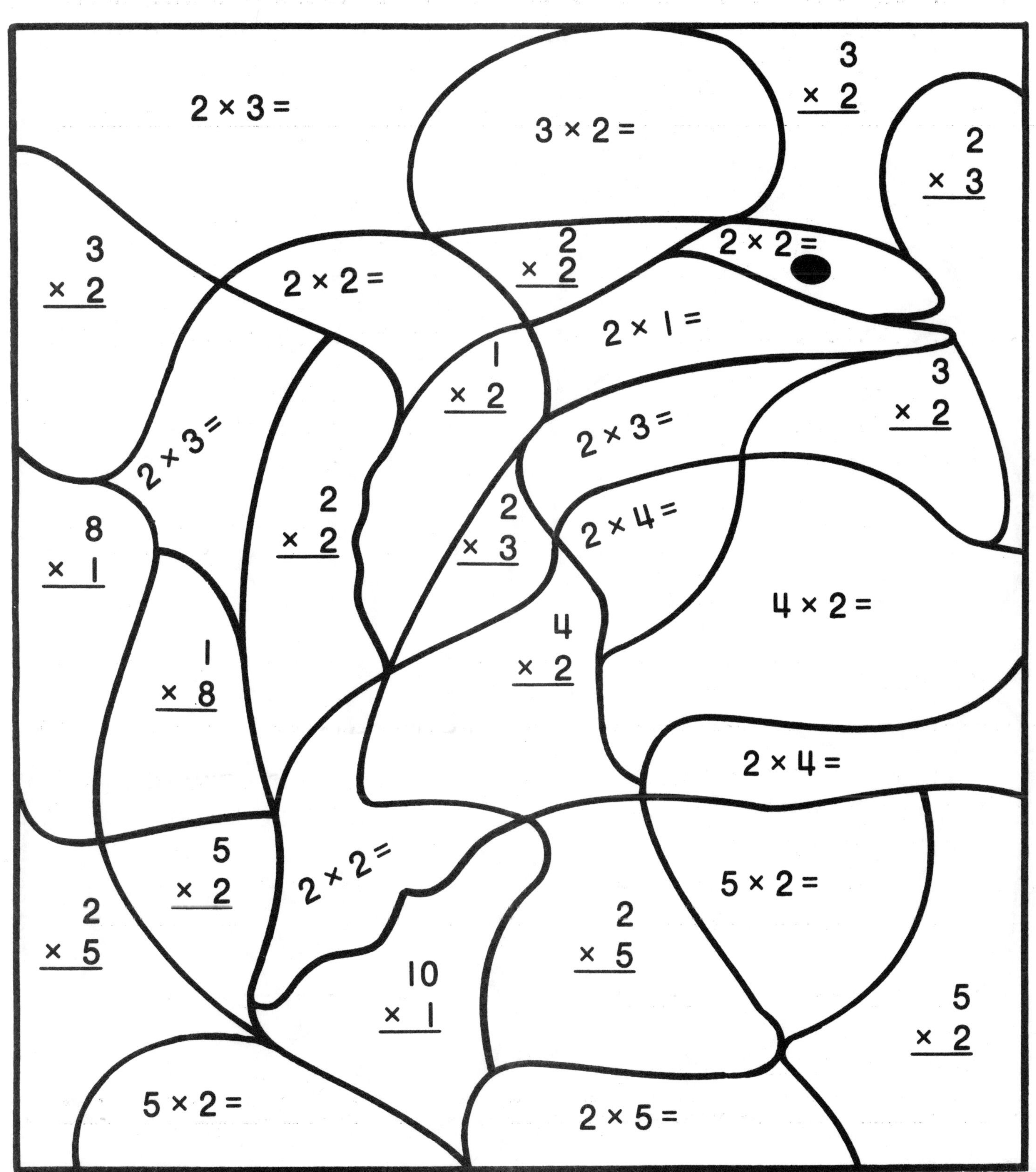

Name ______________________________ Skill: Multiplying by 2

| 12 | 14 | 16 | 18 | 20 |
|---|---|---|---|---|
| red | orange | yellow | green | blue |

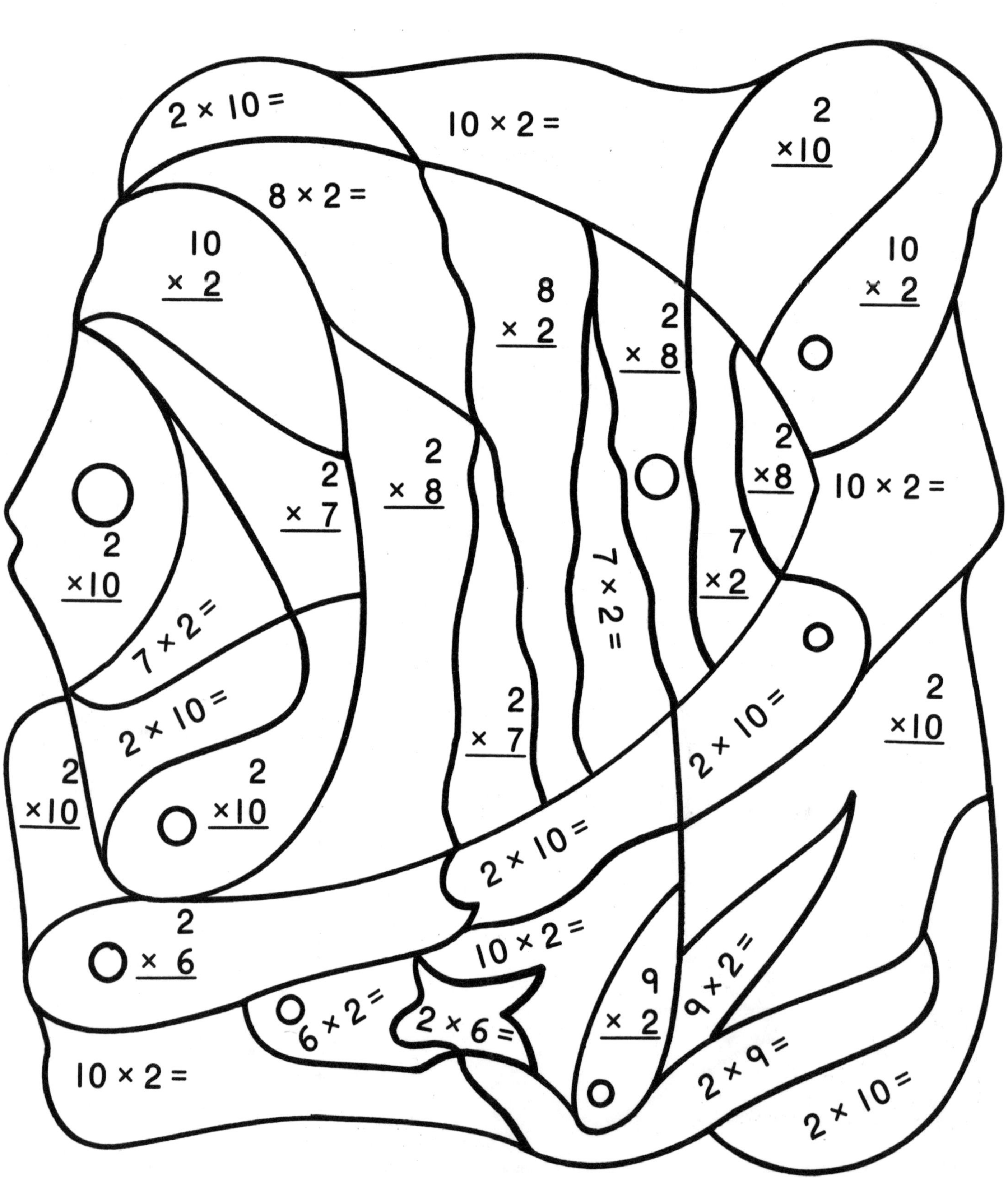

Name ______________________________ Skill: Multiplying by 3

| 3 | 6 | 9 | 12 | 15 |
|---|---|---|---|---|
| brown | orange | red | green | blue |

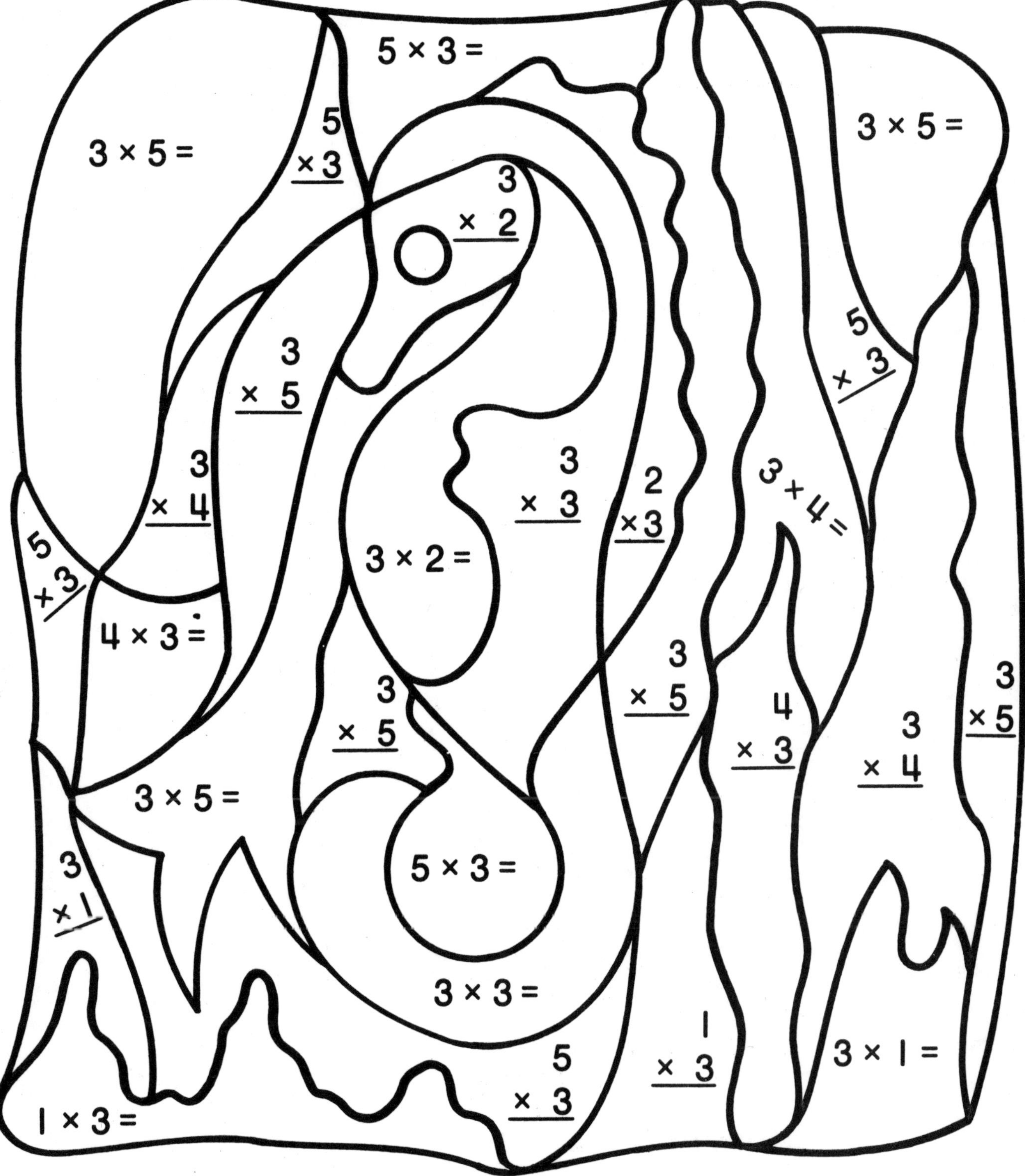

Name ______________________________ Skill: Multiplying by 3

| 18 | 21 | 24 | 27 | 30 |
|---|---|---|---|---|
| black | orange | blue | red | yellow |

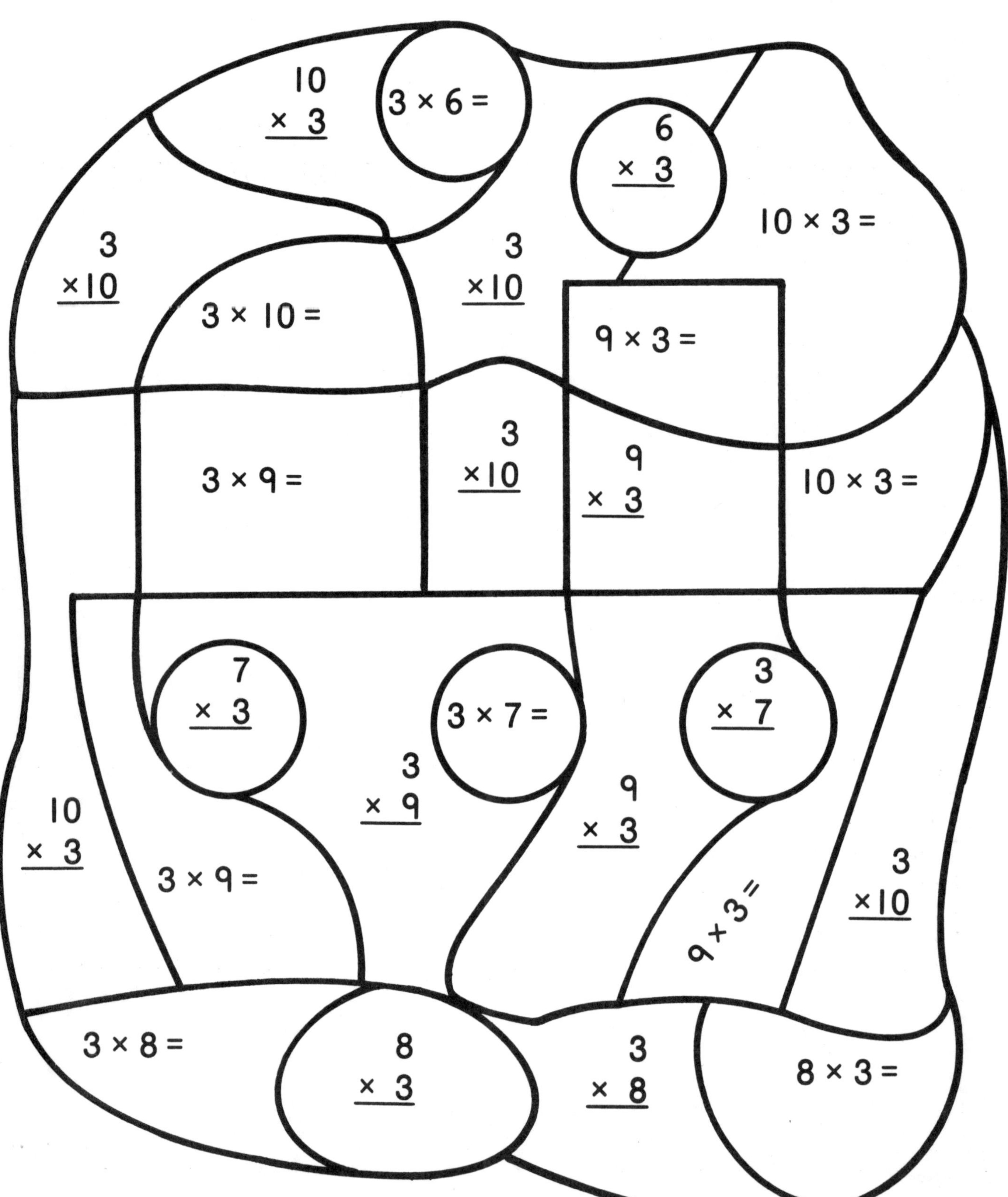

Name ______________________________ Skill: Multiplying by 4

| 4 | 8 | 12 | 16 | 20 |
|---|---|---|---|---|
| black | red | green | blue | yellow |

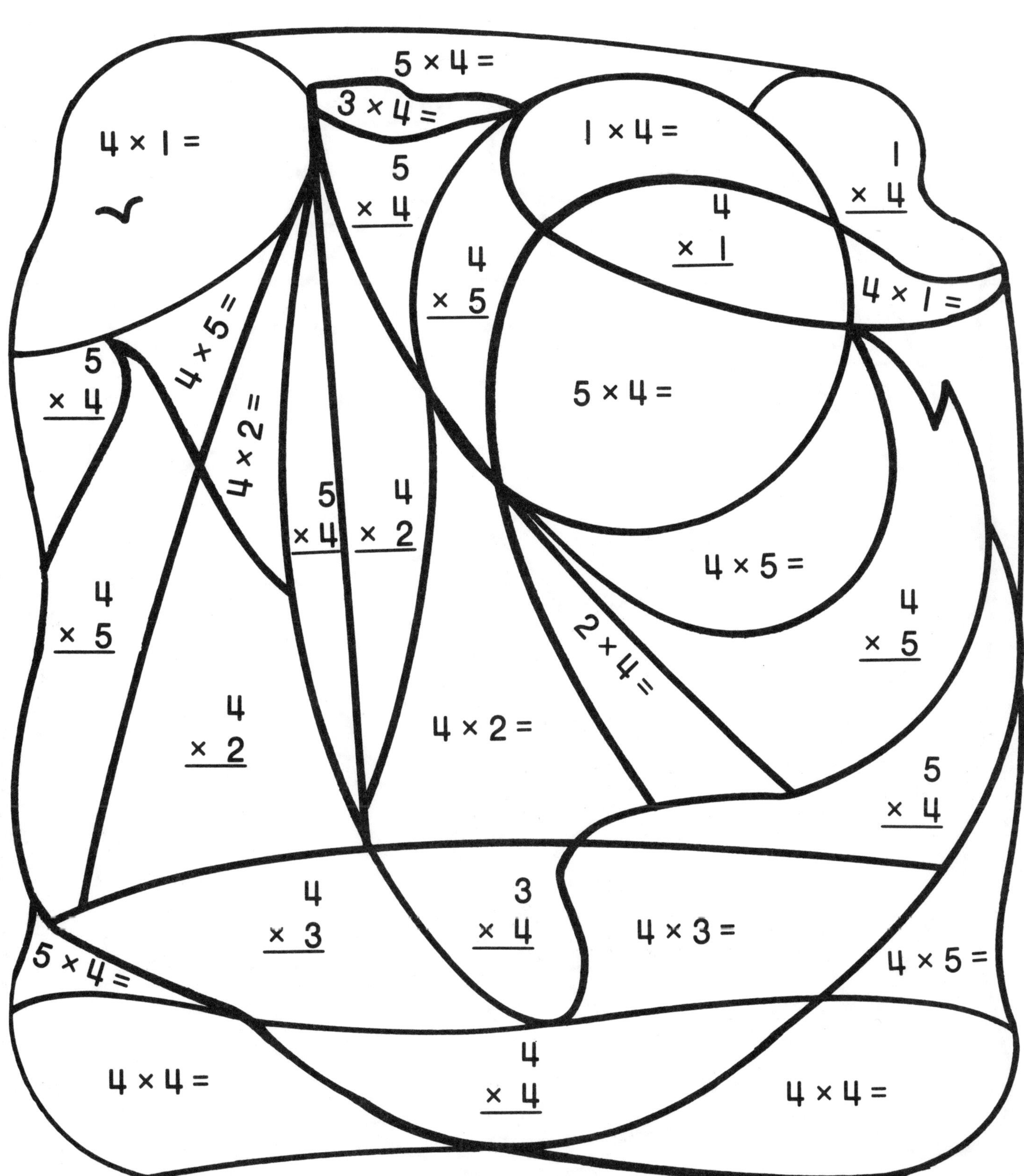

Name ______________________________ Skill: Multiplying by 4

| 24 | 28 | 32 | 36 | 40 |
|---|---|---|---|---|
| orange | yellow | green | blue | red |

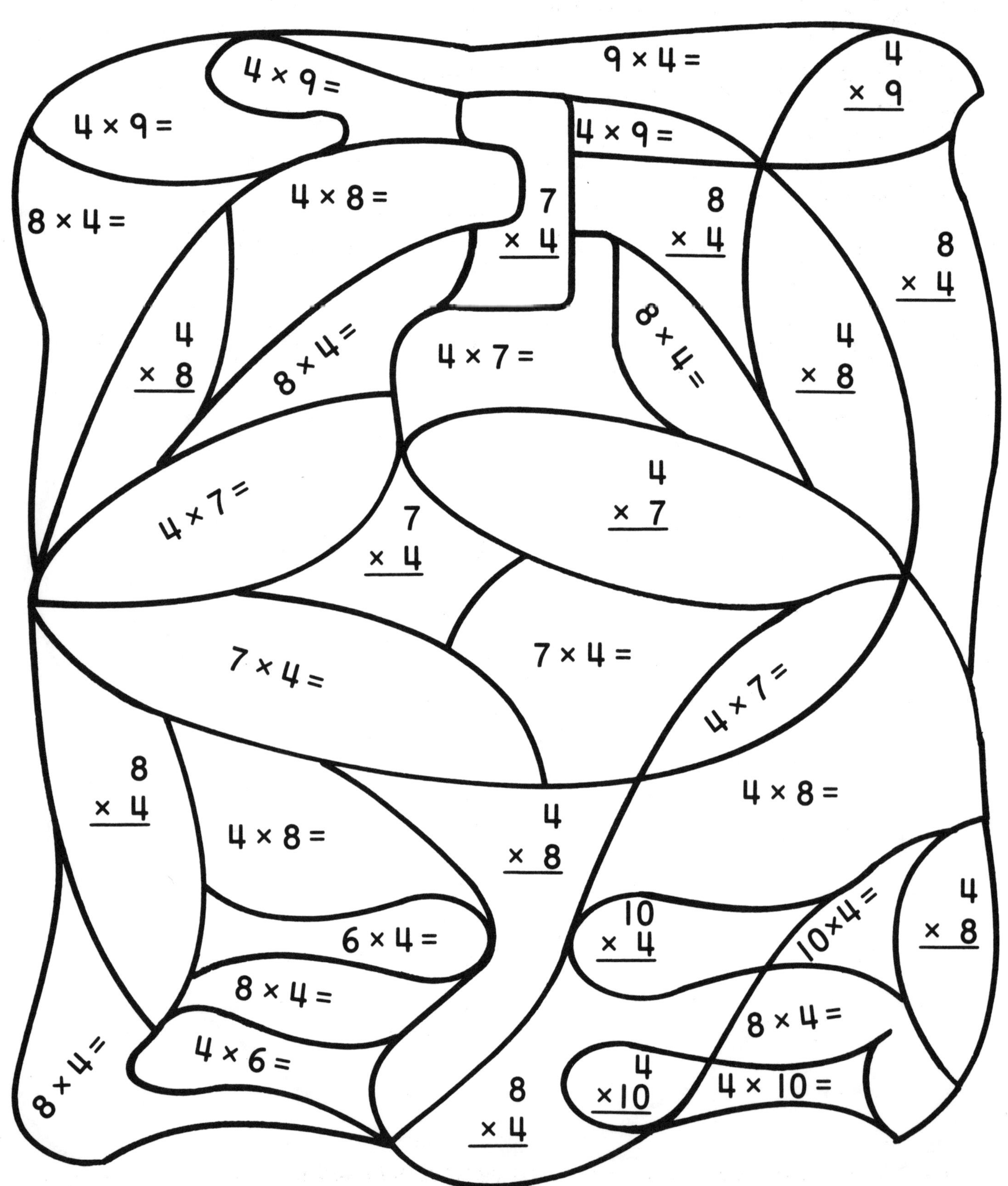

# A Rocket Riddle

How did the rocket lose its job?

To find out, first solve each problem. Then write the letter of the problem on the line above its matching answer.

___ ___    ___ ___ ___    ___ ___ ___ ___ ___

16 9    20 0 9    14 16 32 25 10

| | | | | |
|---|---|---|---|---|
| (B) $3 \times 4$ | (A) $2 \times 2$ | (K) $5 \times 1$ | (T) $3 \times 3$ | |
| (G) $4 \times 5$ | (M) $2 \times 4$ | (D) $5 \times 2$ | (E) $5 \times 5$ | (O) $0 \times 2$ |
| (L) $3 \times 2$ | (I) $4 \times 4$ | (N) $2 \times 9$ | (F) $2 \times 7$ | (C) $3 \times 5$ |
| (S) $4 \times 6$ | (B) $1 \times 7$ | (R) $4 \times 8$ | (Y) $5 \times 6$ | (F) $5 \times 7$ |

**Try This!** Write problems whose answers would spell the word *ROCKET.*

Name



# Thirsty?

What's a robot's favorite drink? To find its picture, solve each division problem. Color spaces with answers 1, 3, or 5 **green** and spaces with answers 2 or 4 **yellow**.

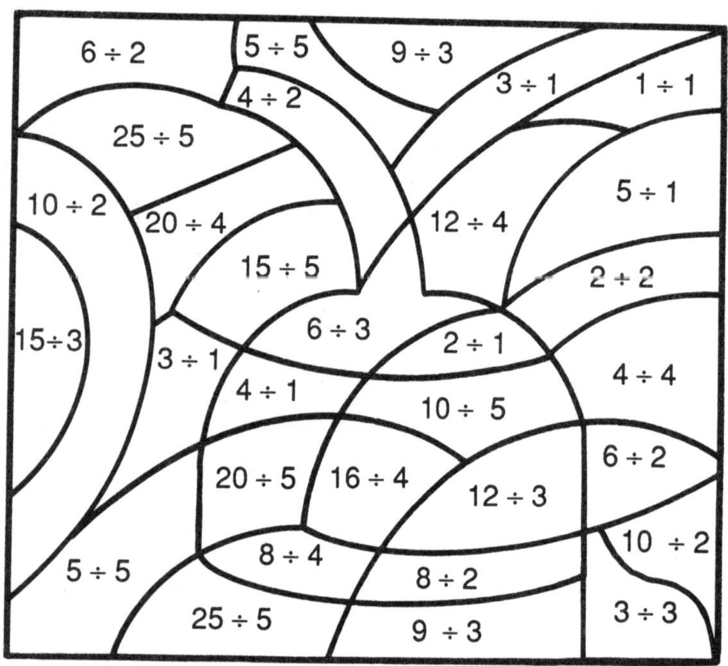

To find the drink's name, color spaces with answers 1, 3, or 5 **blue** and spaces with answers 2 or 4 **red**.

25 ÷ 5
5 ÷ 5
3 ÷ 3
20 ÷ 4
9 ÷ 3
20 ÷ 5
3 ÷ 1
8 ÷ 2
15 ÷ 3
6 ÷ 2
15 ÷ 5
10 ÷ 5
10 ÷ 2
4 ÷ 4
10 ÷ 2
9 ÷ 3
25 ÷ 5
16 ÷ 4
4 ÷ 1
12 ÷ 3
6 ÷ 2
12 ÷ 4
15 ÷ 3
5 ÷ 1
15 ÷ 3

**Try This!** You can write a division problem two different ways. For example 25 ÷ 5 or $5\overline{)25}$. Write three other division facts two different ways.

# Let's Add

| | | | | | | | |
|---|---|---|---|---|---|---|---|
| 1. 6 + 4 | 2. 2 + 3 | 3. 7 + 1 | 4. 9 + 2 | 5. 5 + 5 | 6. 2 + 6 | 7. 4 + 7 | 8. 5 + 8 |
| 9. 9 + 4 | 10. 5 + 1 | 11. 6 + 3 | 12. 8 + 8 | 13. 4 + 1 | 14. 7 + 5 | 15. 8 + 6 | 16. 3 + 3 |
| 17. 7 + 7 | 18. 2 + 8 | 19. 7 + 3 | 20. 6 + 5 | 21. 4 + 0 | 22. 1 + 8 | 23. 3 + 5 | 24. 9 + 8 |
| 25. 4 + 4 | 26. 3 + 6 | 27. 10 + 2 | 28. 5 + 9 | 29. 2 + 2 | 30. 8 + 7 | 31. 3 + 9 | 32. 3 + 8 |
| 33. 7 + 9 | 34. 9 + 9 | 35. 4 + 3 | 36. 6 + 7 | | | | |

I got ____ right out of 36 in ____ minutes.

ADDITRON

Name ____________________ Skill: Sums to 18

# Addition Facts Test

Score ____ / 100

Write the answers.

| | | | | | |
|---|---|---|---|---|---|
| A. | 8 + 2 = ____ | 9 + 4 = ____ | 3 + 8 = ____ | 6 + 6 = ____ | 1 + 4 = ____ |
| B. | 5 + 7 = ____ | 2 + 8 = ____ | 9 + 3 = ____ | 0 + 6 = ____ | 3 + 0 = ____ |
| C. | 1 + 0 = ____ | 6 + 7 = ____ | 0 + 5 = ____ | 6 + 3 = ____ | 4 + 1 = ____ |
| D. | 7 + 3 = ____ | 3 + 1 = ____ | 4 + 9 = ____ | 2 + 3 = ____ | 8 + 3 = ____ |
| E. | 5 + 0 = ____ | 8 + 9 = ____ | 4 + 0 = ____ | 1 + 6 = ____ | 2 + 0 = ____ |
| F. | 9 + 1 = ____ | 0 + 0 = ____ | 2 + 7 = ____ | 5 + 9 = ____ | 4 + 8 = ____ |
| G. | 2 + 2 = ____ | 6 + 4 = ____ | 5 + 1 = ____ | 9 + 3 = ____ | 9 + 6 = ____ |
| H. | 6 + 8 = ____ | 1 + 7 = ____ | 7 + 2 = ____ | 1 + 1 = ____ | 3 + 2 = ____ |
| I. | 9 + 0 = ____ | 3 + 9 = ____ | 1 + 5 = ____ | 5 + 6 = ____ | 0 + 2 = ____ |
| J. | 2 + 4 = ____ | 8 + 7 = ____ | 6 + 2 = ____ | 5 + 8 = ____ | 7 + 5 = ____ |
| K. | 8 + 0 = ____ | 0 + 9 = ____ | 3 + 3 = ____ | 4 + 2 = ____ | 9 + 2 = ____ |
| L. | 6 + 1 = ____ | 8 + 1 = ____ | 0 + 7 = ____ | 7 + 9 = ____ | 3 + 7 = ____ |
| M. | 7 + 8 = ____ | 3 + 4 = ____ | 6 + 0 = ____ | 5 + 2 = ____ | 1 + 9 = ____ |
| N. | 2 + 1 = ____ | 7 + 1 = ____ | 1 + 2 = ____ | 0 + 1 = ____ | 4 + 7 = ____ |
| O. | 6 + 5 = ____ | 4 + 3 = ____ | 8 + 4 = ____ | 4 + 6 = ____ | 0 + 8 = ____ |
| P. | 3 + 5 = ____ | 9 + 7 = ____ | 9 + 8 = ____ | 1 + 3 = ____ | 7 + 0 = ____ |
| Q. | 7 + 7 = ____ | 0 + 3 = ____ | 5 + 4 = ____ | 3 + 6 = ____ | 6 + 9 = ____ |
| R. | 2 + 9 = ____ | 8 + 8 = ____ | 2 + 5 = ____ | 4 + 4 = ____ | 2 + 6 = ____ |
| S. | 8 + 6 = ____ | 5 + 3 = ____ | 7 + 4 = ____ | 1 + 8 = ____ | 8 + 5 = ____ |
| T. | 0 + 4 = ____ | 9 + 9 = ____ | 5 + 5 = ____ | 7 + 6 = ____ | 4 + 5 = ____ |

# Let's Subtract

| 1. 12 − 3 | 2. 8 − 2 | 3. 14 − 5 | 4. 9 − 4 | 5. 10 − 2 | 6. 7 − 5 | 7. 13 − 4 | 8. 9 − 3 |
|---|---|---|---|---|---|---|---|
| 9. 3 − 2 | 10. 16 − 7 | 11. 8 − 5 | 12. 15 − 7 | 13. 6 − 3 | 14. 17 − 8 | 15. 13 − 6 | 16. 5 − 3 |
| 17. 5 − 1 | 18. 11 − 2 | 19. 12 − 6 | 20. 18 − 9 | 21. 13 − 5 | 22. 7 − 2 | 23. 8 − 4 | 24. 12 − 5 |
| 25. 11 − 6 | 26. 12 − 4 | 27. 10 − 3 | 28. 9 − 1 | 29. 11 − 7 | 30. 15 − 6 | 31. 9 − 5 | 32. 12 − 7 |
| 33. 7 − 4 | 34. 16 − 8 | 35. 6 − 2 | 36. 14 − 6 | | | | |

I got ____ right out of 36 in ____ minutes.

SUBTRACTRON

Name ________________ Skill: Subtracting from 18 or less

# Subtraction Facts Test

Score ____ / 100

Write the answers.

| | | | | | |
|---|---|---|---|---|---|
| A. | 6 – 0 = ____ | 12 – 6 = ____ | 13 – 7 = ____ | 10 – 0 = ____ | 9 – 0 = ____ |
| B. | 5 – 5 = ____ | 10 – 7 = ____ | 8 – 5 = ____ | 11 – 6 = ____ | 2 – 2 = ____ |
| C. | 2 – 0 = ____ | 8 – 0 = ____ | 11 – 9 = ____ | 3 – 0 = ____ | 15 – 8 = ____ |
| D. | 1 – 0 = ____ | 16 – 9 = ____ | 9 – 8 = ____ | 8 – 3 = ____ | 5 – 4 = ____ |
| E. | 14 – 9 = ____ | 8 – 4 = ____ | 13 – 5 = ____ | 10 – 1 = ____ | 8 – 2 = ____ |
| F. | 3 – 1 = ____ | 12 – 8 = ____ | 10 – 9 = ____ | 13 – 6 = ____ | 11 – 2 = ____ |
| G. | 10 – 6 = ____ | 8 – 1 = ____ | 9 – 1 = ____ | 8 – 6 = ____ | 16 – 7 = ____ |
| H. | 1 – 1 = ____ | 14 – 5 = ____ | 10 – 2 = ____ | 7 – 5 = ____ | 7 – 2 = ____ |
| I. | 12 – 9 = ____ | 9 – 7 = ____ | 15 – 7 = ____ | 7 – 1 = ____ | 9 – 9 = ____ |
| J. | 6 – 3 = ____ | 7 – 7 = ____ | 12 – 3 = ____ | 11 – 8 = ____ | 7 – 6 = ____ |
| K. | 5 – 3 = ____ | 10 – 3 = ____ | 7 – 4 = ____ | 18 – 9 = ____ | 10 – 5 = ____ |
| L. | 15 – 6 = ____ | 17 – 9 = ____ | 9 – 2 = ____ | 10 – 8 = ____ | 13 – 9 = ____ |
| M. | 6 – 2 = ____ | 11 – 3 = ____ | 12 – 5 = ____ | 6 – 4 = ____ | 7 – 3 = ____ |
| N. | 11 – 7 = ____ | 6 – 5 = ____ | 8 – 7 = ____ | 9 – 3 = ____ | 17 – 8 = ____ |
| O. | 4 – 3 = ____ | 14 – 7 = ____ | 9 – 4 = ____ | 13 – 8 = ____ | 6 – 1 = ____ |
| P. | 10 – 4 = ____ | 3 – 2 = ____ | 11 – 4 = ____ | 12 – 4 = ____ | 14 – 6 = ____ |
| Q. | 16 – 8 = ____ | 11 – 5 = ____ | 4 – 4 = ____ | 5 – 0 = ____ | 7 – 0 = ____ |
| R. | 3 – 3 = ____ | 5 – 1 = ____ | 6 – 6 = ____ | 9 – 6 = ____ | 15 – 9 = ____ |
| S. | 4 – 0 = ____ | 13 – 4 = ____ | 4 – 2 = ____ | 2 – 1 = ____ | 5 – 2 = ____ |
| T. | 8 – 8 = ____ | 4 – 1 = ____ | 9 – 5 = ____ | 12 – 7 = ____ | 14 – 8 = ____ |

# Let's Review the Facts

Write the sums . . .

or differences.

**A.**

| 2 | 9 | 4 |
|---|---|---|
| + 8 | − 5 | + 4 |

**B.**

| 3 | 10 | 2 | 8 | 1 |
|---|---|---|---|---|
| + 6 | − 3 | + 5 | − 5 | + 9 |

**C.**

| 7 | 5 | 6 | 4 | 5 |
|---|---|---|---|---|
| + 3 | − 3 | + 2 | − 1 | + 4 |

**D.** 7 − 3 = ______ 3 + 4 = ______ 3 − 1 = ______

**E.** 1 + 2 = ______ 8 − 2 = ______ 0 + 8 = ______

**F.** 10 − 8 = ______ 5 + 5 = ______ 9 − 3 = ______

**G.** 4 + 6 = ______ 6 − 4 = ______ 2 + 4 = ______

**H.** 9 − 6 = ______ 7 + 2 = ______ 2 − 2 = ______

**Try This!** Do you find it easier to add or subtract? Write to explain why.

Name



# Add and Subtract to 10

| 1. | 2. | 3. | 4. | 5. | 6. | 7. | 8. |
|---|---|---|---|---|---|---|---|
| 7 − 5 | 4 + 6 | 3 + 3 | 10 − 3 | 7 − 6 | 0 + 9 | 7 + 2 | 9 − 4 |
| **9.** | **10.** | **11.** | **12.** | **13.** | **14.** | **15.** | **16.** |
| 5 + 3 | 4 − 2 | 5 + 5 | 2 + 6 | 9 − 7 | 8 − 0 | 5 + 4 | 6 − 4 |
| **17.** | **18.** | **19.** | **20.** | **21.** | **22.** | **23.** | **24.** |
| 10 − 8 | 4 + 4 | 8 − 5 | 3 + 6 | 2 + 8 | 5 − 3 | 10 − 6 | 1 + 5 |
| **25.** | **26.** | **27.** | **28.** | **29.** | **30.** | **31.** | **32.** |
| 4 + 2 | 9 − 3 | 5 + 2 | 8 − 6 | 7 + 1 | 8 − 2 | 3 + 4 | 10 − 5 |
| **33.** | **34.** | **35.** | **36.** | | | | |
| 9 − 2 | 4 + 4 | 7 − 4 | 3 + 2 | | | | |



I got _____ right out of 36 in _____ minutes.

# Add and Subtract to 18

| | | | | | | | |
|---|---|---|---|---|---|---|---|
| 1. 7 − 5 | 2. 2 + 9 | 3. 13 − 8 | 4. 6 + 6 | 5. 9 − 5 | 6. 5 + 2 | 7. 11 − 9 | 8. 8 + 8 |
| 9. 12 − 4 | 10. 3 + 4 | 11. 17 − 8 | 12. 0 + 6 | 13. 8 − 3 | 14. 10 + 4 | 15. 3 + 5 | 16. 16 − 7 |
| 17. 10 − 7 | 18. 6 + 7 | 19. 8 + 3 | 20. 3 − 1 | 21. 18 − 9 | 22. 7 − 5 | 23. 9 + 6 | 24. 4 − 3 |
| 25. 3 + 7 | 26. 15 − 9 | 27. 4 + 8 | 28. 7 + 9 | 29. 6 − 4 | 30. 8 + 5 | 31. 12 − 3 | 32. 7 + 8 |
| 33. 13 − 7 | 34. 6 + 3 | 35. 5 − 3 | 36. 1 + 8 | | | | |

SUBTRACTRON

I got _____ right out of 36 in _____ minutes.

ADDITRON

Name ______________________________ Skill: Two-digit addition review

# Turtle Sums

Score ____
40

Add.

A.

| 43 | 24 | 6 | 28 |
|---|---|---|---|
| + 17 | + 34 | + 67 | + 51 |

B. 25 + 33 = ____ 44 + 32 = ____ 80 + 17 = ____ 64 + 27 = ____

---

C.

| 38 | 17 | 51 | 47 | 83 |
|---|---|---|---|---|
| + 33 | + 42 | + 19 | + 17 | + 10 |

D. 18 + 37 = ____ 22 + 19 = ____ 31 + 36 = ____ 20 + 20 = ____

---

E.

| 28 | 28 | 55 | 49 | 24 |
|---|---|---|---|---|
| + 45 | + 68 | + 6 | + 49 | + 13 |

F. 29 + 26 = ____ 45 + 32 = ____ 36 + 38 = ____ 24 + 14 = ____

---

G.

| 47 | 18 | 33 | 45 | 61 |
|---|---|---|---|---|
| + 40 | + 39 | + 16 | + 17 | + 18 |

H. 28 + 49 = ____ 23 + 34 = ____ 39 + 4 = ____ 66 + 21 = ____

I.

| 25 | 75 | 78 | 59 | 49 |
|---|---|---|---|---|
| + 23 | + 15 | + 17 | + 37 | + 35 |

Name ______________________ Skill: Two-digit subtraction review

# Prizewinning Pig

Score ____ / 40

Find the path that leads to the prize Petunia won at the fair. First subtract and write the answers. Then color the boxes with odd answers.

| | | | | | |
|---|---|---|---|---|---|
| → START | | 78 − 57 | 94 − 9 | 55 − 17 | 58 − 10 |
| 73 − 19 | 39 − 11 | 67 − 17 | 58 − 33 | 97 − 19 | 62 − 6 |
| 81 − 29 | 45 − 9 | 98 − 22 | 88 − 23 | 70 − 26 | 36 − 18 |
| 42 − 17 | 58 − 41 | 62 − 59 | 96 − 45 | 74 − 16 | 82 − 20 |
| 60 − 15 | 87 − 11 | 57 − 9 | 81 − 17 | 48 − 10 | 61 − 7 |
| 74 − 13 | 36 − 29 | 28 − 13 | 43 − 35 | 74 − 26 | 98 − 46 |
| 84 − 26 | 47 − 31 | 57 − 24 | 99 − 27 | 44 − 18 | 72 − 18 |

**Brainwork!** Write at least three subtraction problems that have 45 as their answer.

Name ______________________________ Skill: Three-digit addition review

# Answers on Ice

Score ____ / 30

Add and write the answers. Then cross off each answer on the iceberg. All answers on the iceberg should be crossed off.

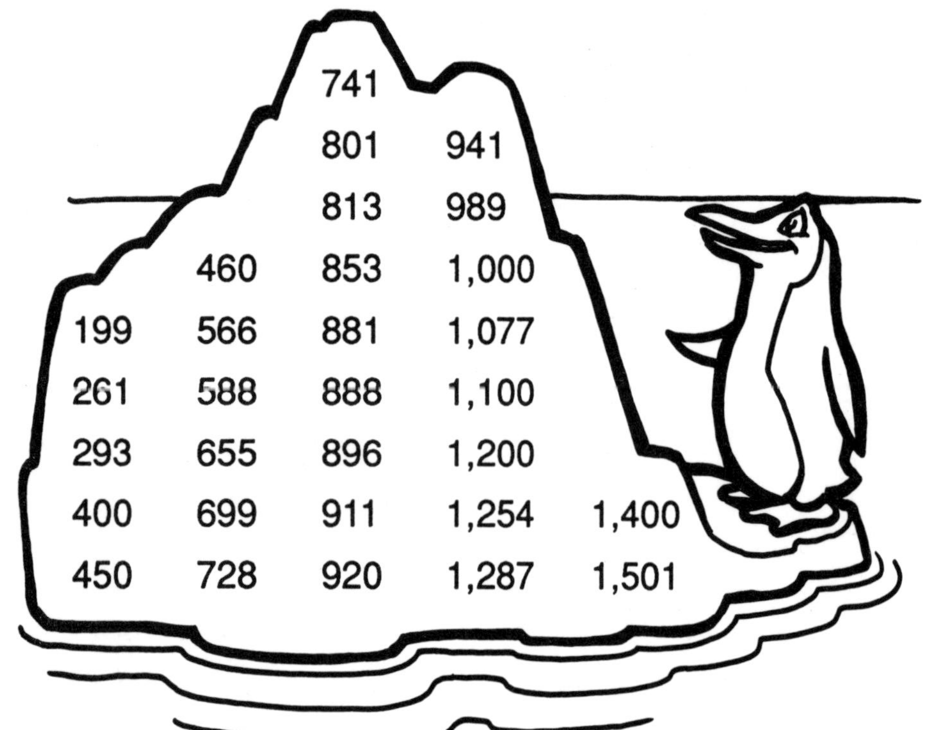


A. 414 + 36 = ______

B. 596 + 300 = ______

C. 800 + 200 = ______

D. 67 + 194 = ______

E. 352 + 461 = ______

F. 862 + 639 = ______

| | | | | | | |
|---|---|---|---|---|---|---|
| G. | 348 + 52 | 88 + 640 | 333 + 656 | 100 + 360 | 809 + 72 | 394 + 305 |
| H. | 626 + 628 | 470 + 271 | 555 + 246 | 437 + 451 | 900 + 20 | 762 + 525 |
| I. | 700 + 400 | 344 + 597 | 285 + 281 | 177 + 676 | 500 + 900 | 574 + 503 |
| J. | 206 + 87 | 348 + 240 | 854 + 57 | 88 + 111 | 162 + 493 | 874 + 326 |

**Brainwork!** Choose a pair of numbers from the iceberg. Write an addition problem with these numbers and solve it.

Name ____________________ Skill: Addition review

# Chipmunk Puzzle Time

Score ____ / 30

Solve each problem. Use the answers to complete the crossword.

**Across**

**A.** $5 + 5 =$ ____

**B.** $3{,}000 + 69 =$ ____

**D.** $50 + 25 =$ ____

**F.** $234 + 624 =$ ____

**H.** $252 + 233 =$ ____

**I.** $7{,}618 + 51 =$ ____

**J.** $12 + 85 =$ ____

**K.** $310 + 409 =$ ____

**M.** $26 + 38 =$ ____

**N.** $437 + 500 =$ ____

**P.** $362 + 343 =$ ____

**Q.** $9 + 8 =$ ____

**S.** $500 + 380 =$ ____

**U.** $8{,}191 + 66 =$ ____

**X.** $100 + 50 + 50 =$ ____

**Down**

**A.** $80 + 30$

**C.** $82 + 16$

**E.** $247 + 299$

**G.** $48 + 6$

**H.** $3{,}550 + 1{,}227$

**I.** $572 + 165$

**L.** $9 + 7$

**N.** $892 + 26$

**O.** $351 + 429$

**P.** $334 + 433$

**R.** $27 + 47$

**T.** $3{,}145 + 5{,}226$

**U.** $45 + 35$

**V.** $6 + 6$

**W.** $400 + 500$

Name ______________________________ 

# Packed for Adventure

Score ____ / 30

Write the answers. Cross off each answer on the camel's pack.

| | | | |
|---|---|---|---|
| | 27 | 32 | 37 |
| | 43 | 47 | 66 |
| | 73 | 75 | 99 |
| 103 | 124 | 207 | 225 |
| 237 | 266 | 325 | 328 |
| 336 | 414 | 422 | 460 |
| 483 | 488 | 522 | |
| 544 | 548 | 579 | |
| 674 | 689 | 879 | |

| | | | | | |
|---|---|---|---|---|---|
| A. | 89 − 42 | 74 − 47 | 656 − 173 | 313 − 76 | 652 − 192 |
| B. | 905 − 26 | 821 − 299 | 376 − 151 | 406 − 81 | 90 − 15 |
| C. | 80 − 37 | 884 − 556 | 506 − 92 | 99 − 26 | 412 − 205 |
| D. | 600 − 21 | 85 − 48 | 726 − 178 | 887 − 213 | 155 − 89 |
| E. | 433 − 167 | 706 − 603 | 687 − 199 | 443 − 107 | 600 − 56 |
| F. | 807 − 118 | 874 − 452 | 337 − 213 | 94 − 62 | 908 − 809 |

**Brainwork!** Choose one of the answers in the camel's pack. Write three different subtraction problems for it.

Name ______________________________ Skill: Subtraction review

# Math to Hoot About!

Solve each problem below. Use the answers to complete the puzzle.

## Across

B. 328 – 120 = ________

D. 7,498 – 2,744 = ________

E. 8,067 – 2,332 = ________

G. 900 – 60 = ________

I. 989 – 346 = ________

K. 50 – 22 = ________

L. 92 – 15 = ________

N. 425 – 205 = ________

O. 881 – 770 = ________

R. 819 – 149 = ________

S. 900 – 318 = ________

U. 897 – 434 = ________

W. 347 – 305 = ________

X. 900 – 840 = ________

## Down

A. 90 – 20

B. 82 – 58

C. 100 – 15

D. 1,100 – 700

F. 823 – 257

G. 97 – 9

H. 66 – 18

J. 94 – 57

K. 408 – 129

M. 952 – 191

P. 1,300 – 800

Q. 474 – 190

R. 71 – 9

S. 800 – 253

T. 1,000 – 800

V. 111 – 75

Name ______________________________ 

Write the number sentence and answer.

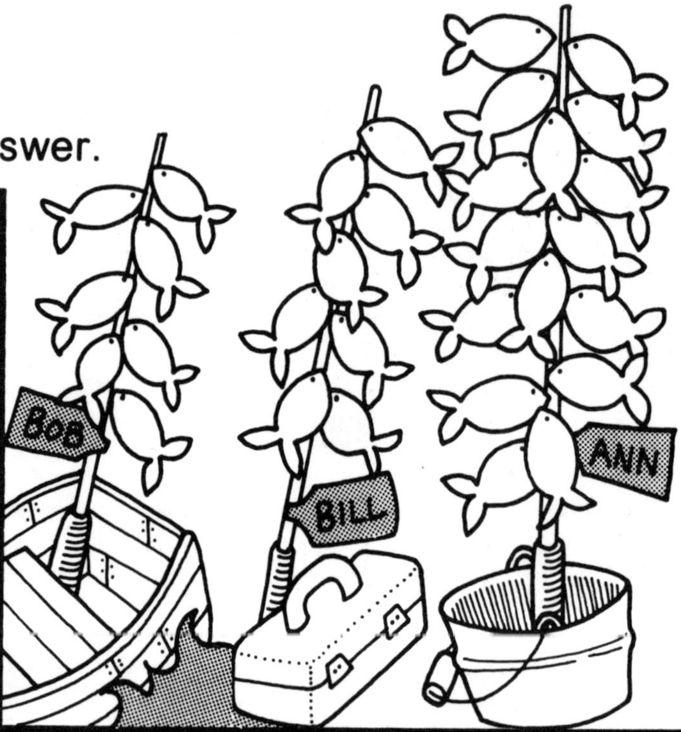

1. How many fish did Bob and Bill catch between them?

______________________________

They caught ______ fish.

2. Ann gave 9 of her fish to her cat. How many did she have left?

______________________________

Ann had ______ fish left.

3. How many more fish did Ann catch than Bill?

______________________________

Ann caught ______ more fish.

4. If Bill caught 4 more fish the next day, how many would that be in all?

______________________________

That would be ______ fish.

5. Bob caught how many less fish than Ann?

______________________________

Bob caught ______ less fish.

Name ______________________ Skill: Review—2 digits

Write the number sentence and answer.

1. How many more children are in Miss Smith's class than Mrs. Brown's class?

   ______________________

   There are ______ more.

2. How many children are there in Mr. West's class and Ms. Jones' class all together?

   ______________________

   There are ______ children.

3. How many less children does Ms. Jones have in her class than Mrs. Brown?

   ______________________

   Ms. Jones has ______ less.

4. How many children are there in Miss Smith's class and Mrs. Brown's class in all?

   ______________________

   There are ______ children.

5. Five children in Miss Smith's class moved. How many children does she have left?

   ______________________

   She has ______ children left.

Name ______________________________ Skill: 2 digit regrouping-review

Write the number sentence and answer.

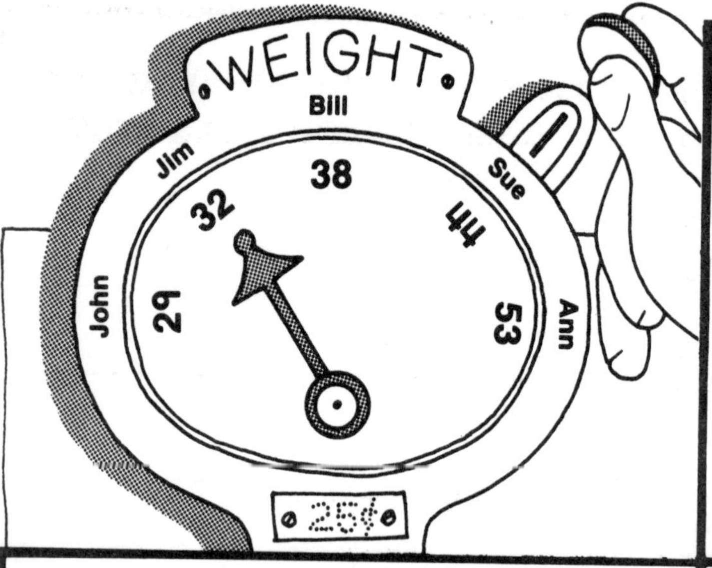


1. How much do Bill and Sue weigh together?

______________________________

They weigh ______ pounds.

2. How much more than John does Sue weigh?

______________________________

______ pounds more.

3. What would the scale show if John, Jim, and Bill all got on?

______________________________

It would show ______ pounds.

4. If Sue were to lose 9 pounds, how much would she weigh?

______________________________

______ pounds.

5. How much less does Bill weigh than Ann?

______________________________

______ pounds less.

Name ______________________________ 

Write the number sentence and answer.

1. Sam bought a yo-yo, a car, and a teddy bear. How much did he spend?

______________________________

Sam spent ______¢.

2. Linda had 70¢. If she bought a necklace, how much did she have left?

______________________________

Linda had ______¢ left.

3. How much less are the glasses than the book?

______________________________

The glasses are ______¢ less.

4. Jim bought a teddy bear. Ann bought a necklace. How much did they spend between them?

______________________________

They spent ______¢.

5. How much difference in price is there between the yo-yo and the book?

______________________________

A difference of ______¢.

Name ______________________________ Skill: Review

Circle the letter of the correct number sentence. Fill in **all** answers.

1. The school library has 26 old books about cats and 38 new ones. How many cat books does the library have?

   a. 38–26= ______ books
   b. 26+38= ______ books
   c. 38+26= ______ bananas

2. The library has 52 books about dinosaurs. If 13 are checked out, how many are left?

   a. 52–13= ______ apples
   b. 42–23= ______ dinosaurs
   c. 52–13= ______ books

3. Mrs. Smith gave 17 new books to the library, Mr. Brown gave 24, and Ms. Jones gave 38. How many new books were given in all?

   a. 17+24+38= ______ books
   b. 38+17+24= ______ trees
   c. 38–24= ______ books

4. Mrs. Black brings her class of 32 students to the library. Mr. Black brings 28. How much difference in class size is there?

   a. 32+28= ______ books
   b. 32–28= ______ students
   c. 32–28= ______ books

5. There were 82 books on the top shelf. 14 of them fell off. How many were on the shelf then?

   a. 82–14= ______ children
   b. 82+14= ______ books
   c. 82–14= ______ books

# Answer Key

Name ______ Skill: Sums to 10

## Try These Facts!

Score ___ / 50

Write the answers.

| | | | | | | |
|---|---|---|---|---|---|---|
| A. | 5 + 2 = 7 | 1 + 6 = 7 | 0 + 6 = 6 | 4 + 6 = 10 | 9 + 1 = 10 | 1 + 4 = 5 |
| B. | 6 + 3 = 9 | 2 + 5 = 7 | 1 + 1 = 2 | 3 + 4 = 7 | 7 + 2 = 9 | 4 + 3 = 7 |
| C. | 1 + 3 = 4 | 3 + 5 = 8 | 6 + 2 = 8 | 3 + 1 = 4 | 1 + 8 = 9 | 5 + 4 = 9 |
| D. | 0 + 7 = 7 | 3 + 7 = 10 | 1 + 9 = 10 | 2 + 6 = 8 | 2 + 2 = 4 | 8 + 0 = 8 |
| E. | 3 + 0 = 3 | 4 + 4 = 8 | 2 + 3 = 5 | 0 + 8 = 8 | 8 + 1 = 9 | 2 + 8 = 10 |
| F. | 1 + 5 = 6 | 7 + 3 = 10 | 0 + 0 = 0 | 8 + 2 = 10 | 5 + 3 = 8 | 4 + 2 = 6 |
| G. | 3 + 2 = 5 | 4 + 1 = 5 | 4 + 5 = 9 | 2 + 1 = 3 | 2 + 7 = 9 | 1 + 7 = 8 |
| H. | 2 + 4 = 6 | 0 + 1 = 1 | 6 + 4 = 10 | 0 + 5 = 5 | | |
| I. | 5 + 5 = 10 | 1 + 2 = 3 | 3 + 6 = 9 | 3 + 3 = 6 | | |

Page 1

Name ______ Skill: Sums to 12

## Addition Facts-s-s-s

Score ___ / 50

Write the answers.

| | | | | | | |
|---|---|---|---|---|---|---|
| A. | 8 + 1 = 9 | 5 + 5 = 10 | 8 + 0 = 8 | 1 + 9 = 10 | 6 + 1 = 7 | 3 + 5 = 8 |
| B. | 3 + 9 = 12 | 2 + 7 = 9 | 6 + 2 = 8 | 7 + 3 = 10 | 5 + 0 = 5 | 7 + 0 = 7 |
| C. | 8 + 2 = 10 | 5 + 6 = 11 | 9 + 2 = 11 | 0 + 9 = 9 | 7 + 2 = 9 | 2 + 5 = 7 |
| D. | 4 + 2 = 6 | 3 + 6 = 9 | 6 + 3 = 9 | 5 + 3 = 8 | 4 + 5 = 9 | 3 + 8 = 11 |
| E. | 3 + 7 = 10 | 4 + 4 = 8 | 7 + 1 = 8 | 9 + 1 = 10 | 5 + 4 = 9 | 1 + 8 = 9 |
| F. | 7 + 4 = 11 | 8 + 4 = 12 | 6 + 5 = 11 | 5 + 2 = 7 | 4 + 6 = 10 | 2 + 4 = 6 |
| G. | 6 + 6 = 12 | 2 + 6 = 8 | 9 + 3 = 12 | 7 + 5 = 12 | 2 + 8 = 10 | 4 + 8 = 12 |
| H. | 6 + 0 = 6 | 8 + 3 = 11 | 5 + 7 = 12 | 4 + 7 = 11 | | |
| I. | 3 + 4 = 7 | 6 + 4 = 10 | 4 + 3 = 7 | 2 + 9 = 11 | | |

Page 2

Name ______ Skill: Sums to 18

## Think and Write

Score ___ / 50

Write the answers.

| | | | | | | |
|---|---|---|---|---|---|---|
| A. | 6 + 6 = 12 | 9 + 2 = 11 | 6 + 4 = 10 | 7 + 7 = 14 | 2 + 7 = 9 | 3 + 8 = 11 |
| B. | 3 + 9 = 12 | 7 + 6 = 13 | 4 + 6 = 10 | 6 + 9 = 15 | 4 + 4 = 8 | 9 + 9 = 18 |
| C. | 9 + 5 = 14 | 3 + 5 = 8 | 8 + 2 = 10 | 8 + 5 = 13 | 9 + 3 = 12 | 6 + 3 = 9 |
| D. | 4 + 5 = 9 | 9 + 1 = 10 | 6 + 8 = 14 | 4 + 9 = 13 | 6 + 7 = 13 | 9 + 4 = 13 |
| E. | 8 + 6 = 14 | 6 + 5 = 11 | 7 + 8 = 15 | 9 + 6 = 15 | 8 + 3 = 11 | 7 + 4 = 11 |
| F. | 3 + 7 = 10 | 8 + 4 = 12 | 5 + 7 = 12 | 3 + 6 = 9 | 7 + 5 = 12 | 5 + 6 = 11 |
| G. | 9 + 7 = 16 | 4 + 7 = 11 | 1 + 9 = 10 | 8 + 7 = 15 | 2 + 9 = 11 | 5 + 8 = 13 |
| H. | 2 + 8 = 10 | 7 + 9 = 16 | 4 + 8 = 12 | 7 + 3 = 10 | | |
| I. | 8 + 9 = 17 | 8 + 8 = 16 | 5 + 9 = 14 | 9 + 8 = 17 | | |

Page 3

Name ______ Sums 11 to 18

## Lost Spaceship

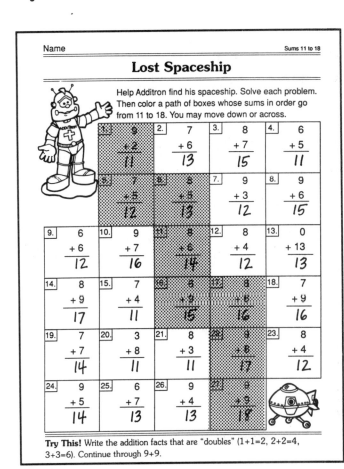

Help Additron find his spaceship. Solve each problem. Then color a path of boxes whose sums in order go from 11 to 18. You may move down or across.

| | | | | |
|---|---|---|---|---|
| | 1. 9 + 2 = 11 | 2. 7 + 6 = 13 | 3. 8 + 7 = 15 | 4. 6 + 5 = 11 |
| | 5. 7 + 5 = 12 | 6. 8 + 5 = 13 | 7. 9 + 3 = 12 | 8. 9 + 6 = 15 |
| 9. 6 + 6 = 12 | 10. 9 + 7 = 16 | 11. 8 + 6 = 14 | 12. 8 + 4 = 12 | 13. 0 + 13 = 13 |
| 14. 8 + 9 = 17 | 15. 7 + 4 = 11 | 16. 6 + 9 = 15 | 17. 8 + 8 = 16 | 18. 7 + 9 = 16 |
| 19. 7 + 7 = 14 | 20. 3 + 8 = 11 | 21. 8 + 3 = 11 | 22. 9 + 8 = 17 | 23. 8 + 4 = 12 |
| 24. 9 + 5 = 14 | 25. 6 + 7 = 13 | 26. 9 + 4 = 13 | 27. 9 + 9 = 18 | |

**Try This!** Write the addition facts that are "doubles" (1+1=2, 2+2=4, 3+3=6). Continue through 9+9.

Page 4

# Answer Key

Name Score /20 | Name Score /20

**Twenty Team** (Sums to 18) — 5a

| Problem | Answer | Problem | Answer |
|---|---|---|---|
| 2 + 1 = | 3 | 7 + 8 = | 15 |
| 6 + 3 = | 9 | 1 + 1 = | 2 |
| 1 + 0 = | 1 | 5 + 9 = | 14 |
| 4 + 7 = | 11 | 6 + 4 = | 10 |
| 6 + 7 = | 13 | 5 + 4 = | 9 |
| 8 + 9 = | 17 | 0 + 0 = | 0 |
| 4 + 3 = | 7 | 3 + 1 = | 4 |
| 4 + 2 = | 6 | 5 + 6 = | 11 |
| 8 + 8 = | 16 | 7 + 3 = | 10 |
| 9 + 4 = | 13 | 3 + 3 = | 6 |

**Twenty Team** (Sums to 18) — 5b

| Problem | Answer | Problem | Answer |
|---|---|---|---|
| 8 + 2 = | 10 | 5 + 5 = | 10 |
| 1 + 2 = | 3 | 3 + 5 = | 8 |
| 6 + 6 = | 12 | 9 + 9 = | 18 |
| 8 + 5 = | 13 | 2 + 0 = | 2 |
| 2 + 3 = | 5 | 2 + 2 = | 4 |
| 9 + 3 = | 12 | 7 + 7 = | 14 |
| 2 + 5 = | 7 | 5 + 2 = | 7 |
| 9 + 7 = | 16 | 6 + 9 = | 15 |
| 6 + 2 = | 8 | 7 + 5 = | 12 |
| 4 + 5 = | 9 | 4 + 1 = | 5 |

5a 5b

**Page 5**

Name Score /30 | Name Score /30

**Thirty Thinkers** (Sums to 18) — 6a

| Problem | Answer | Problem | Answer |
|---|---|---|---|
| 8 + 9 = | 17 | 7 + 5 = | 12 |
| 6 + 2 = | 8 | 5 + 0 = | 5 |
| 3 + 1 = | 4 | 6 + 3 = | 9 |
| 8 + 2 = | 10 | 8 + 9 = | 17 |
| 0 + 8 = | 8 | 4 + 2 = | 6 |
| 5 + 4 = | 9 | 7 + 8 = | 15 |
| 5 + 3 = | 8 | 2 + 7 = | 9 |
| 2 + 5 = | 7 | 2 + 4 = | 6 |
| 7 + 2 = | 9 | 8 + 6 = | 14 |
| 9 + 5 = | 14 | 4 + 7 = | 11 |
| 7 + 1 = | 8 | 9 + 7 = | 16 |
| 5 + 6 = | 11 | 7 + 6 = | 13 |
| 7 + 3 = | 10 | 8 + 8 = | 16 |
| 4 + 9 = | 13 | 2 + 9 = | 11 |
| 8 + 5 = | 13 | 9 + 1 = | 10 |

**Thirty Thinkers** (Sums to 18) — 6b

| Problem | Answer | Problem | Answer |
|---|---|---|---|
| 4 + 6 = | 10 | 8 + 1 = | 9 |
| 6 + 5 = | 11 | 5 + 0 = | 5 |
| 7 + 5 = | 12 | 8 + 6 = | 14 |
| 8 + 3 = | 11 | 8 + 9 = | 17 |
| 2 + 6 = | 8 | 4 + 2 = | 6 |
| 7 + 7 = | 14 | 5 + 3 = | 8 |
| 1 + 1 = | 2 | 3 + 3 = | 6 |
| 3 + 6 = | 9 | 2 + 4 = | 6 |
| 4 + 4 = | 8 | 8 + 6 = | 14 |
| 9 + 9 = | 18 | 4 + 7 = | 11 |
| 6 + 3 = | 9 | 9 + 7 = | 16 |
| 3 + 8 = | 11 | 7 + 6 = | 13 |
| 4 + 6 = | 10 | 8 + 8 = | 16 |
| 2 + 2 = | 4 | 2 + 9 = | 11 |
| 9 + 3 = | 12 | 9 + 1 = | 10 |

6a 6b

**Page 6**

Name Score /40 | Name Score /40

**Forty Force** (Sums to 18) — 7a

| Problem | Answer | Problem | Answer |
|---|---|---|---|
| 5 + 5 = | 10 | 9 + 6 = | 15 |
| 3 + 5 = | 8 | 4 + 9 = | 13 |
| 9 + 9 = | 18 | 1 + 7 = | 8 |
| 2 + 0 = | 2 | 8 + 8 = | 16 |
| 2 + 2 = | 4 | 3 + 6 = | 9 |
| 9 + 8 = | 17 | 8 + 3 = | 11 |
| 7 + 9 = | 16 | 7 + 6 = | 13 |
| 6 + 9 = | 15 | 9 + 2 = | 11 |
| 7 + 5 = | 12 | 7 + 7 = | 14 |
| 1 + 4 = | 5 | 8 + 6 = | 14 |
| 6 + 8 = | 14 | 1 + 8 = | 9 |
| 6 + 3 = | 9 | 4 + 6 = | 10 |
| 6 + 6 = | 12 | 7 + 4 = | 11 |
| 4 + 7 = | 11 | 1 + 9 = | 10 |
| 6 + 7 = | 13 | 7 + 2 = | 9 |
| 8 + 9 = | 17 | 4 + 8 = | 12 |
| 4 + 3 = | 7 | 5 + 5 = | 10 |
| 4 + 2 = | 6 | 4 + 4 = | 8 |
| 8 + 8 = | 16 | 2 + 8 = | 10 |
| 9 + 4 = | 13 | 5 + 7 = | 12 |

**Forty Force** (Sums to 18) — 7b

| Problem | Answer | Problem | Answer |
|---|---|---|---|
| 7 + 8 = | 15 | 3 + 9 = | 12 |
| 1 + 1 = | 2 | 8 + 2 = | 10 |
| 5 + 9 = | 14 | 4 + 8 = | 12 |
| 1 + 0 = | 1 | 1 + 6 = | 7 |
| 8 + 9 = | 17 | 6 + 2 = | 8 |
| 0 + 0 = | 0 | 8 + 4 = | 12 |
| 3 + 1 = | 4 | 9 + 5 = | 14 |
| 5 + 6 = | 11 | 6 + 4 = | 10 |
| 7 + 3 = | 10 | 2 + 3 = | 5 |
| 3 + 3 = | 6 | 5 + 1 = | 6 |
| 9 + 9 = | 18 | 3 + 7 = | 10 |
| 1 + 5 = | 6 | 8 + 7 = | 15 |
| 6 + 6 = | 12 | 5 + 4 = | 9 |
| 8 + 5 = | 13 | 7 + 2 = | 9 |
| 2 + 3 = | 5 | 2 + 5 = | 7 |
| 9 + 3 = | 12 | 5 + 8 = | 13 |
| 5 + 2 = | 7 | 5 + 9 = | 14 |
| 9 + 7 = | 16 | 4 + 4 = | 8 |
| 6 + 2 = | 8 | 2 + 9 = | 11 |
| 4 + 5 = | 9 | 3 + 8 = | 11 |

7a 7b

**Page 7**

Name ______ Skill: Subtracting from 10 or less

## Fishing for Facts!

Write the answers.

Score ___ /50

| | | | | | | |
|---|---|---|---|---|---|---|
| A. | 9 − 9 = 0 | 7 − 5 = 2 | 8 − 8 = 0 | 9 − 2 = 7 | 10 − 7 = 3 | 2 − 1 = 1 |
| B. | 7 − 4 = 3 | 10 − 9 = 1 | 7 − 6 = 1 | 7 − 3 = 4 | 6 − 5 = 1 | 4 − 1 = 3 |
| C. | 8 − 2 = 6 | 10 − 2 = 8 | 9 − 8 = 1 | 10 − 3 = 7 | 9 − 5 = 4 | 3 − 2 = 1 |
| D. | 8 − 7 = 1 | 9 − 1 = 8 | 7 − 2 = 5 | 8 − 3 = 5 | 6 − 4 = 2 | 5 − 1 = 4 |
| E. | 6 − 3 = 3 | 7 − 1 = 6 | 4 − 3 = 1 | 9 − 0 = 9 | 8 − 5 = 3 | 9 − 6 = 3 |
| F. | 5 − 4 = 1 | 9 − 4 = 5 | 8 − 1 = 7 | 6 − 2 = 4 | 10 − 1 = 9 | 5 − 5 = 0 |
| G. | 10 − 8 = 2 | 5 − 3 = 2 | 8 − 6 = 2 | 10 − 4 = 6 | 9 − 3 = 6 | 10 − 6 = 4 |
| H. | 4 − 2 = 2 | 7 − 7 = 0 | 9 − 7 = 2 | 6 − 1 = 5 | | |
| I. | 3 − 1 = 2 | 10 − 5 = 5 | 5 − 2 = 3 | 8 − 4 = 4 | | |

**Page 8**

# Answer Key

Name ______ Skill: Subtracting from 12 or less

## Think and Subtract

Score ____ / 50

Write the answers.

| | | | | | | |
|---|---|---|---|---|---|---|
| A. | 3 − 2 = 1 | 4 − 1 = 3 | 7 − 2 = 5 | 5 − 2 = 3 | 8 − 1 = 7 | 10 − 9 = 1 |
| B. | 6 − 4 = 2 | 9 − 6 = 3 | 10 − 5 = 5 | 7 − 6 = 1 | 11 − 2 = 9 | 6 − 3 = 3 |
| C. | 7 − 5 = 2 | 11 − 3 = 8 | 9 − 8 = 1 | 12 − 3 = 9 | 10 − 3 = 7 | 9 − 4 = 5 |
| D. | 10 − 4 = 6 | 6 − 5 = 1 | 7 − 3 = 4 | 8 − 2 = 6 | 8 − 6 = 2 | 5 − 3 = 2 |
| E. | 7 − 4 = 3 | 11 − 7 = 4 | 8 − 5 = 3 | 6 − 2 = 4 | 10 − 6 = 4 | 8 − 4 = 4 |
| F. | 9 − 7 = 2 | 12 − 8 = 4 | 9 − 3 = 6 | 11 − 4 = 7 | 8 − 3 = 5 | 9 − 2 = 7 |
| G. | 11 − 5 = 6 | 12 − 6 = 6 | 10 − 7 = 3 | 9 − 5 = 4 | 11 − 9 = 2 | 8 − 7 = 1 |
| H. | 12 − 7 = 5 | 10 − 2 = 8 | 11 − 6 = 5 | 12 − 4 = 8 | | |
| I. | 10 − 8 = 2 | 12 − 5 = 7 | 12 − 9 = 3 | 11 − 8 = 3 | | |

Page 9

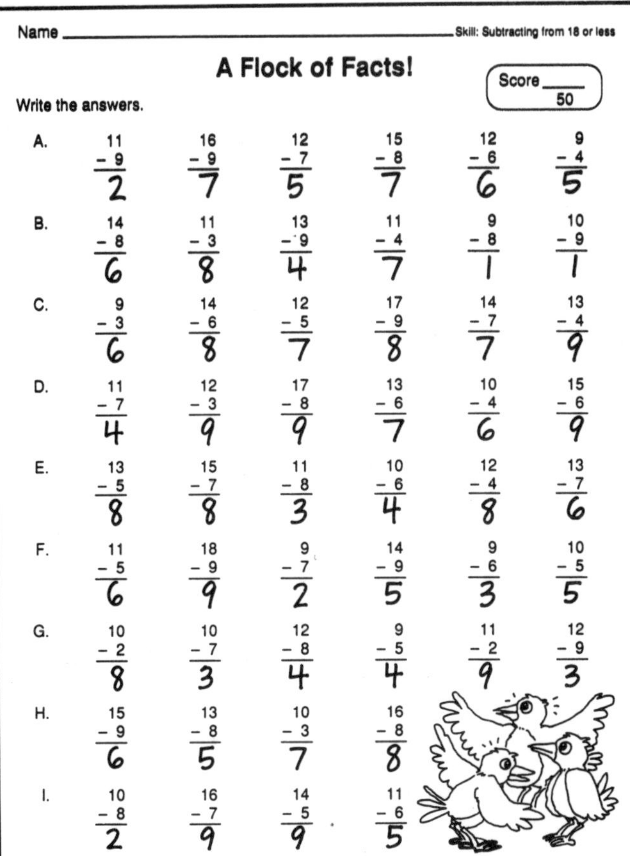

Name ______ Skill: Subtracting from 18 or less

## A Flock of Facts!

Score ____ / 50

Write the answers.

| | | | | | | |
|---|---|---|---|---|---|---|
| A. | 11 − 9 = 2 | 16 − 9 = 7 | 12 − 7 = 5 | 15 − 8 = 7 | 12 − 6 = 6 | 9 − 4 = 5 |
| B. | 14 − 8 = 6 | 11 − 3 = 8 | 13 − 9 = 4 | 11 − 4 = 7 | 9 − 8 = 1 | 10 − 9 = 1 |
| C. | 9 − 3 = 6 | 14 − 6 = 8 | 12 − 5 = 7 | 17 − 9 = 8 | 14 − 7 = 7 | 13 − 4 = 9 |
| D. | 11 − 7 = 4 | 12 − 3 = 9 | 17 − 8 = 9 | 13 − 6 = 7 | 10 − 4 = 6 | 15 − 6 = 9 |
| E. | 13 − 5 = 8 | 15 − 7 = 8 | 11 − 8 = 3 | 10 − 6 = 4 | 12 − 4 = 8 | 13 − 7 = 6 |
| F. | 11 − 5 = 6 | 18 − 9 = 9 | 9 − 7 = 2 | 14 − 9 = 5 | 9 − 6 = 3 | 10 − 5 = 5 |
| G. | 10 − 2 = 8 | 10 − 7 = 3 | 12 − 8 = 4 | 9 − 5 = 4 | 11 − 2 = 9 | 12 − 9 = 3 |
| H. | 15 − 9 = 6 | 13 − 8 = 5 | 10 − 3 = 7 | 16 − 8 = 8 | | |
| I. | 10 − 8 = 2 | 16 − 7 = 9 | 14 − 5 = 9 | 11 − 6 = 5 | | |

Page 10

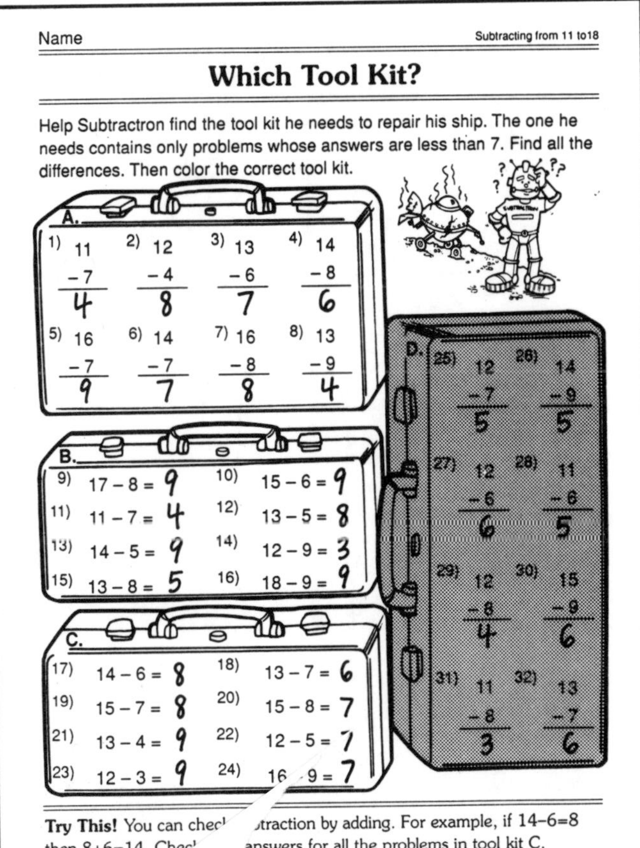

Name ______ Subtracting from 11 to18

## Which Tool Kit?

Help Subtractron find the tool kit he needs to repair his ship. The one he needs contains only problems whose answers are less than 7. Find all the differences. Then color the correct tool kit.

**A.**

1) 11 − 7 = 4
2) 12 − 4 = 8
3) 13 − 6 = 7
4) 14 − 8 = 6
5) 16 − 7 = 9
6) 14 − 7 = 7
7) 16 − 8 = 8
8) 13 − 9 = 4

**B.**

9) 17 − 8 = 9
10) 15 − 6 = 9
11) 11 − 7 = 4
12) 13 − 5 = 8
13) 14 − 5 = 9
14) 12 − 9 = 3
15) 13 − 8 = 5
16) 18 − 9 = 9

**C.**

17) 14 − 6 = 8
18) 13 − 7 = 6
19) 15 − 7 = 8
20) 15 − 8 = 7
21) 13 − 4 = 9
22) 12 − 5 = 7
23) 12 − 3 = 9
24) 16 − 9 = 7

**D.**

25) 12 − 7 = 5
26) 14 − 9 = 5
27) 12 − 6 = 6
28) 11 − 6 = 5
29) 12 − 8 = 4
30) 15 − 9 = 6
31) 11 − 8 = 3
32) 13 − 7 = 6

**Try This!** You can chec[illegible]traction by adding. For example, if 14−6=8 then 8+6=14. Chec[illegible] answers for all the problems in tool kit C.

Page 11

Name ______ Score ____ /20

## Twenty Team

Subtracting from 18 or less

| | |
|---|---|
| 7 − 2 = 5 | 6 − 0 = 6 |
| 10 − 2 = 8 | 10 − 3 = 7 |
| 7 − 4 = 3 | 4 − 2 = 2 |
| 9 − 8 = 1 | 9 − 4 = 5 |
| 12 − 3 = 9 | 10 − 6 = 4 |
| 9 − 3 = 6 | 5 − 2 = 3 |
| 11 − 7 = 4 | 16 − 8 = 8 |
| 6 − 4 = 2 | 12 − 6 = 6 |
| 12 − 4 = 8 | 10 − 9 = 1 |
| 7 − 0 = 7 | 15 − 7 = 8 |

12a

Name ______ Score ____ /20

## Twenty Team

Subtracting from 18 or less

| | |
|---|---|
| 18 − 9 = 9 | 14 − 6 = 8 |
| 3 − 2 = 1 | 7 − 6 = 1 |
| 10 − 4 = 6 | 11 − 5 = 6 |
| 11 − 8 = 3 | 6 − 3 = 3 |
| 12 − 8 = 4 | 10 − 5 = 5 |
| 8 − 3 = 5 | 3 − 1 = 2 |
| 8 − 6 = 2 | 13 − 6 = 7 |
| 17 − 9 = 8 | 11 − 2 = 9 |
| 9 − 0 = 9 | 8 − 4 = 4 |
| 13 − 4 = 9 | 0 − 0 = 0 |

12b

Page 12

# Answer Key

Name Score /30

## Thirty Thinkers

Subtracting from 18 or less

| | |
|---|---|
| 9 − 3 = 6 | 6 − 0 = 6 |
| 11 − 7 = 4 | 10 − 3 = 7 |
| 6 − 4 = 2 | 4 − 2 = 2 |
| 12 − 4 = 8 | 9 − 4 = 5 |
| 7 − 0 = 7 | 10 − 6 = 4 |
| 10 − 7 = 3 | 5 − 2 = 3 |
| 9 − 6 = 3 | 16 − 8 = 8 |
| 8 − 3 = 5 | 12 − 6 = 6 |
| 6 − 2 = 4 | 10 − 9 = 1 |
| 10 − 9 = 1 | 15 − 7 = 8 |
| 6 − 5 = 1 | 18 − 9 = 9 |
| 5 − 5 = 0 | 3 − 2 = 1 |
| 9 − 1 = 8 | 10 − 4 = 6 |
| 7 − 4 = 3 | 11 − 8 = 3 |
| 5 − 3 = 2 | 12 − 8 = 4 |

13a

Name Score /30

## Thirty Thinkers

Subtracting from 18 or less

| | |
|---|---|
| 10 − 2 = 8 | 3 − 3 = 0 |
| 7 − 6 = 1 | 8 − 6 = 2 |
| 11 − 5 = 6 | 12 − 5 = 7 |
| 6 − 3 = 3 | 9 − 0 = 9 |
| 10 − 5 = 5 | 13 − 4 = 9 |
| 3 − 1 = 2 | 9 − 5 = 4 |
| 13 − 6 = 7 | 18 − 9 = 9 |
| 11 − 2 = 9 | 11 − 3 = 8 |
| 8 − 4 = 4 | 4 − 2 = 2 |
| 0 − 0 = 0 | 17 − 9 = 8 |
| 7 − 2 = 5 | 8 − 4 = 4 |
| 14 − 7 = 7 | 2 − 1 = 1 |
| 7 − 4 = 3 | 4 − 0 = 4 |
| 9 − 8 = 1 | 7 − 5 = 2 |
| 12 − 3 = 9 | 10 − 8 = 2 |

13b

**Page 13**

Name Score /40

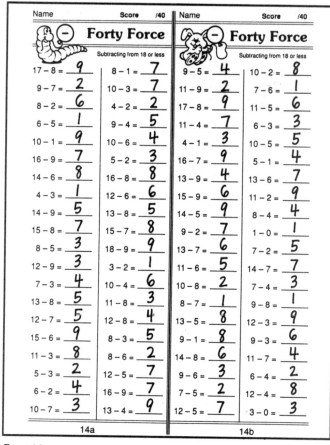

## Forty Force

Subtracting from 18 or less

| | |
|---|---|
| 17 − 8 = 9 | 8 − 1 = 7 |
| 9 − 7 = 2 | 10 − 3 = 7 |
| 8 − 2 = 6 | 4 − 2 = 2 |
| 6 − 5 = 1 | 9 − 4 = 5 |
| 10 − 1 = 9 | 10 − 6 = 4 |
| 16 − 9 = 7 | 5 − 2 = 3 |
| 14 − 6 = 8 | 16 − 8 = 8 |
| 4 − 3 = 1 | 12 − 6 = 6 |
| 14 − 9 = 5 | 13 − 8 = 5 |
| 15 − 8 = 7 | 15 − 7 = 8 |
| 8 − 5 = 3 | 18 − 9 = 9 |
| 12 − 9 = 3 | 3 − 2 = 1 |
| 7 − 3 = 4 | 10 − 4 = 6 |
| 13 − 8 = 5 | 11 − 8 = 3 |
| 12 − 7 = 5 | 12 − 8 = 4 |
| 15 − 6 = 9 | 8 − 3 = 5 |
| 11 − 3 = 8 | 8 − 6 = 2 |
| 5 − 3 = 2 | 12 − 5 = 7 |
| 6 − 2 = 4 | 16 − 9 = 7 |
| 10 − 7 = 3 | 13 − 4 = 9 |

14a

Name Score /40

## Forty Force

Subtracting from 18 or less

| | |
|---|---|
| 9 − 5 = 4 | 10 − 2 = 8 |
| 11 − 9 = 2 | 7 − 6 = 1 |
| 17 − 8 = 9 | 11 − 5 = 6 |
| 11 − 4 = 7 | 6 − 3 = 3 |
| 4 − 1 = 3 | 10 − 5 = 5 |
| 16 − 7 = 9 | 5 − 1 = 4 |
| 13 − 9 = 4 | 13 − 6 = 7 |
| 15 − 9 = 6 | 11 − 2 = 9 |
| 14 − 5 = 9 | 8 − 4 = 4 |
| 9 − 2 = 7 | 1 − 0 = 1 |
| 13 − 7 = 6 | 7 − 2 = 5 |
| 11 − 6 = 5 | 14 − 7 = 7 |
| 10 − 8 = 2 | 7 − 4 = 3 |
| 8 − 7 = 1 | 9 − 8 = 1 |
| 13 − 5 = 8 | 12 − 3 = 9 |
| 9 − 1 = 8 | 9 − 3 = 6 |
| 14 − 8 = 6 | 11 − 7 = 4 |
| 9 − 6 = 3 | 6 − 4 = 2 |
| 7 − 5 = 2 | 12 − 4 = 8 |
| 12 − 5 = 7 | 3 − 0 = 3 |

14b

**Page 14**

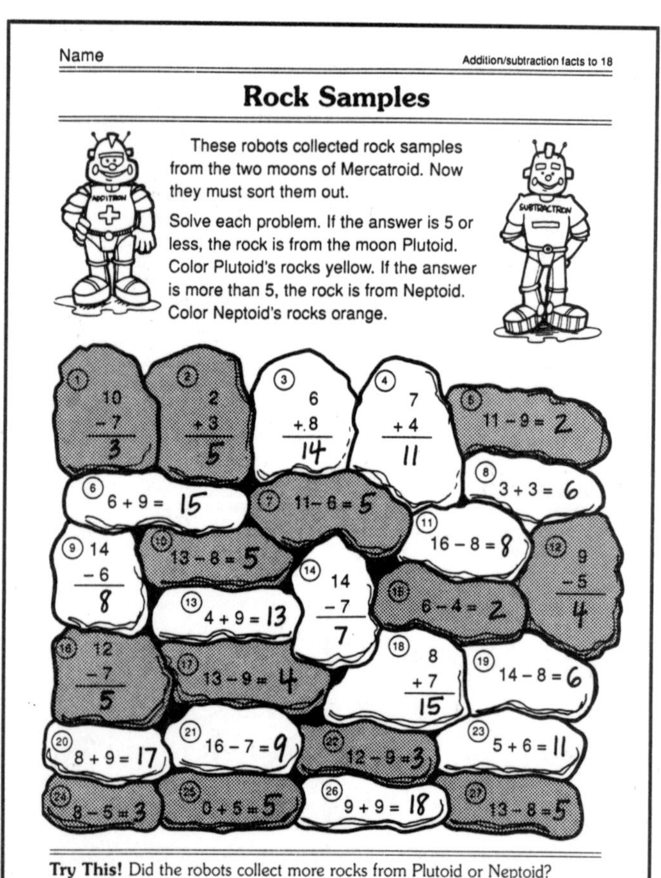

Name Addition/subtraction facts to 18

## Rock Samples

These robots collected rock samples from the two moons of Mercatroid. Now they must sort them out.

Solve each problem. If the answer is 5 or less, the rock is from the moon Plutoid. Color Plutoid's rocks yellow. If the answer is more than 5, the rock is from Neptoid. Color Neptoid's rocks orange.



**Try This!** Did the robots collect more rocks from Plutoid or Neptoid?

**Page 15**

Name Score /20

## Twenty Team

Sums and differences 0–18

| | |
|---|---|
| 10 − 2 = 8 | 7 + 2 = 9 |
| 11 − 3 = 8 | 8 + 3 = 11 |
| 4 + 3 = 7 | 11 − 5 = 6 |
| 9 + 6 = 15 | 4 + 4 = 8 |
| 7 − 5 = 2 | 7 + 6 = 13 |
| 8 − 0 = 8 | 4 + 2 = 6 |
| 18 − 9 = 9 | 9 − 5 = 4 |
| 6 + 5 = 11 | 3 + 9 = 12 |
| 2 + 3 = 5 | 10 − 5 = 5 |
| 6 − 4 = 2 | 13 − 4 = 9 |

16a

Name Score /20

## Twenty Team

Sums and differences 0–18

| | |
|---|---|
| 15 − 8 = 7 | 15 − 7 = 8 |
| 8 + 8 = 16 | 18 − 9 = 9 |
| 9 − 6 = 3 | 4 + 6 = 10 |
| 1 + 8 = 9 | 12 − 7 = 5 |
| 12 − 6 = 6 | 17 − 8 = 9 |
| 7 + 7 = 14 | 9 + 3 = 12 |
| 13 − 5 = 8 | 0 + 5 = 5 |
| 3 + 7 = 10 | 5 + 8 = 13 |
| 5 + 9 = 14 | 14 − 6 = 8 |
| 7 + 1 = 8 | 16 − 7 = 9 |

16b

**Page 16**

# Answer Key

Name Score /30

## Thirty Thinkers

Sums and differences 0–18

| | |
|---|---|
| 8 + 7 = 15 | 6 + 9 = 15 |
| 3 + 6 = 9 | 13 − 8 = 5 |
| 12 − 5 = 7 | 8 − 6 = 2 |
| 6 − 2 = 4 | 4 + 7 = 11 |
| 3 + 4 = 7 | 11 − 4 = 7 |
| 8 + 2 = 10 | 5 − 3 = 2 |
| 11 − 7 = 4 | 6 + 2 = 8 |
| 8 − 5 = 3 | 2 + 9 = 11 |
| 3 − 2 = 1 | 9 − 3 = 6 |
| 5 + 3 = 8 | 10 − 4 = 6 |
| 1 + 6 = 7 | 6 + 7 = 13 |
| 14 − 8 = 6 | 15 − 6 = 9 |
| 5 + 6 = 11 | 18 − 9 = 9 |
| 12 − 3 = 9 | 7 + 5 = 12 |
| 7 − 2 = 5 | 8 + 4 = 12 |

17a

Name Score /30

## Thirty Thinkers

Sums and differences 0–18

| | |
|---|---|
| 3 + 2 = 5 | 14 − 7 = 7 |
| 13 − 9 = 4 | 15 − 9 = 6 |
| 8 + 6 = 14 | 6 − 3 = 3 |
| 10 − 8 = 2 | 3 + 5 = 8 |
| 6 − 5 = 1 | 2 + 6 = 8 |
| 9 + 4 = 13 | 5 + 2 = 7 |
| 5 + 7 = 12 | 8 + 9 = 17 |
| 4 + 8 = 12 | 9 + 5 = 14 |
| 0 + 6 = 6 | 13 − 7 = 6 |
| 17 − 8 = 9 | 8 − 4 = 4 |
| 11 − 9 = 2 | 17 − 9 = 8 |
| 10 − 7 = 3 | 2 − 2 = 0 |
| 5 + 4 = 9 | 7 + 8 = 15 |
| 6 + 6 = 12 | 4 + 9 = 13 |
| 8 + 1 = 9 | 5 + 5 = 10 |

17b

Page 17

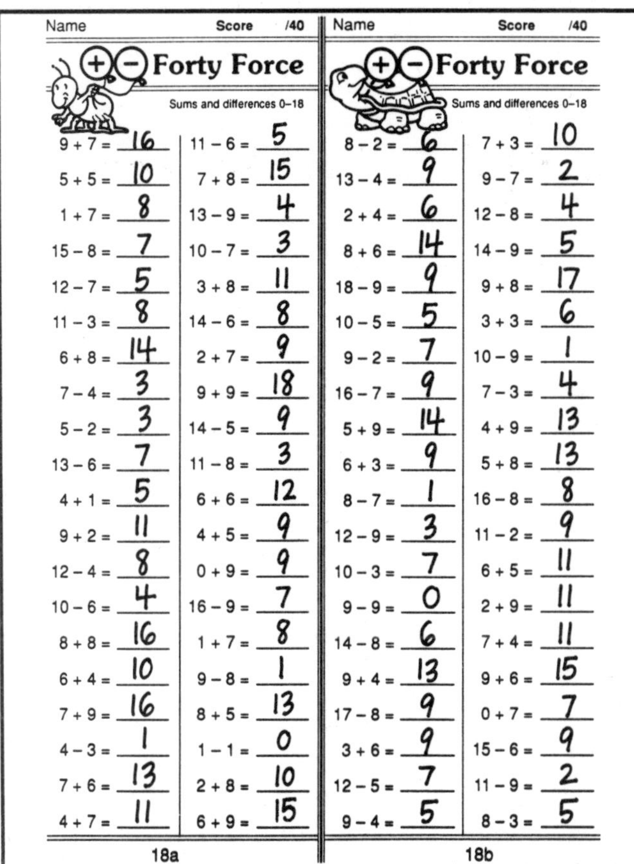

Name Score /40

## Forty Force

Sums and differences 0–18

| | |
|---|---|
| 9 + 7 = 16 | 11 − 6 = 5 |
| 5 + 5 = 10 | 7 + 8 = 15 |
| 1 + 7 = 8 | 13 − 9 = 4 |
| 15 − 8 = 7 | 10 − 7 = 3 |
| 12 − 7 = 5 | 3 + 8 = 11 |
| 11 − 3 = 8 | 14 − 6 = 8 |
| 6 + 8 = 14 | 2 + 7 = 9 |
| 7 − 4 = 3 | 9 + 9 = 18 |
| 5 − 2 = 3 | 14 − 5 = 9 |
| 13 − 6 = 7 | 11 − 8 = 3 |
| 4 + 1 = 5 | 6 + 6 = 12 |
| 9 + 2 = 11 | 4 + 5 = 9 |
| 12 − 4 = 8 | 0 + 9 = 9 |
| 10 − 6 = 4 | 16 − 9 = 7 |
| 8 + 8 = 16 | 1 + 7 = 8 |
| 6 + 4 = 10 | 9 − 8 = 1 |
| 7 + 9 = 16 | 8 + 5 = 13 |
| 4 − 3 = 1 | 1 − 1 = 0 |
| 7 + 6 = 13 | 2 + 8 = 10 |
| 4 + 7 = 11 | 6 + 9 = 15 |

18a

Name Score /40

## Forty Force

Sums and differences 0–18

| | |
|---|---|
| 8 − 2 = 6 | 7 + 3 = 10 |
| 13 − 4 = 9 | 9 − 7 = 2 |
| 2 + 4 = 6 | 12 − 8 = 4 |
| 8 + 6 = 14 | 14 − 9 = 5 |
| 18 − 9 = 9 | 9 + 8 = 17 |
| 10 − 5 = 5 | 3 + 3 = 6 |
| 9 − 2 = 7 | 10 − 9 = 1 |
| 16 − 7 = 9 | 7 − 3 = 4 |
| 5 + 9 = 14 | 4 + 9 = 13 |
| 6 + 3 = 9 | 5 + 8 = 13 |
| 8 − 7 = 1 | 16 − 8 = 8 |
| 12 − 9 = 3 | 11 − 2 = 9 |
| 10 − 3 = 7 | 6 + 5 = 11 |
| 9 − 9 = 0 | 2 + 9 = 11 |
| 14 − 8 = 6 | 7 + 4 = 11 |
| 9 + 4 = 13 | 9 + 6 = 15 |
| 17 − 8 = 9 | 0 + 7 = 7 |
| 3 + 6 = 9 | 15 − 6 = 9 |
| 12 − 5 = 7 | 11 − 9 = 2 |
| 9 − 4 = 5 | 8 − 3 = 5 |

18b

Page 18

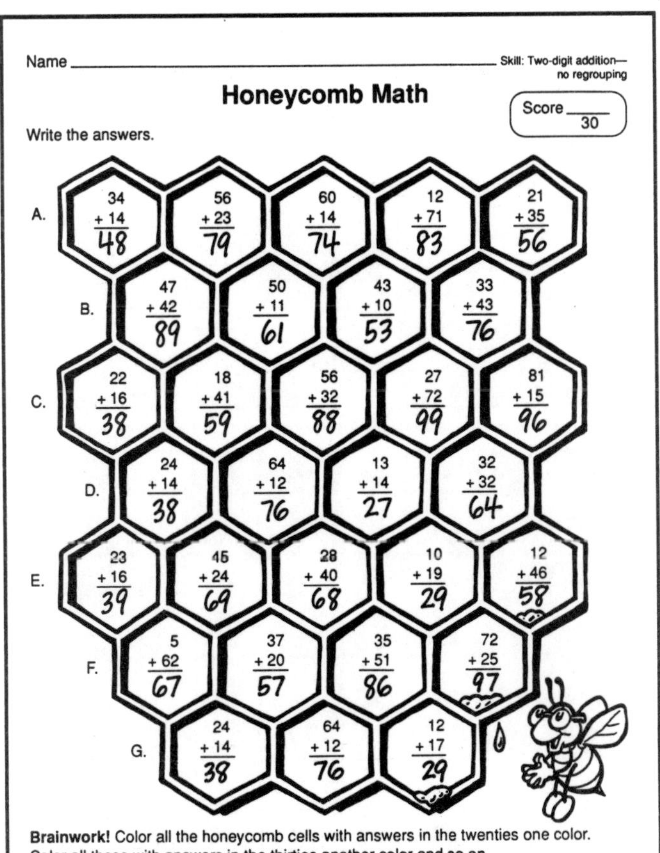

Name ______ Skill: Two-digit addition—no regrouping

## Honeycomb Math

Score ___ 30

Write the answers.

| | | | | | |
|---|---|---|---|---|---|
| A. | 34 + 14 = 48 | 56 + 23 = 79 | 60 + 14 = 74 | 12 + 71 = 83 | 21 + 35 = 56 |
| B. | 47 + 42 = 89 | 50 + 11 = 61 | 43 + 10 = 53 | 33 + 43 = 76 | |
| C. | 22 + 16 = 38 | 18 + 41 = 59 | 56 + 32 = 88 | 27 + 72 = 99 | 81 + 15 = 96 |
| D. | 24 + 14 = 38 | 64 + 12 = 76 | 13 + 14 = 27 | 32 + 32 = 64 | |
| E. | 23 + 16 = 39 | 45 + 24 = 69 | 28 + 40 = 68 | 10 + 19 = 29 | 12 + 46 = 58 |
| F. | 5 + 62 = 67 | 37 + 20 = 57 | 35 + 51 = 86 | 72 + 25 = 97 | |
| G. | 24 + 14 = 38 | 64 + 12 = 76 | 12 + 17 = 29 | | |

**Brainwork!** Color all the honeycomb cells with answers in the twenties one color. Color all those with answers in the thirties another color and so on.

Page 19

Name ______ Skill: Adding multiples of 10

## Snail Sums

Score ___ 40

Write the answers in the shells.

A. Center + 40; inner: 50, 80, 30, 60, 40, 10, 20, 70; answers: 90, 120, 70, 100, 80, 50, 60, 110

B. Center + 70; inner: 90, 30, 70, 40, 50, 80, 20, 60; answers: 160, 100, 140, 110, 120, 150, 90, 130

C. Center + 50; inner: 50, 10, 70, 60, 80, 30, 20, 90; answers: 100, 60, 120, 110, 130, 80, 70, 140

D. Center + 80; inner: 40, 80, 30, 60, 70, 20, 90, 50; answers: 120, 160, 110, 140, 150, 100, 170, 130

E. Center + 60; inner: 30, 10, 70, 40, 90, 80, 50, 60; answers: 90, 70, 130, 100, 150, 140, 110, 120

**Brainwork!** Draw your own snail for sums. Write *+ 90* in the center. Trade snails with a friend. Do the addition.

Page 20

# Answer Key

Name ______________________ Skill: Two-digit subtraction—no regrouping

## Taking a Bite

Score ____ 35

Subtract and write the answers. To find where the worm bit the apple, color the box with the greatest answer.

| | | | | | |
|---|---|---|---|---|---|
| A. 24<br>− 13<br>11 | 86<br>− 52<br>34 | 89<br>− 36<br>53 | 77<br>− 5<br>72 | | |
| B. 57<br>− 22<br>35 | 19<br>− 5<br>14 | 68<br>− 24<br>44 | 71<br>− 50<br>21 | 86<br>− 13<br>73 | 50<br>− 10<br>40 |
| C. 69<br>− 23<br>46 | 88<br>− 12<br>76 | 45<br>− 13<br>32 | 28<br>− 12<br>16 | 94<br>− 24<br>70 | 76<br>− 73<br>3 |
| D. 52<br>− 10<br>42 | 79<br>− 61<br>18 | 49<br>− 22<br>27 | 70<br>− 40<br>30 | 95<br>− 4<br>91 | 87<br>− 12<br>75 |
| E. 79<br>− 70<br>9 | 39<br>− 11<br>28 | 36<br>− 32<br>4 | 28<br>− 2<br>26 | 99<br>− 55<br>44 | 98<br>− 15<br>83 |
| | F. 77<br>− 45<br>32 | 68<br>− 20<br>48 | 49<br>− 32<br>17 | 87<br>− 30<br>57 | |
| | G. 88<br>− 72<br>16 | 76<br>− 21<br>55 | 99<br>− 68<br>31 | | |

**Brainwork!** Write five of your answers in order from the least to the greatest.

Page 21

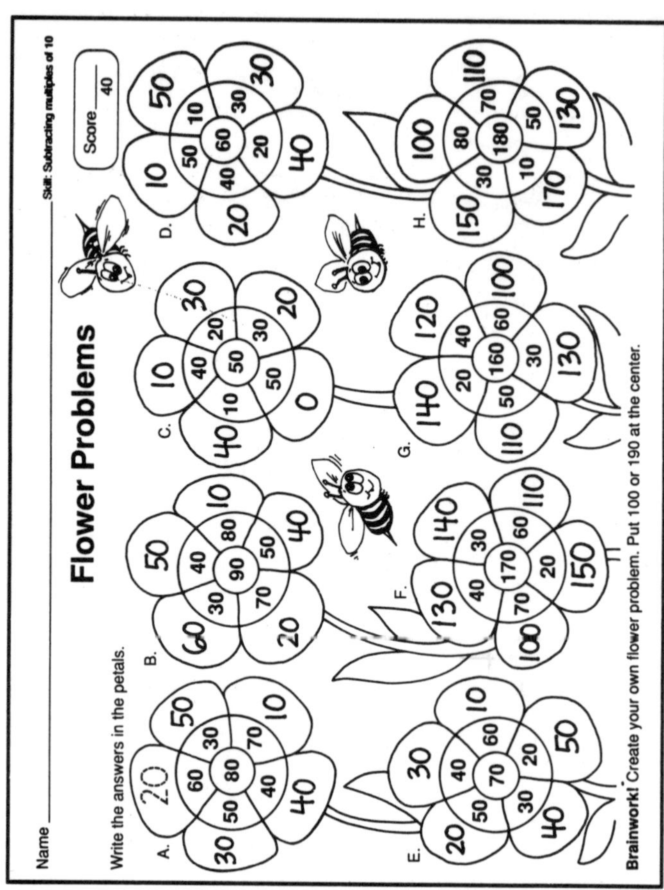

Name ______________________ Skill: Subtracting multiples of 10

Score ____ 40

## Flower Problems

Write the answers in the petals.

**Brainwork!** Create your own flower problem. Put 100 or 190 at the center.

Page 22

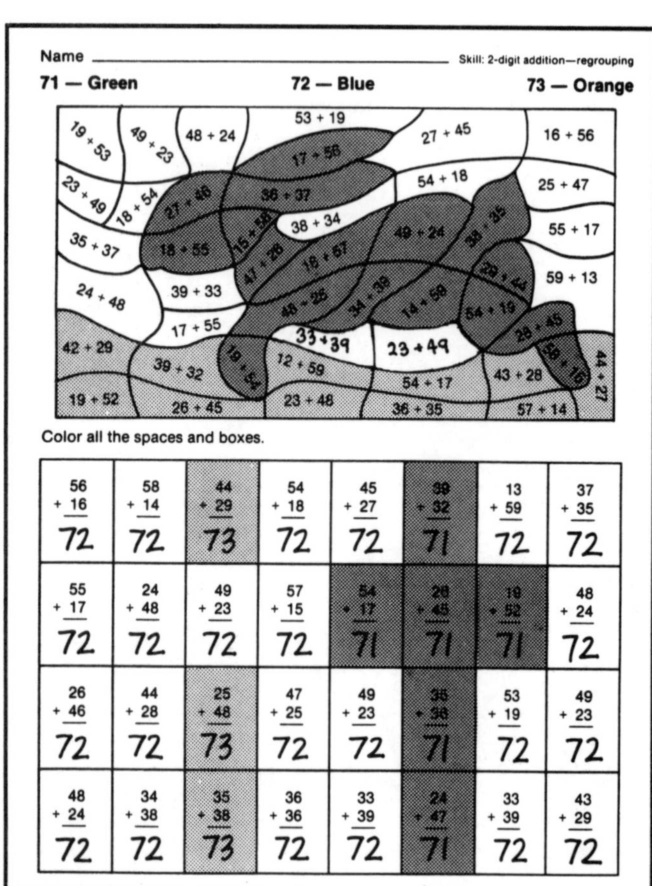

Name ______________________ Skill: 2-digit addition—regrouping

**71 — Green** **72 — Blue** **73 — Orange**

Color all the spaces and boxes.

| | | | | | | | |
|---|---|---|---|---|---|---|---|
| 56<br>+ 16<br>72 | 58<br>+ 14<br>72 | 44<br>+ 29<br>73 | 54<br>+ 18<br>72 | 45<br>+ 27<br>72 | 39<br>+ 32<br>71 | 13<br>+ 59<br>72 | 37<br>+ 35<br>72 |
| 55<br>+ 17<br>72 | 24<br>+ 48<br>72 | 49<br>+ 23<br>72 | 57<br>+ 15<br>72 | 54<br>+ 17<br>71 | 26<br>+ 45<br>71 | 19<br>+ 52<br>71 | 48<br>+ 24<br>72 |
| 26<br>+ 46<br>72 | 44<br>+ 28<br>72 | 25<br>+ 48<br>73 | 47<br>+ 25<br>72 | 49<br>+ 23<br>72 | 35<br>+ 36<br>71 | 53<br>+ 19<br>72 | 49<br>+ 23<br>72 |
| 48<br>+ 24<br>72 | 34<br>+ 38<br>72 | 35<br>+ 38<br>73 | 36<br>+ 36<br>72 | 33<br>+ 39<br>72 | 24<br>+ 47<br>71 | 33<br>+ 39<br>72 | 43<br>+ 29<br>72 |

Page 23

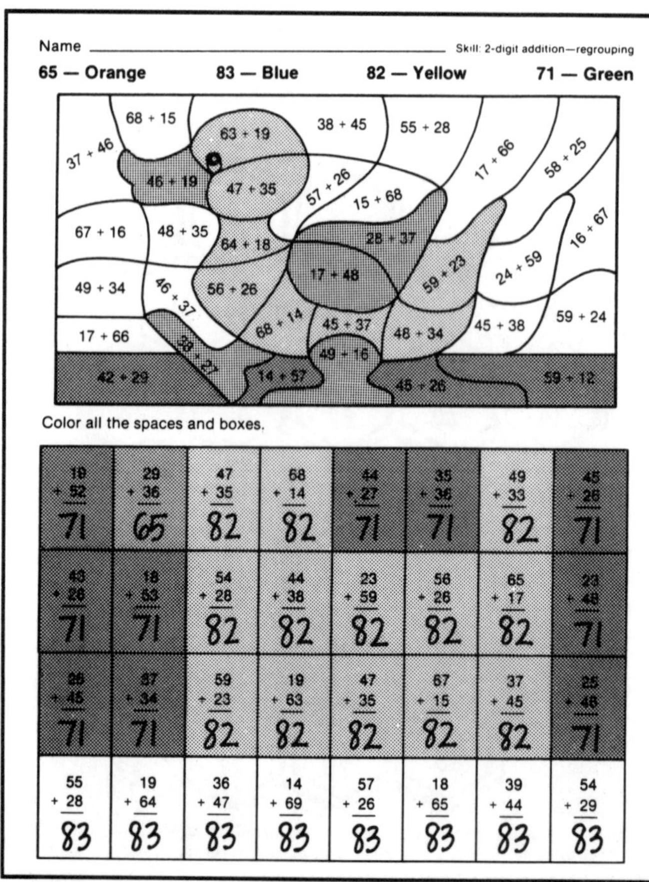

Name ______________________ Skill: 2-digit addition—regrouping

**65 — Orange** **83 — Blue** **82 — Yellow** **71 — Green**

Color all the spaces and boxes.

| | | | | | | | |
|---|---|---|---|---|---|---|---|
| 19<br>+ 52<br>71 | 29<br>+ 36<br>65 | 47<br>+ 35<br>82 | 68<br>+ 14<br>82 | 44<br>+ 27<br>71 | 35<br>+ 36<br>71 | 49<br>+ 33<br>82 | 45<br>+ 26<br>71 |
| 43<br>+ 28<br>71 | 18<br>+ 53<br>71 | 54<br>+ 28<br>82 | 44<br>+ 38<br>82 | 23<br>+ 59<br>82 | 56<br>+ 26<br>82 | 65<br>+ 17<br>82 | 23<br>+ 48<br>71 |
| 26<br>+ 45<br>71 | 37<br>+ 34<br>71 | 59<br>+ 23<br>82 | 19<br>+ 63<br>82 | 47<br>+ 35<br>82 | 67<br>+ 15<br>82 | 37<br>+ 45<br>82 | 25<br>+ 46<br>71 |
| 55<br>+ 28<br>83 | 19<br>+ 64<br>83 | 36<br>+ 47<br>83 | 14<br>+ 69<br>83 | 57<br>+ 26<br>83 | 18<br>+ 65<br>83 | 39<br>+ 44<br>83 | 54<br>+ 29<br>83 |

Page 24

# Answer Key

Name ______________________ Skill: 2-digit addition—regrouping

**61 and 83 - Red**
**71 and 64 - Yellow**
**82 and 63 - Orange**

Color all the spaces and boxes.

| | | | | | | | |
|---|---|---|---|---|---|---|---|
| 42 + 29 = 71 | 55 + 27 = 82 | 44 + 27 = 71 | 48 + 15 = 63 | 26 + 45 = 71 | 68 + 15 = 83 | 49 + 15 = 64 | 35 + 29 = 64 |
| 52 + 19 = 71 | 16 + 47 = 63 | 33 + 38 = 71 | 63 + 19 = 82 | 29 + 42 = 71 | 57 + 14 = 71 | 16 + 55 = 71 | 43 + 28 = 71 |
| 28 + 36 = 64 | 47 + 35 = 82 | 38 + 25 = 63 | 67 + 15 = 82 | 48 + 16 = 64 | 27 + 34 = 61 | 45 + 19 = 64 | 45 + 26 = 71 |
| 12 + 59 = 71 | 54 + 28 = 82 | 49 + 15 = 64 | 39 + 24 = 63 | 47 + 17 = 64 | 28 + 55 = 83 | 14 + 57 = 71 | 18 + 46 = 64 |
| 38 + 26 = 64 | 35 + 28 = 63 | 18 + 46 = 64 | 68 + 14 = 82 | 39 + 32 = 71 | 14 + 47 = 61 | 36 + 35 = 71 | 25 + 46 = 71 |

Page 25

Name ______________________ Skill: 2-digit addition—regrouping

**81 and 52 — Yellow**
**82 and 63 — Brown**
**83 and 71 — Red**

Color all the spaces and boxes.

| | | | | | | | |
|---|---|---|---|---|---|---|---|
| 17 + 66 = 83 | 59 + 12 = 71 | 48 + 23 = 71 | 49 + 32 = 81 | 38 + 44 = 82 | 64 + 17 = 81 | 29 + 42 = 71 | 58 + 23 = 81 |
| 54 + 17 = 71 | 23 + 29 = 52 | 56 + 25 = 81 | 44 + 37 = 81 | 39 + 13 = 52 | 43 + 28 = 71 | 28 + 55 = 83 | 45 + 38 = 83 |
| 26 + 57 = 83 | 43 + 28 = 71 | 59 + 24 = 83 | 22 + 59 = 81 | 35 + 28 = 63 | 36 + 16 = 52 | 33 + 38 = 71 | 68 + 13 = 81 |
| 16 + 65 = 81 | 38 + 14 = 52 | 55 + 28 = 83 | 54 + 27 = 81 | 13 + 69 = 82 | 33 + 48 = 81 | 46 + 25 = 71 | 34 + 47 = 81 |
| 38 + 45 = 83 | 65 + 18 = 83 | 29 + 42 = 71 | 52 + 29 = 81 | 49 + 14 = 63 | 14 + 67 = 81 | 42 + 29 = 71 | 24 + 28 = 52 |

Page 26

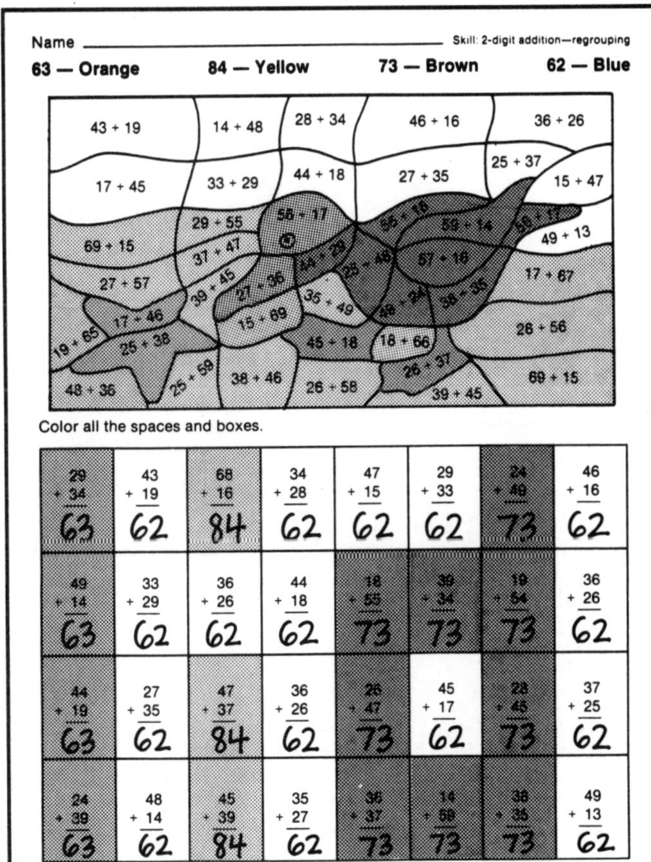


Name ______________________ Skill: 2-digit addition—regrouping

**63 — Orange** **84 — Yellow** **73 — Brown** **62 — Blue**

Color all the spaces and boxes.

| | | | | | | | |
|---|---|---|---|---|---|---|---|
| 29 + 34 = 63 | 43 + 19 = 62 | 68 + 16 = 84 | 34 + 28 = 62 | 47 + 15 = 62 | 29 + 33 = 62 | 24 + 49 = 73 | 46 + 16 = 62 |
| 49 + 14 = 63 | 33 + 29 = 62 | 36 + 26 = 62 | 44 + 18 = 62 | 18 + 55 = 73 | 39 + 34 = 73 | 19 + 54 = 73 | 36 + 26 = 62 |
| 44 + 19 = 63 | 27 + 35 = 62 | 47 + 37 = 84 | 36 + 26 = 62 | 26 + 47 = 73 | 45 + 17 = 62 | 28 + 45 = 73 | 37 + 25 = 62 |
| 24 + 39 = 63 | 48 + 14 = 62 | 45 + 39 = 84 | 35 + 27 = 62 | 36 + 37 = 73 | 14 + 59 = 73 | 38 + 35 = 73 | 49 + 13 = 62 |

Page 27

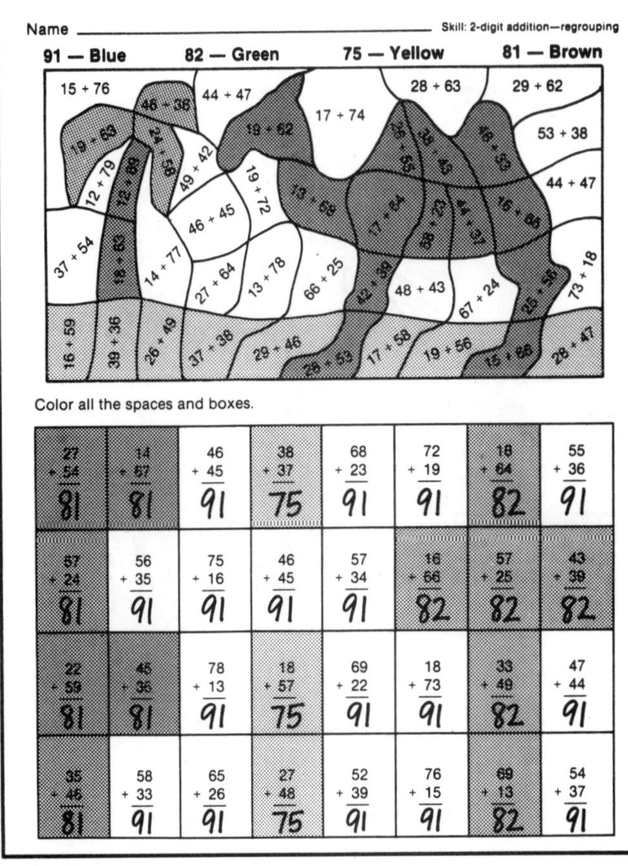


Name ______________________ Skill: 2-digit addition—regrouping

**91 — Blue** **82 — Green** **75 — Yellow** **81 — Brown**

Color all the spaces and boxes.

| | | | | | | | |
|---|---|---|---|---|---|---|---|
| 27 + 54 = 81 | 14 + 67 = 81 | 46 + 45 = 91 | 38 + 37 = 75 | 68 + 23 = 91 | 72 + 19 = 91 | 18 + 64 = 82 | 55 + 36 = 91 |
| 57 + 24 = 81 | 56 + 35 = 91 | 75 + 16 = 91 | 46 + 45 = 91 | 57 + 34 = 91 | 16 + 66 = 82 | 57 + 25 = 82 | 43 + 39 = 82 |
| 22 + 59 = 81 | 45 + 36 = 81 | 78 + 13 = 91 | 18 + 57 = 75 | 69 + 22 = 91 | 18 + 73 = 91 | 33 + 49 = 82 | 47 + 44 = 91 |
| 35 + 46 = 81 | 58 + 33 = 91 | 65 + 26 = 91 | 27 + 48 = 75 | 52 + 39 = 91 | 76 + 15 = 91 | 69 + 13 = 82 | 54 + 37 = 91 |

Page 28

# Answer Key

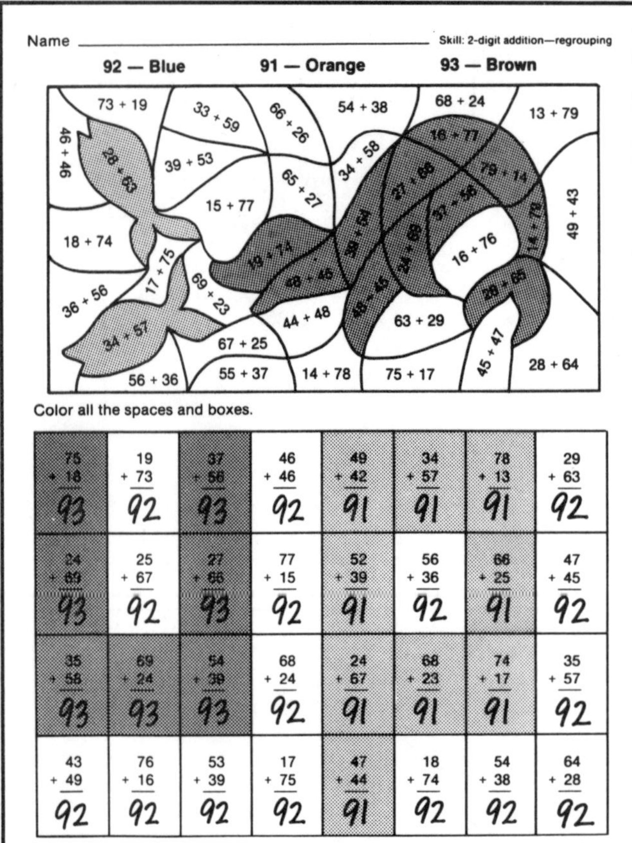

Name ______________________ Skill: 2-digit addition—regrouping

**92 — Blue** **91 — Orange** **93 — Brown**



Color all the spaces and boxes.

| 75 + 18<br>93 | 19 + 73<br>92 | 37 + 56<br>93 | 46 + 46<br>92 | 49 + 42<br>91 | 34 + 57<br>91 | 78 + 13<br>91 | 29 + 63<br>92 |
|---|---|---|---|---|---|---|---|
| 24 + 69<br>93 | 25 + 67<br>92 | 27 + 66<br>93 | 77 + 15<br>92 | 52 + 39<br>91 | 56 + 36<br>92 | 66 + 25<br>91 | 47 + 45<br>92 |
| 35 + 58<br>93 | 69 + 24<br>93 | 54 + 39<br>93 | 68 + 24<br>92 | 24 + 67<br>91 | 68 + 23<br>91 | 74 + 17<br>91 | 35 + 57<br>92 |
| 43 + 49<br>92 | 76 + 16<br>92 | 53 + 39<br>92 | 17 + 75<br>92 | 47 + 44<br>91 | 18 + 74<br>92 | 54 + 38<br>92 | 64 + 28<br>92 |

**Page 29**

Name ______________________ Skill: 2-digit addition—regrouping

**72 and 65 — Yellow**
**93 and 74 — Red**
**81 and 71 — Brown**



Color all the spaces and boxes.

| 29 + 42<br>71 | 28 + 43<br>71 | 25 + 56<br>81 | 48 + 33<br>81 | 47 + 18<br>65 | 38 + 27<br>65 | 54 + 18<br>72 | 49 + 16<br>65 |
|---|---|---|---|---|---|---|---|
| 52 + 19<br>71 | 39 + 33<br>72 | 38 + 27<br>65 | 46 + 26<br>72 | 38 + 34<br>72 | 33 + 39<br>72 | 48 + 17<br>65 | 35 + 37<br>72 |
| 35 + 36<br>71 | 58 + 13<br>71 | 64 + 17<br>81 | 46 + 25<br>71 | 16 + 56<br>72 | 39 + 35<br>74 | 25 + 49<br>74 | 19 + 55<br>74 |
| 15 + 57<br>72 | 28 + 37<br>65 | 56 + 16<br>72 | 63 + 18<br>81 | 23 + 49<br>72 | 14 + 79<br>93 | 29 + 43<br>72 | 18 + 75<br>93 |
| 37 + 44<br>81 | 59 + 22<br>81 | 43 + 38<br>81 | 39 + 32<br>71 | 28 + 44<br>72 | 25 + 68<br>93 | 37 + 37<br>74 | 26 + 48<br>74 |

**Page 30**

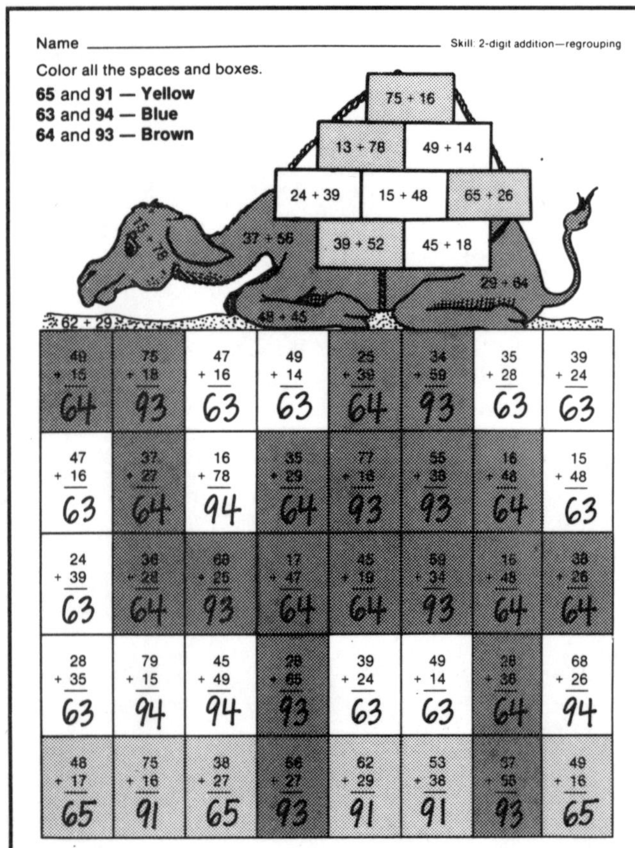

Name ______________________ Skill: 2-digit addition—regrouping

Color all the spaces and boxes.

**65 and 91 — Yellow**
**63 and 94 — Blue**
**64 and 93 — Brown**



| 49 + 15<br>64 | 75 + 18<br>93 | 47 + 16<br>63 | 49 + 14<br>63 | 25 + 39<br>64 | 34 + 59<br>93 | 35 + 28<br>63 | 39 + 24<br>63 |
|---|---|---|---|---|---|---|---|
| 47 + 16<br>63 | 37 + 27<br>64 | 16 + 78<br>94 | 35 + 29<br>64 | 77 + 16<br>93 | 55 + 38<br>93 | 16 + 48<br>64 | 15 + 48<br>63 |
| 24 + 39<br>63 | 36 + 28<br>64 | 68 + 25<br>93 | 17 + 47<br>64 | 45 + 19<br>64 | 59 + 34<br>93 | 16 + 48<br>64 | 38 + 26<br>64 |
| 28 + 35<br>63 | 79 + 15<br>94 | 45 + 49<br>94 | 28 + 65<br>93 | 39 + 24<br>63 | 49 + 14<br>63 | 28 + 36<br>64 | 68 + 26<br>94 |
| 48 + 17<br>65 | 75 + 16<br>91 | 38 + 27<br>65 | 66 + 27<br>93 | 62 + 29<br>91 | 53 + 38<br>91 | 57 + 36<br>93 | 49 + 16<br>65 |

**Page 31**

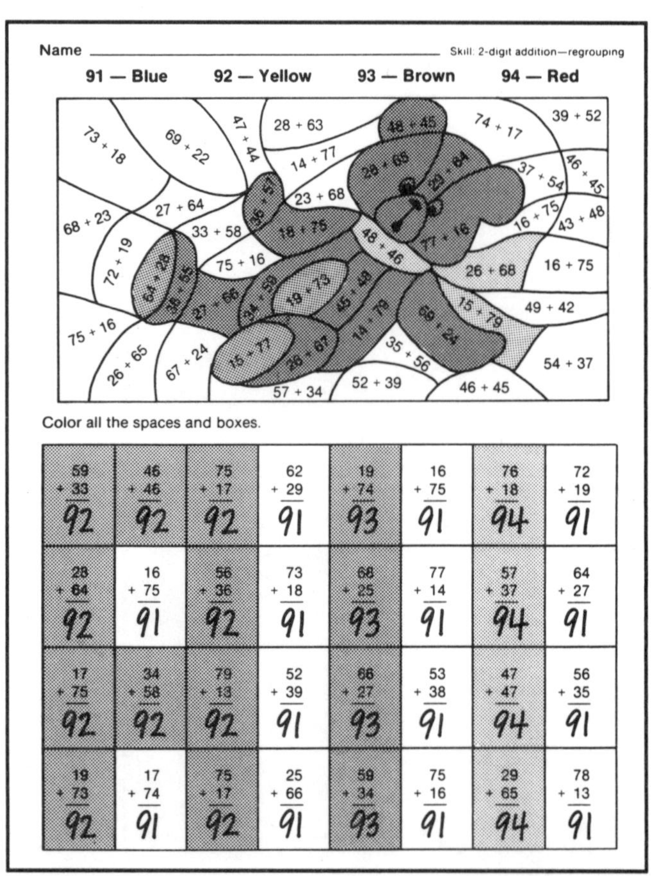

Name ______________________ Skill: 2-digit addition—regrouping

**91 — Blue** **92 — Yellow** **93 — Brown** **94 — Red**



Color all the spaces and boxes.

| 59 + 33<br>92 | 46 + 46<br>92 | 75 + 17<br>92 | 62 + 29<br>91 | 19 + 74<br>93 | 16 + 75<br>91 | 76 + 18<br>94 | 72 + 19<br>91 |
|---|---|---|---|---|---|---|---|
| 28 + 64<br>92 | 16 + 75<br>91 | 56 + 36<br>92 | 73 + 18<br>91 | 68 + 25<br>93 | 77 + 14<br>91 | 57 + 37<br>94 | 64 + 27<br>91 |
| 17 + 75<br>92 | 34 + 58<br>92 | 79 + 13<br>92 | 52 + 39<br>91 | 66 + 27<br>93 | 53 + 38<br>91 | 47 + 47<br>94 | 56 + 35<br>91 |
| 19 + 73<br>92 | 17 + 74<br>91 | 75 + 17<br>92 | 25 + 66<br>91 | 59 + 34<br>93 | 75 + 16<br>91 | 29 + 65<br>94 | 78 + 13<br>91 |

**Page 32**

# Answer Key

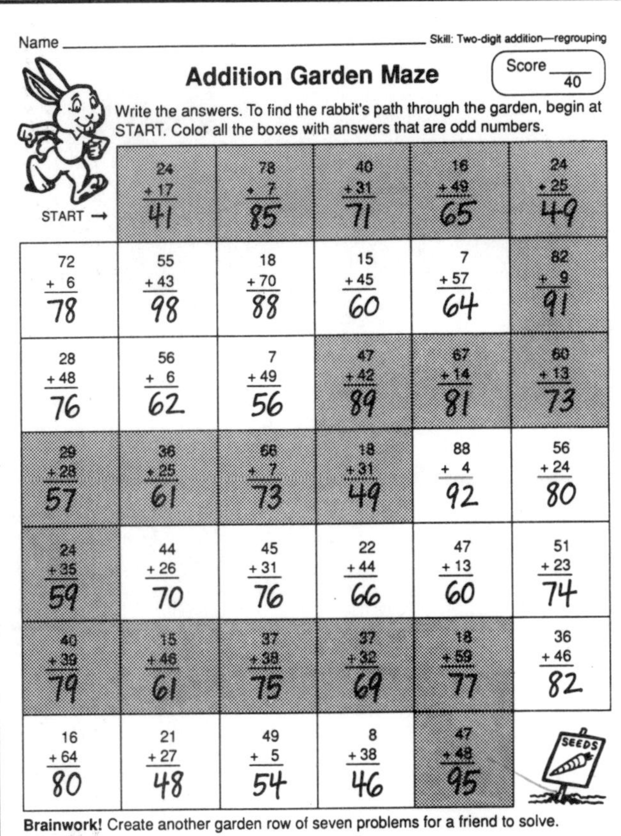

Name ______________________ Skill: Two-digit addition—regrouping

## Addition Garden Maze

Score ___ / 40

Write the answers. To find the rabbit's path through the garden, begin at START. Color all the boxes with answers that are odd numbers.

| | | | | | |
|---|---|---|---|---|---|
| START → | 24 + 17 = 41 | 78 + 7 = 85 | 40 + 31 = 71 | 16 + 49 = 65 | 24 + 25 = 49 |
| 72 + 6 = 78 | 55 + 43 = 98 | 18 + 70 = 88 | 15 + 45 = 60 | 7 + 57 = 64 | 82 + 9 = 91 |
| 28 + 48 = 76 | 56 + 6 = 62 | 7 + 49 = 56 | 47 + 42 = 89 | 67 + 14 = 81 | 60 + 13 = 73 |
| 29 + 28 = 57 | 36 + 25 = 61 | 66 + 7 = 73 | 18 + 31 = 49 | 88 + 4 = 92 | 56 + 24 = 80 |
| 24 + 35 = 59 | 44 + 26 = 70 | 45 + 31 = 76 | 22 + 44 = 66 | 47 + 13 = 60 | 51 + 23 = 74 |
| 40 + 39 = 79 | 15 + 46 = 61 | 37 + 38 = 75 | 37 + 32 = 69 | 18 + 59 = 77 | 36 + 46 = 82 |
| 16 + 64 = 80 | 21 + 27 = 48 | 49 + 5 = 54 | 8 + 38 = 46 | 47 + 48 = 95 | |



**Brainwork!** Create another garden row of seven problems for a friend to solve.

Page 33

Name ______________________ Skill: 2-digit subtraction—regrouping

**25 and 14 — Black**
**26 and 15 — Red**
**27 and 16 — Blue**



Color all the spaces and boxes.

| | | | | | | | |
|---|---|---|---|---|---|---|---|
| 71 - 55 = 16 | 83 - 56 = 27 | 91 - 75 = 16 | 65 - 49 = 16 | 82 - 66 = 16 | 64 - 37 = 27 | 74 - 58 = 16 | 62 - 35 = 27 |
| 73 - 46 = 27 | 41 - 16 = 25 | 41 - 15 = 26 | 74 - 59 = 15 | 52 - 26 = 26 | 80 - 54 = 26 | 61 - 46 = 15 | 80 - 53 = 27 |
| 51 - 35 = 16 | 71 - 45 = 26 | 82 - 67 = 15 | 54 - 28 = 26 | 63 - 48 = 15 | 83 - 57 = 26 | 73 - 47 = 26 | 61 - 45 = 16 |
| 42 - 15 = 27 | 61 - 45 = 16 | 50 - 25 = 25 | 83 - 67 = 16 | 92 - 65 = 27 | 75 - 48 = 27 | 42 - 28 = 14 | 62 - 46 = 16 |
| 61 - 34 = 27 | 72 - 56 = 16 | 84 - 57 = 27 | 45 - 29 = 16 | 55 - 39 = 16 | 53 - 26 = 27 | 74 - 58 = 16 | 62 - 35 = 27 |

Page 34

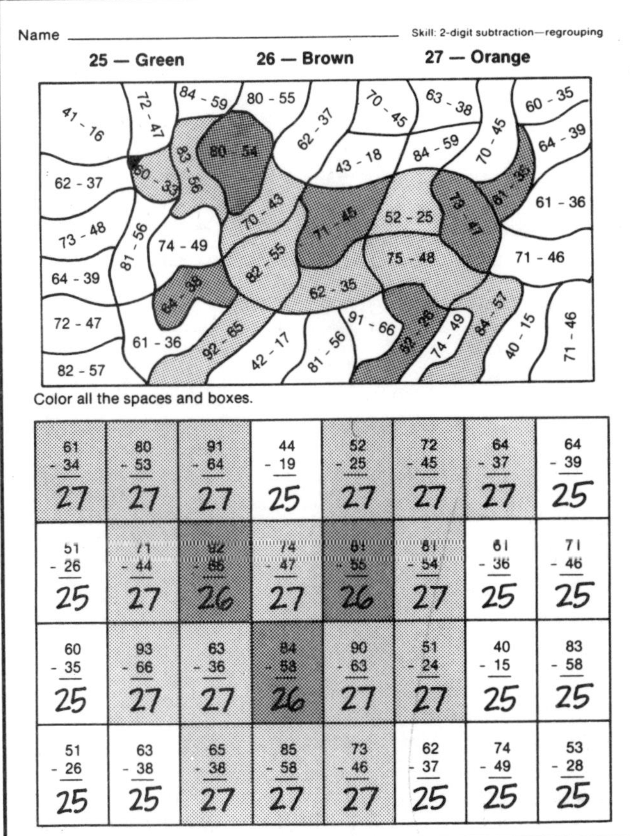

Name ______________________ Skill: 2-digit subtraction—regrouping

**25 — Green** **26 — Brown** **27 — Orange**



Color all the spaces and boxes.

| | | | | | | | |
|---|---|---|---|---|---|---|---|
| 61 - 34 = 27 | 80 - 53 = 27 | 91 - 64 = 27 | 44 - 19 = 25 | 52 - 25 = 27 | 72 - 45 = 27 | 64 - 37 = 27 | 64 - 39 = 25 |
| 51 - 26 = 25 | 71 - 44 = 27 | 92 - 66 = 26 | 74 - 47 = 27 | 81 - 55 = 26 | 81 - 54 = 27 | 61 - 36 = 25 | 71 - 46 = 25 |
| 60 - 35 = 25 | 93 - 66 = 27 | 63 - 36 = 27 | 84 - 58 = 26 | 90 - 63 = 27 | 51 - 24 = 27 | 40 - 15 = 25 | 83 - 58 = 25 |
| 51 - 26 = 25 | 63 - 38 = 25 | 65 - 38 = 27 | 85 - 58 = 27 | 73 - 46 = 27 | 62 - 37 = 25 | 74 - 49 = 25 | 53 - 28 = 25 |

Page 35

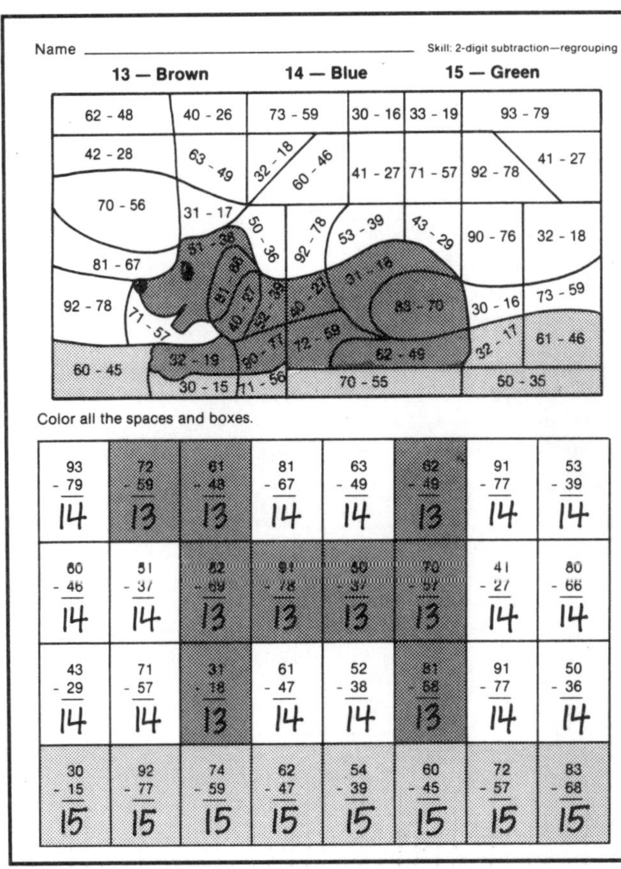

Name ______________________ Skill: 2-digit subtraction—regrouping

**13 — Brown** **14 — Blue** **15 — Green**



Color all the spaces and boxes.

| | | | | | | | |
|---|---|---|---|---|---|---|---|
| 93 - 79 = 14 | 72 - 59 = 13 | 61 - 48 = 13 | 81 - 67 = 14 | 63 - 49 = 14 | 62 - 49 = 13 | 91 - 77 = 14 | 53 - 39 = 14 |
| 60 - 46 = 14 | 51 - 37 = 14 | 82 - 69 = 13 | 91 - 78 = 13 | 50 - 37 = 13 | 70 - 57 = 13 | 41 - 27 = 14 | 80 - 66 = 14 |
| 43 - 29 = 14 | 71 - 57 = 14 | 31 - 18 = 13 | 61 - 47 = 14 | 52 - 38 = 14 | 81 - 68 = 13 | 91 - 77 = 14 | 50 - 36 = 14 |
| 30 - 15 = 15 | 92 - 77 = 15 | 74 - 59 = 15 | 62 - 47 = 15 | 54 - 39 = 15 | 60 - 45 = 15 | 72 - 57 = 15 | 83 - 68 = 15 |

Page 36

# Answer Key

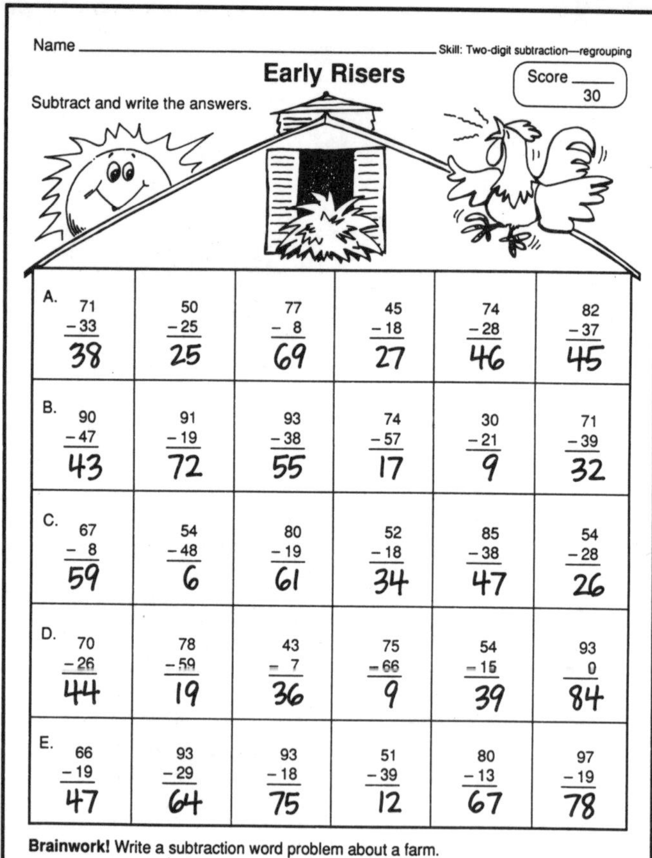

Name ____________________ Skill: Two-digit subtraction—regrouping

## Early Risers

Score ___ / 30

Subtract and write the answers.

| | | | | | |
|---|---|---|---|---|---|
| A. 71<br>− 33<br>38 | 50<br>− 25<br>25 | 77<br>− 8<br>69 | 45<br>− 18<br>27 | 74<br>− 28<br>46 | 82<br>− 37<br>45 |
| B. 90<br>− 47<br>43 | 91<br>− 19<br>72 | 93<br>− 38<br>55 | 74<br>− 57<br>17 | 30<br>− 21<br>9 | 71<br>− 39<br>32 |
| C. 67<br>− 8<br>59 | 54<br>− 48<br>6 | 80<br>− 19<br>61 | 52<br>− 18<br>34 | 85<br>− 38<br>47 | 54<br>− 28<br>26 |
| D. 70<br>− 26<br>44 | 78<br>− 59<br>19 | 43<br>− 7<br>36 | 75<br>− 66<br>9 | 54<br>− 15<br>39 | 93<br>0<br>84 |
| E. 66<br>− 19<br>47 | 93<br>− 29<br>64 | 93<br>− 18<br>75 | 51<br>− 39<br>12 | 80<br>− 13<br>67 | 97<br>− 19<br>78 |

**Brainwork!** Write a subtraction word problem about a farm.

Page 37

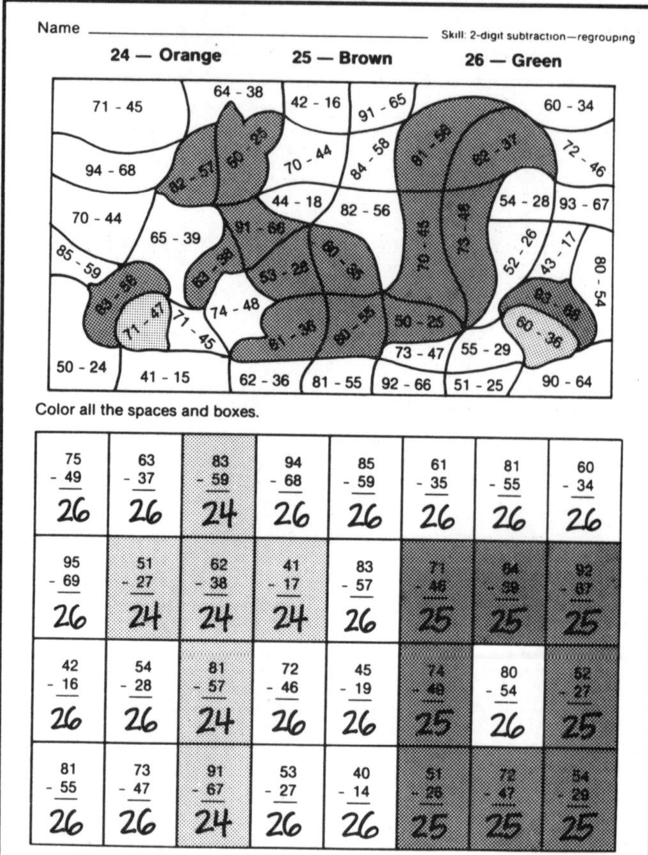

Name ____________________ Skill: 2-digit subtraction—regrouping

**24 — Orange** **25 — Brown** **26 — Green**



Color all the spaces and boxes.

| | | | | | | | |
|---|---|---|---|---|---|---|---|
| 75<br>- 49<br>26 | 63<br>- 37<br>26 | 83<br>- 59<br>24 | 94<br>- 68<br>26 | 85<br>- 59<br>26 | 61<br>- 35<br>26 | 81<br>- 55<br>26 | 60<br>- 34<br>26 |
| 95<br>- 69<br>26 | 51<br>- 27<br>24 | 62<br>- 38<br>24 | 41<br>- 17<br>24 | 83<br>- 57<br>26 | 71<br>- 46<br>25 | 84<br>- 59<br>25 | 92<br>- 67<br>25 |
| 42<br>- 16<br>26 | 54<br>- 28<br>26 | 81<br>- 57<br>24 | 72<br>- 46<br>26 | 45<br>- 19<br>26 | 74<br>- 49<br>25 | 80<br>- 54<br>26 | 52<br>- 27<br>25 |
| 81<br>- 55<br>26 | 73<br>- 47<br>26 | 91<br>- 67<br>24 | 53<br>- 27<br>26 | 40<br>- 14<br>26 | 51<br>- 26<br>25 | 72<br>- 47<br>25 | 54<br>- 29<br>25 |

Page 38

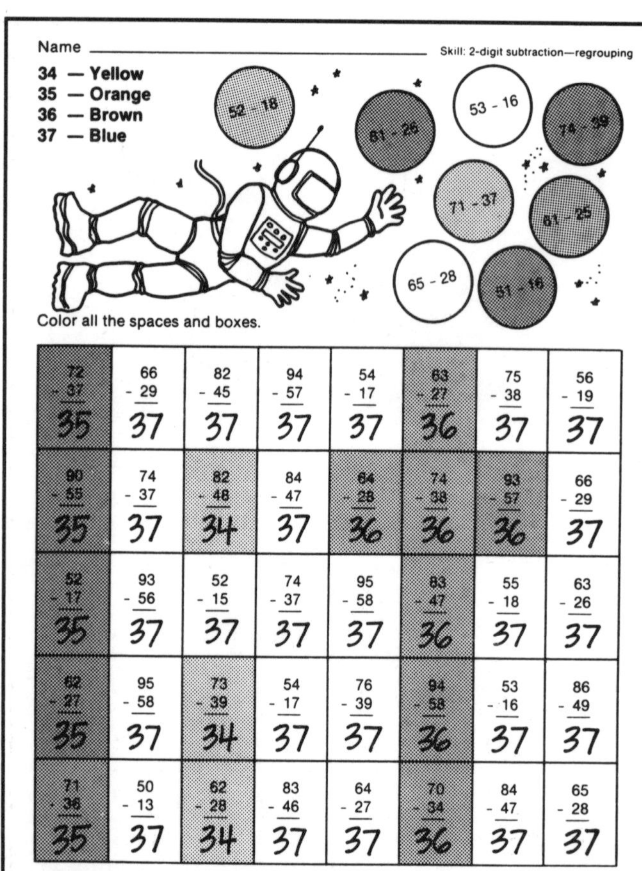

Name ____________________ Skill: 2-digit subtraction—regrouping

**34 — Yellow**
**35 — Orange**
**36 — Brown**
**37 — Blue**



Color all the spaces and boxes.

| | | | | | | | |
|---|---|---|---|---|---|---|---|
| 72<br>- 37<br>35 | 66<br>- 29<br>37 | 82<br>- 45<br>37 | 94<br>- 57<br>37 | 54<br>- 17<br>37 | 63<br>- 27<br>36 | 75<br>- 38<br>37 | 56<br>- 19<br>37 |
| 90<br>- 55<br>35 | 74<br>- 37<br>37 | 82<br>- 48<br>34 | 84<br>- 47<br>37 | 64<br>- 28<br>36 | 74<br>- 38<br>36 | 93<br>- 57<br>36 | 66<br>- 29<br>37 |
| 52<br>- 17<br>35 | 93<br>- 56<br>37 | 52<br>- 15<br>37 | 74<br>- 37<br>37 | 95<br>- 58<br>37 | 83<br>- 47<br>36 | 55<br>- 18<br>37 | 63<br>- 26<br>37 |
| 62<br>- 27<br>35 | 95<br>- 58<br>37 | 73<br>- 39<br>34 | 54<br>- 17<br>37 | 76<br>- 39<br>37 | 94<br>- 58<br>36 | 53<br>- 16<br>37 | 86<br>- 49<br>37 |
| 71<br>- 36<br>35 | 50<br>- 13<br>37 | 62<br>- 28<br>34 | 83<br>- 46<br>37 | 64<br>- 27<br>37 | 70<br>- 34<br>36 | 84<br>- 47<br>37 | 65<br>- 28<br>37 |

Page 39

Name ____________________ Skill: 2-digit subtraction—regrouping

Color all the spaces and boxes.

**16 — Red**
**17 — Orange**
**18 — Yellow**



| | | | | | | | |
|---|---|---|---|---|---|---|---|
| 95<br>- 79<br>16 | 45<br>- 29<br>16 | 70<br>- 54<br>16 | 65<br>- 49<br>16 | 32<br>- 14<br>18 | 94<br>- 76<br>18 | 54<br>- 36<br>18 | 84<br>- 66<br>18 |
| 91<br>- 75<br>16 | 42<br>- 24<br>18 | 71<br>- 53<br>18 | 57<br>- 39<br>18 | 72<br>- 54<br>18 | 91<br>- 73<br>18 | 35<br>- 17<br>18 | 92<br>- 74<br>18 |
| 51<br>- 35<br>16 | 42<br>- 24<br>18 | 82<br>- 66<br>16 | 55<br>- 39<br>16 | 93<br>- 75<br>18 | 60<br>- 43<br>17 | 71<br>- 54<br>17 | 95<br>- 78<br>17 |
| 83<br>- 67<br>16 | 45<br>- 27<br>18 | 54<br>- 36<br>18 | 95<br>- 79<br>16 | 44<br>- 26<br>18 | 62<br>- 45<br>17 | 77<br>- 59<br>18 | 90<br>- 73<br>17 |
| 61<br>- 45<br>16 | 83<br>- 67<br>16 | 41<br>- 25<br>16 | 80<br>- 64<br>16 | 93<br>- 75<br>18 | 74<br>- 57<br>17 | 40<br>- 23<br>17 | 75<br>- 58<br>17 |

Page 40

# Answer Key

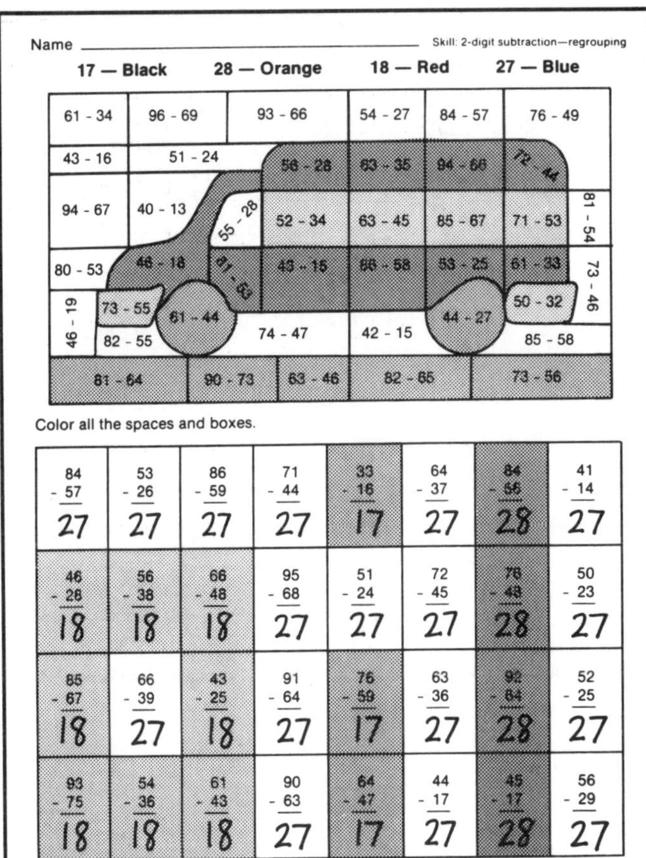
Name ______ Skill: 2-digit subtraction—regrouping

**17 — Black** **28 — Orange** **18 — Red** **27 — Blue**



Color all the spaces and boxes.

| 84<br>- 57<br>27 | 53<br>- 26<br>27 | 86<br>- 59<br>27 | 71<br>- 44<br>27 | 33<br>- 16<br>17 | 64<br>- 37<br>27 | 84<br>- 56<br>28 | 41<br>- 14<br>27 |
|---|---|---|---|---|---|---|---|
| 46<br>- 28<br>18 | 56<br>- 38<br>18 | 66<br>- 48<br>18 | 95<br>- 68<br>27 | 51<br>- 24<br>27 | 72<br>- 45<br>27 | 76<br>- 48<br>28 | 50<br>- 23<br>27 |
| 85<br>- 67<br>18 | 66<br>- 39<br>27 | 43<br>- 25<br>18 | 91<br>- 64<br>27 | 76<br>- 59<br>17 | 63<br>- 36<br>27 | 92<br>- 64<br>28 | 52<br>- 25<br>27 |
| 93<br>- 75<br>18 | 54<br>- 36<br>18 | 61<br>- 43<br>18 | 90<br>- 63<br>27 | 64<br>- 47<br>17 | 44<br>- 17<br>27 | 45<br>- 17<br>28 | 56<br>- 29<br>27 |

**Page 41**

Name ______ Skill: 2-digit subtraction—regrouping

Color all the spaces and boxes.
**13 and 27 — Brown**
**14 and 28 — Yellow**
**15 and 29 — Orange**



| 73<br>- 59<br>14 | 47<br>- 19<br>28 | 61<br>- 32<br>29 | 50<br>- 36<br>14 | 52<br>- 24<br>28 | 41<br>- 13<br>28 | 82<br>- 68<br>14 | 74<br>- 46<br>28 |
|---|---|---|---|---|---|---|---|
| 91<br>- 63<br>28 | 33<br>- 19<br>14 | 82<br>- 67<br>15 | 73<br>- 45<br>28 | 82<br>- 54<br>28 | 71<br>- 57<br>14 | 50<br>- 22<br>28 | 51<br>- 37<br>14 |
| 44<br>- 29<br>15 | 51<br>- 22<br>29 | 43<br>- 14<br>29 | 52<br>- 38<br>14 | 92<br>- 79<br>13 | 84<br>- 57<br>27 | 41<br>- 28<br>13 | 87<br>- 59<br>28 |
| 72<br>- 43<br>29 | 61<br>- 47<br>14 | 73<br>- 58<br>15 | 62<br>- 34<br>28 | 72<br>- 45<br>27 | 96<br>- 68<br>28 | 41<br>- 14<br>27 | 51<br>- 23<br>28 |
| 91<br>- 62<br>29 | 50<br>- 35<br>15 | 84<br>- 55<br>29 | 80<br>- 66<br>14 | 50<br>- 23<br>27 | 31<br>- 18<br>13 | 54<br>- 27<br>27 | 42<br>- 28<br>14 |

**Page 42**

Name ______ Skill: 2-digit subtraction—regrouping

**34 — Red**
**35 — Blue**
**36 — Brown**
**37 — Green**



Color all the spaces and boxes.

| 72<br>- 38<br>34 | 80<br>- 45<br>35 | 52<br>- 17<br>35 | 54<br>- 19<br>35 | 84<br>- 49<br>35 | 63<br>- 28<br>35 | 50<br>- 13<br>37 | 70<br>- 35<br>35 |
|---|---|---|---|---|---|---|---|
| 53<br>- 19<br>34 | 90<br>- 55<br>35 | 51<br>- 16<br>35 | 92<br>- 57<br>35 | 50<br>- 15<br>35 | 85<br>- 48<br>37 | 63<br>- 26<br>37 | 96<br>- 59<br>37 |
| 60<br>- 26<br>34 | 82<br>- 47<br>35 | 82<br>- 46<br>36 | 65<br>- 29<br>36 | 62<br>- 26<br>36 | 93<br>- 58<br>35 | 83<br>- 46<br>37 | 61<br>- 26<br>35 |
| 83<br>- 49<br>34 | 71<br>- 36<br>35 | 62<br>- 26<br>36 | 81<br>- 46<br>35 | 73<br>- 37<br>36 | 53<br>- 18<br>35 | 71<br>- 34<br>37 | 62<br>- 27<br>35 |
| 92<br>- 58<br>34 | 83<br>- 48<br>35 | 71<br>- 35<br>36 | 85<br>- 49<br>36 | 84<br>- 48<br>36 | 64<br>- 29<br>35 | 51<br>- 14<br>37 | 74<br>- 39<br>35 |

**Page 43**

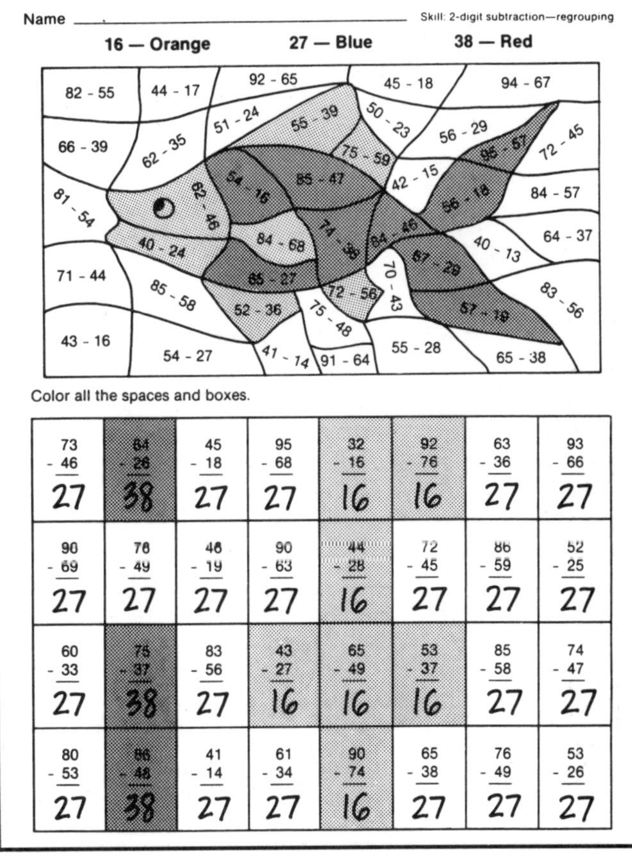
Name ______ Skill: 2-digit subtraction—regrouping

**16 — Orange** **27 — Blue** **38 — Red**



Color all the spaces and boxes.

| 73<br>- 46<br>27 | 64<br>- 26<br>38 | 45<br>- 18<br>27 | 95<br>- 68<br>27 | 32<br>- 16<br>16 | 92<br>- 76<br>16 | 63<br>- 36<br>27 | 93<br>- 66<br>27 |
|---|---|---|---|---|---|---|---|
| 96<br>- 69<br>27 | 76<br>- 49<br>27 | 46<br>- 19<br>27 | 90<br>- 63<br>27 | 44<br>- 28<br>16 | 72<br>- 45<br>27 | 86<br>- 59<br>27 | 52<br>- 25<br>27 |
| 60<br>- 33<br>27 | 75<br>- 37<br>38 | 83<br>- 56<br>27 | 43<br>- 27<br>16 | 65<br>- 49<br>16 | 53<br>- 37<br>16 | 85<br>- 58<br>27 | 74<br>- 47<br>27 |
| 80<br>- 53<br>27 | 86<br>- 48<br>38 | 41<br>- 14<br>27 | 61<br>- 34<br>27 | 90<br>- 74<br>16 | 65<br>- 38<br>27 | 76<br>- 49<br>27 | 53<br>- 26<br>27 |

**Page 44**

# Answer Key

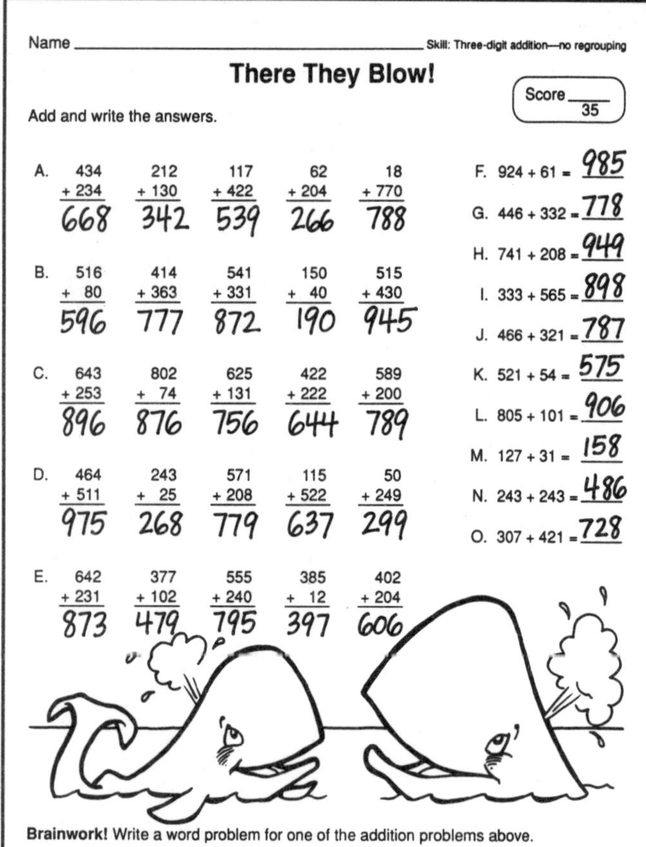

Name ______________________ Skill: Three-digit addition—no regrouping

## There They Blow!

Score ___ / 35

Add and write the answers.

| | | | | | |
|---|---|---|---|---|---|
| A. | 434 + 234 = 668 | 212 + 130 = 342 | 117 + 422 = 539 | 62 + 204 = 266 | 18 + 770 = 788 |
| B. | 516 + 80 = 596 | 414 + 363 = 777 | 541 + 331 = 872 | 150 + 40 = 190 | 515 + 430 = 945 |
| C. | 643 + 253 = 896 | 802 + 74 = 876 | 625 + 131 = 756 | 422 + 222 = 644 | 589 + 200 = 789 |
| D. | 464 + 511 = 975 | 243 + 25 = 268 | 571 + 208 = 779 | 115 + 522 = 637 | 50 + 249 = 299 |
| E. | 642 + 231 = 873 | 377 + 102 = 479 | 555 + 240 = 795 | 385 + 12 = 397 | 402 + 204 = 606 |

F. 924 + 61 = 985
G. 446 + 332 = 778
H. 741 + 208 = 949
I. 333 + 565 = 898
J. 466 + 321 = 787
K. 521 + 54 = 575
L. 805 + 101 = 906
M. 127 + 31 = 158
N. 243 + 243 = 486
O. 307 + 421 = 728

**Brainwork!** Write a word problem for one of the addition problems above.

Page 45

Name ______________________ Skill: Adding multiples of 100

## For the Birds

Score ___ / 45

Add.

| A. + 400 | | B. + 700 | | C. + 900 | |
|---|---|---|---|---|---|
| 700 | 1,100 | 700 | 1,400 | 400 | 1,300 |
| 500 | 900 | 300 | 1,000 | 200 | 1,100 |
| 200 | 600 | 100 | 800 | 800 | 1,700 |
| 800 | 1,200 | 900 | 1,600 | 600 | 1,500 |
| 600 | 1,000 | 500 | 1,200 | 700 | 1,600 |
| 900 | 1,300 | 200 | 900 | 900 | 1,800 |
| 400 | 800 | 400 | 1,100 | 300 | 1,200 |
| 300 | 700 | 800 | 1,500 | 500 | 1,400 |

| D. + 600 | | E. + 500 | | F. + 800 | |
|---|---|---|---|---|---|
| 700 | 1,300 | 700 | 1,200 | 700 | 1,500 |
| 500 | 1,100 | 500 | 1,000 | 500 | 1,300 |
| 200 | 800 | 100 | 600 | 200 | 1,000 |
| 800 | 1,400 | 900 | 1,400 | 800 | 1,600 |
| 600 | 1,200 | 300 | 800 | 600 | 1,400 |
| 900 | 1,500 | 200 | 700 | 900 | 1,700 |
| 400 | 1,000 | 400 | 900 | 400 | 1,200 |

**Brainwork!** Draw a *+1000* birdhouse like the ones above. Have a friend write the answers. Check your friend's work.

Page 46

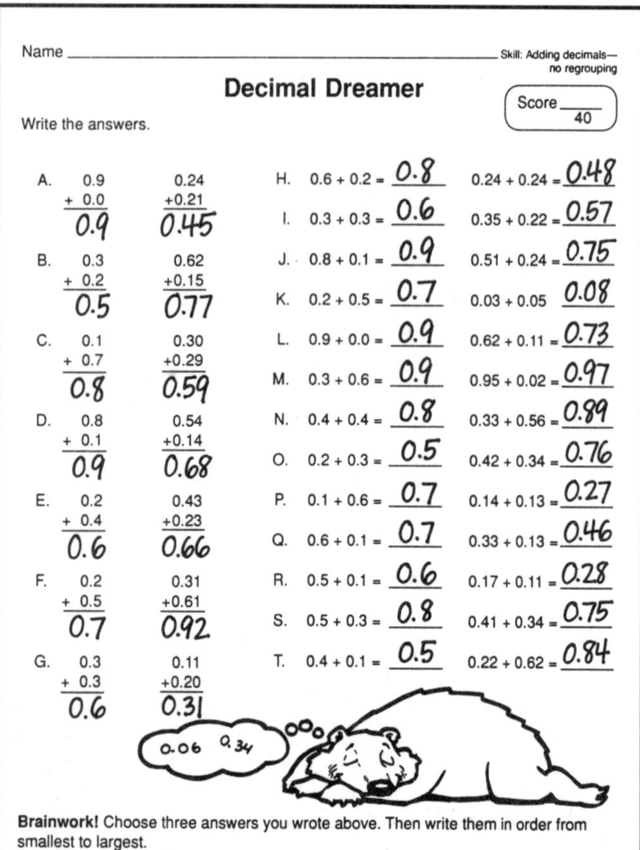

Name ______________________ Skill: Adding decimals—no regrouping

## Decimal Dreamer

Score ___ / 40

Write the answers.

| | | |
|---|---|---|
| A. | 0.9 + 0.0 = 0.9 | 0.24 + 0.21 = 0.45 |
| B. | 0.3 + 0.2 = 0.5 | 0.62 + 0.15 = 0.77 |
| C. | 0.1 + 0.7 = 0.8 | 0.30 + 0.29 = 0.59 |
| D. | 0.8 + 0.1 = 0.9 | 0.54 + 0.14 = 0.68 |
| E. | 0.2 + 0.4 = 0.6 | 0.43 + 0.23 = 0.66 |
| F. | 0.2 + 0.5 = 0.7 | 0.31 + 0.61 = 0.92 |
| G. | 0.3 + 0.3 = 0.6 | 0.11 + 0.20 = 0.31 |

| | | |
|---|---|---|
| H. | 0.6 + 0.2 = 0.8 | 0.24 + 0.24 = 0.48 |
| I. | 0.3 + 0.3 = 0.6 | 0.35 + 0.22 = 0.57 |
| J. | 0.8 + 0.1 = 0.9 | 0.51 + 0.24 = 0.75 |
| K. | 0.2 + 0.5 = 0.7 | 0.03 + 0.05 = 0.08 |
| L. | 0.9 + 0.0 = 0.9 | 0.62 + 0.11 = 0.73 |
| M. | 0.3 + 0.6 = 0.9 | 0.95 + 0.02 = 0.97 |
| N. | 0.4 + 0.4 = 0.8 | 0.33 + 0.56 = 0.89 |
| O. | 0.2 + 0.3 = 0.5 | 0.42 + 0.34 = 0.76 |
| P. | 0.1 + 0.6 = 0.7 | 0.14 + 0.13 = 0.27 |
| Q. | 0.6 + 0.1 = 0.7 | 0.33 + 0.13 = 0.46 |
| R. | 0.5 + 0.1 = 0.6 | 0.17 + 0.11 = 0.28 |
| S. | 0.5 + 0.3 = 0.8 | 0.41 + 0.34 = 0.75 |
| T. | 0.4 + 0.1 = 0.5 | 0.22 + 0.62 = 0.84 |



**Brainwork!** Choose three answers you wrote above. Then write them in order from smallest to largest.

Page 47

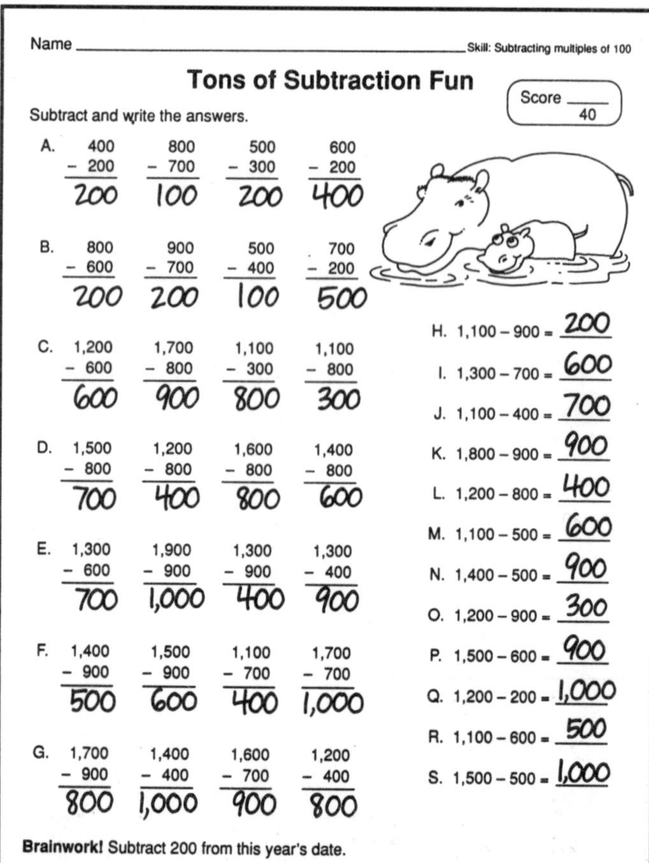

Name ______________________ Skill: Subtracting multiples of 100

## Tons of Subtraction Fun

Score ___ / 40

Subtract and write the answers.

| | | | | |
|---|---|---|---|---|
| A. | 400 − 200 = 200 | 800 − 700 = 100 | 500 − 300 = 200 | 600 − 200 = 400 |
| B. | 800 − 600 = 200 | 900 − 700 = 200 | 500 − 400 = 100 | 700 − 200 = 500 |
| C. | 1,200 − 600 = 600 | 1,700 − 800 = 900 | 1,100 − 300 = 800 | 1,100 − 800 = 300 |
| D. | 1,500 − 800 = 700 | 1,200 − 800 = 400 | 1,600 − 800 = 800 | 1,400 − 800 = 600 |
| E. | 1,300 − 600 = 700 | 1,900 − 900 = 1,000 | 1,300 − 900 = 400 | 1,300 − 400 = 900 |
| F. | 1,400 − 900 = 500 | 1,500 − 900 = 600 | 1,100 − 700 = 400 | 1,700 − 700 = 1,000 |
| G. | 1,700 − 900 = 800 | 1,400 − 400 = 1,000 | 1,600 − 700 = 900 | 1,200 − 400 = 800 |

H. 1,100 − 900 = 200
I. 1,300 − 700 = 600
J. 1,100 − 400 = 700
K. 1,800 − 900 = 900
L. 1,200 − 800 = 400
M. 1,100 − 500 = 600
N. 1,400 − 500 = 900
O. 1,200 − 900 = 300
P. 1,500 − 600 = 900
Q. 1,200 − 200 = 1,000
R. 1,100 − 600 = 500
S. 1,500 − 500 = 1,000

**Brainwork!** Subtract 200 from this year's date.

Page 48

# Answer Key

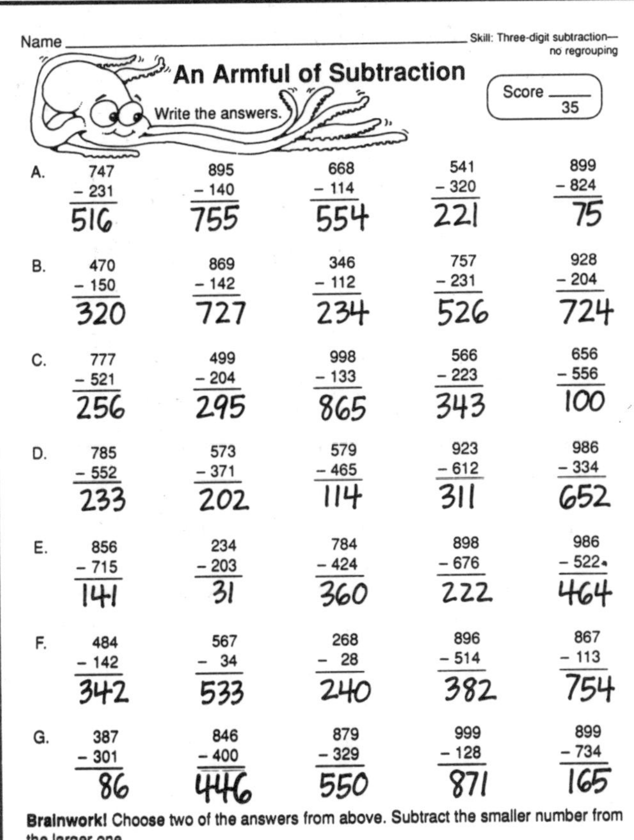

Name ______________________ Skill: Three-digit subtraction—no regrouping

## An Armful of Subtraction

Score ____ 35

Write the answers.

| | | | | | |
|---|---|---|---|---|---|
| A. | 747 − 231 = 516 | 895 − 140 = 755 | 668 − 114 = 554 | 541 − 320 = 221 | 899 − 824 = 75 |
| B. | 470 − 150 = 320 | 869 − 142 = 727 | 346 − 112 = 234 | 757 − 231 = 526 | 928 − 204 = 724 |
| C. | 777 − 521 = 256 | 499 − 204 = 295 | 998 − 133 = 865 | 566 − 223 = 343 | 656 − 556 = 100 |
| D. | 785 − 552 = 233 | 573 − 371 = 202 | 579 − 465 = 114 | 923 − 612 = 311 | 986 − 334 = 652 |
| E. | 856 − 715 = 141 | 234 − 203 = 31 | 784 − 424 = 360 | 898 − 676 = 222 | 986 − 522 = 464 |
| F. | 484 − 142 = 342 | 567 − 34 = 533 | 268 − 28 = 240 | 896 − 514 = 382 | 867 − 113 = 754 |
| G. | 387 − 301 = 86 | 846 − 400 = 446 | 879 − 329 = 550 | 999 − 128 = 871 | 899 − 734 = 165 |

**Brainwork!** Choose two of the answers from above. Subtract the smaller number from the larger one.

**Page 49**

Name ______________________ Skill: Subtracting decimals—no regrouping

## Sunny Subtraction

Score ____ 40

Write the answers.

| | | |
|---|---|---|
| A. | 0.7 − 0.1 = 0.6 | 0.89 − 0.64 = 0.25 |
| B. | 0.5 − 0.4 = 0.1 | 0.34 − 0.24 = 0.10 |
| C. | 0.7 − 0.5 = 0.2 | 0.97 − 0.75 = 0.22 |
| D. | 0.6 − 0.3 = 0.3 | 0.34 − 0.33 = 0.01 |
| E. | 0.5 − 0.2 = 0.3 | 0.69 − 0.42 = 0.27 |
| F. | 0.9 − 0.5 = 0.4 | 0.67 − 0.32 = 0.35 |
| G. | 0.4 − 0.0 = 0.4 | 0.75 − 0.15 = 0.60 |
| H. | 0.9 − 0.7 = 0.2 | 0.46 − 0.26 = 0.20 |
| I. | 0.8 − 0.4 = 0.4 | 0.89 − 0.56 = 0.33 |
| J. | 0.9 − 0.1 = 0.8 | 0.13 − 0.11 = 0.02 |
| K. | 0.6 − 0.3 = 0.3 | 0.79 − 0.40 = 0.39 |
| L. | 0.6 − 0.5 = 0.1 | 0.24 − 0.21 = 0.03 |
| M. | 0.9 − 0.4 = 0.5 | 0.98 − 0.33 = 0.65 |
| N. | 0.6 − 0.2 = 0.4 | 0.56 − 0.42 = 0.14 |

| | | |
|---|---|---|
| O. | 0.7 − 0.3 = 0.4 | 0.79 − 0.68 = 0.11 |
| P. | 0.9 − 0.6 = 0.3 | 0.86 − 0.05 = 0.81 |
| Q. | 0.8 − 0.5 = 0.3 | 0.98 − 0.54 = 0.44 |
| R. | 0.5 − 0.2 = 0.3 | 0.89 − 0.21 = 0.68 |
| S. | 0.9 − 0.2 = 0.7 | 0.78 − 0.31 = 0.47 |
| T. | 0.8 − 0.2 = 0.6 | 0.98 − 0.97 = 0.01 |

**Brainwork!** Write three decimals that are greater than 0.5.

**Page 50**

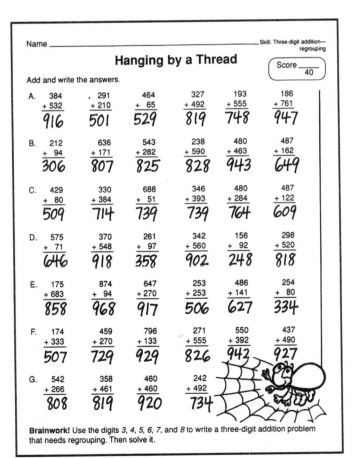

Name ______________________ Skill: Three-digit addition—regrouping

## Hanging by a Thread

Score ____ 40

Add and write the answers.

| | | | | | | |
|---|---|---|---|---|---|---|
| A. | 384 + 532 = 916 | 291 + 210 = 501 | 464 + 65 = 529 | 327 + 492 = 819 | 193 + 555 = 748 | 186 + 761 = 947 |
| B. | 212 + 94 = 306 | 636 + 171 = 807 | 543 + 282 = 825 | 238 + 590 = 828 | 480 + 463 = 943 | 487 + 162 = 649 |
| C. | 429 + 80 = 509 | 330 + 384 = 714 | 688 + 51 = 739 | 346 + 393 = 739 | 480 + 284 = 764 | 487 + 122 = 609 |
| D. | 575 + 71 = 646 | 370 + 548 = 918 | 261 + 97 = 358 | 342 + 560 = 902 | 156 + 92 = 248 | 298 + 520 = 818 |
| E. | 175 + 683 = 858 | 874 + 94 = 968 | 647 + 270 = 917 | 253 + 253 = 506 | 486 + 141 = 627 | 254 + 80 = 334 |
| F. | 174 + 333 = 507 | 459 + 270 = 729 | 796 + 133 = 929 | 271 + 555 = 826 | 550 + 392 = 942 | 437 + 490 = 927 |
| G. | 542 + 266 = 808 | 358 + 461 = 819 | 460 + 460 = 920 | 242 + 492 = 734 | | |

**Brainwork!** Use the digits *3, 4, 5, 6, 7,* and *8* to write a three-digit addition problem that needs regrouping. Then solve it.

**Page 51**

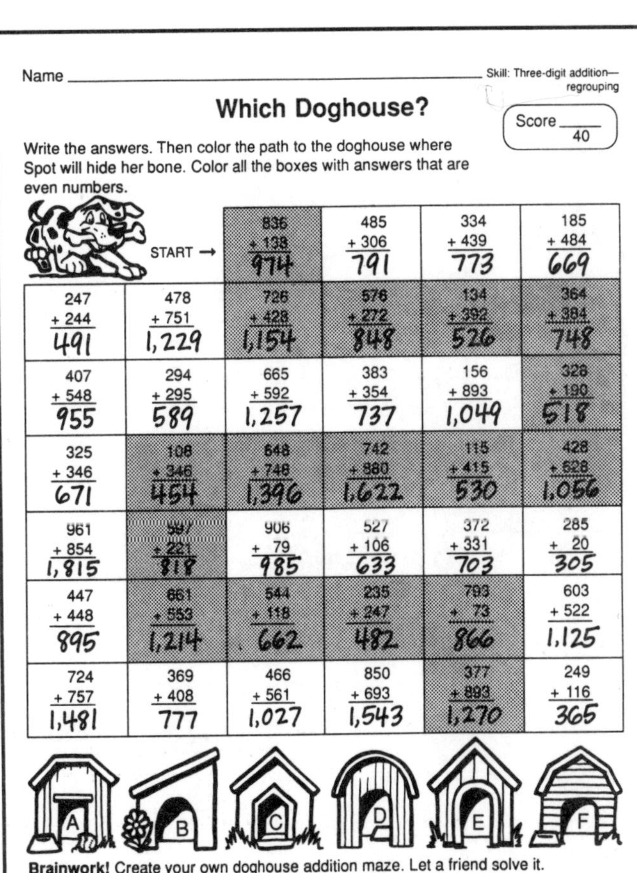

Name ______________________ Skill: Three-digit addition—regrouping

## Which Doghouse?

Score ____ 40

Write the answers. Then color the path to the doghouse where Spot will hide her bone. Color all the boxes with answers that are even numbers.

| | | | | | |
|---|---|---|---|---|---|
| START → | | 836 + 138 = 974 | 485 + 306 = 791 | 334 + 439 = 773 | 185 + 484 = 669 |
| 247 + 244 = 491 | 478 + 751 = 1,229 | 726 + 428 = 1,154 | 576 + 272 = 848 | 134 + 392 = 526 | 364 + 384 = 748 |
| 407 + 548 = 955 | 294 + 295 = 589 | 665 + 592 = 1,257 | 383 + 354 = 737 | 156 + 893 = 1,049 | 328 + 190 = 518 |
| 325 + 346 = 671 | 108 + 346 = 454 | 648 + 748 = 1,396 | 742 + 880 = 1,622 | 115 + 415 = 530 | 428 + 628 = 1,056 |
| 961 + 854 = 1,815 | 597 + 221 = 818 | 906 + 79 = 985 | 527 + 106 = 633 | 372 + 331 = 703 | 285 + 20 = 305 |
| 447 + 448 = 895 | 661 + 553 = 1,214 | 544 + 118 = 662 | 235 + 247 = 482 | 793 + 73 = 866 | 603 + 522 = 1,125 |
| 724 + 757 = 1,481 | 369 + 408 = 777 | 466 + 561 = 1,027 | 850 + 693 = 1,543 | 377 + 893 = 1,270 | 249 + 116 = 365 |



**Brainwork!** Create your own doghouse addition maze. Let a friend solve it.

**Page 52**

# Answer Key

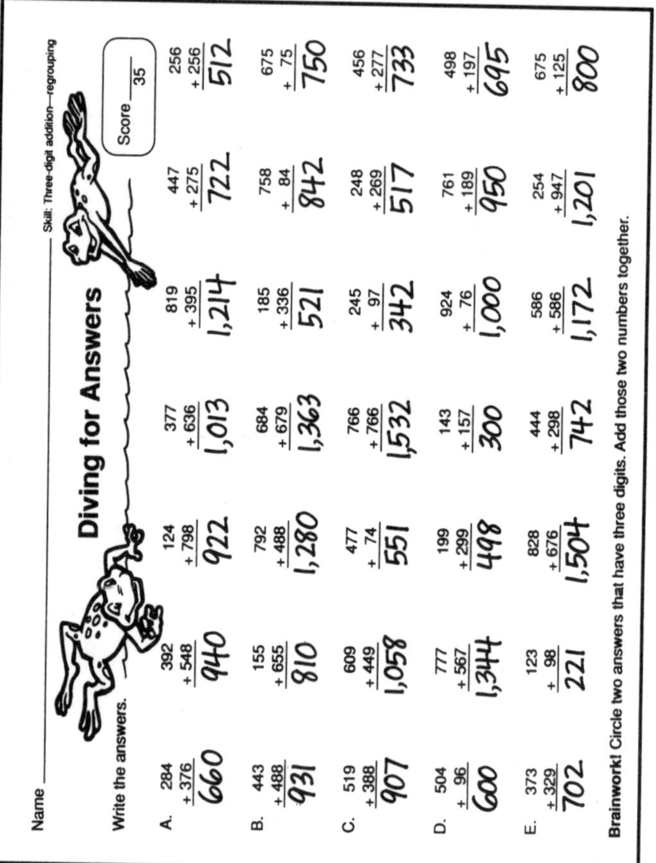

Name ______ Skill: Three-digit addition—regrouping

## Diving for Answers

Score ___ 35

Write the answers.

| | | | | | | | |
|---|---|---|---|---|---|---|---|
| A. | 284 + 376 = 660 | 392 + 548 = 940 | 124 + 798 = 922 | 377 + 636 = 1,013 | 819 + 395 = 1,214 | 447 + 275 = 722 | 256 + 256 = 512 |
| B. | 443 + 488 = 931 | 155 + 655 = 810 | 792 + 488 = 1,280 | 684 + 679 = 1,363 | 185 + 336 = 521 | 758 + 84 = 842 | 675 + 75 = 750 |
| C. | 519 + 388 = 907 | 609 + 449 = 1,058 | 477 + 74 = 551 | 766 + 766 = 1,532 | 245 + 97 = 342 | 248 + 269 = 517 | 456 + 277 = 733 |
| D. | 504 + 96 = 600 | 777 + 567 = 1,344 | 199 + 299 = 498 | 143 + 157 = 300 | 924 + 76 = 1,000 | 761 + 189 = 950 | 498 + 197 = 695 |
| E. | 373 + 329 = 702 | 123 + 98 = 221 | 828 + 676 = 1,504 | 444 + 298 = 742 | 586 + 586 = 1,172 | 254 + 947 = 1,201 | 675 + 125 = 800 |

**Brainwork!** Circle two answers that have three digits. Add those two numbers together.

Page 53

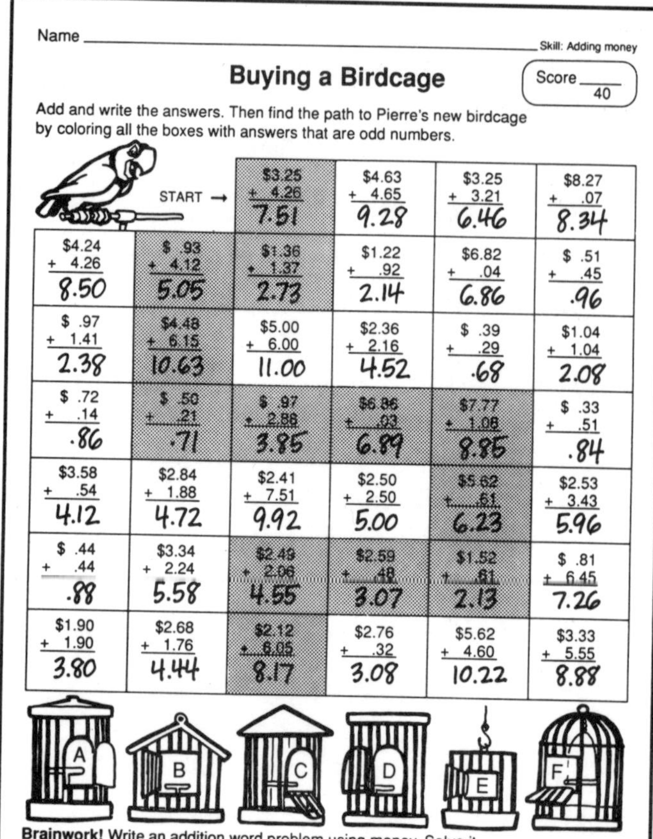

Name ______ Skill: Adding money

## Buying a Birdcage

Score ___ 40

Add and write the answers. Then find the path to Pierre's new birdcage by coloring all the boxes with answers that are odd numbers.

| | | | | | |
|---|---|---|---|---|---|
| | START → | \$3.25 + 4.26 = 7.51 | \$4.63 + 4.65 = 9.28 | \$3.25 + 3.21 = 6.46 | \$8.27 + .07 = 8.34 |
| \$4.24 + 4.26 = 8.50 | \$ .93 + 4.12 = 5.05 | \$1.36 + 1.37 = 2.73 | \$1.22 + .92 = 2.14 | \$6.82 + .04 = 6.86 | \$ .51 + .45 = .96 |
| \$ .97 + 1.41 = 2.38 | \$4.48 + 6.15 = 10.63 | \$5.00 + 6.00 = 11.00 | \$2.36 + 2.16 = 4.52 | \$ .39 + .29 = .68 | \$1.04 + 1.04 = 2.08 |
| \$ .72 + .14 = .86 | \$ .50 + .21 = .71 | \$ .97 + 2.88 = 3.85 | \$6.86 + .03 = 6.89 | \$7.77 + 1.08 = 8.85 | \$ .33 + .51 = .84 |
| \$3.58 + .54 = 4.12 | \$2.84 + 1.88 = 4.72 | \$2.41 + 7.51 = 9.92 | \$2.50 + 2.50 = 5.00 | \$5.62 + .61 = 6.23 | \$2.53 + 3.43 = 5.96 |
| \$ .44 + .44 = .88 | \$3.34 + 2.24 = 5.58 | \$2.49 + 2.06 = 4.55 | \$2.59 + .48 = 3.07 | \$1.52 + .61 = 2.13 | \$ .81 + 6.45 = 7.26 |
| \$1.90 + 1.90 = 3.80 | \$2.68 + 1.76 = 4.44 | \$2.12 + 6.05 = 8.17 | \$2.76 + .32 = 3.08 | \$5.62 + 4.60 = 10.22 | \$3.33 + 5.55 = 8.88 |



**Brainwork!** Write an addition word problem using money. Solve it.

Page 54

Name ______ Skill: Four-digit addition

## Adding Larger Numbers

Score ___ 35



| | | | | | |
|---|---|---|---|---|---|
| A. | 2,714 + 3,281 = 5,995 | 4,265 + 5,135 = 9,400 | 6,223 + 290 = 6,513 | 2,227 + 1,462 = 3,689 | 5,540 + 1,628 = 7,168 |
| B. | 4,175 + 377 = 4,552 | 1,097 + 1,983 = 3,080 | 7,142 + 2,355 = 9,497 | 8,426 + 722 = 9,148 | 1,014 + 792 = 1,806 |
| C. | 6,514 + 1,922 = 8,436 | 3,555 + 1,671 = 5,226 | 892 + 3,419 = 4,311 | 5,001 + 4,232 = 9,233 | 1,660 + 2,237 = 3,897 |
| D. | 1,554 + 667 = 2,221 | 8,817 + 1,012 = 9,829 | 5,572 + 918 = 6,490 | 1,090 + 703 = 1,793 | 2,813 + 2,763 = 5,576 |
| E. | 4,272 + 624 = 4,896 | 1,456 + 1,417 = 2,873 | 5,915 + 1,775 = 7,690 | 1,500 + 1,458 = 2,958 | 7,254 + 746 = 8,000 |
| F. | 2,754 + 2,787 = 5,541 | 2,861 + 668 = 3,529 | 7,565 + 1,907 = 9,472 | 4,841 + 1,827 = 6,668 | 5,817 + 2,062 = 7,879 |
| G. | 1,533 + 1,316 = 2,849 | 2,376 + 1,849 = 4,225 | 4,458 + 998 = 5,456 | 8,814 + 1,092 = 9,906 | 3,464 + 3,721 = 7,185 |

**Brainwork!** Add this year's date to next year's date.

Page 55

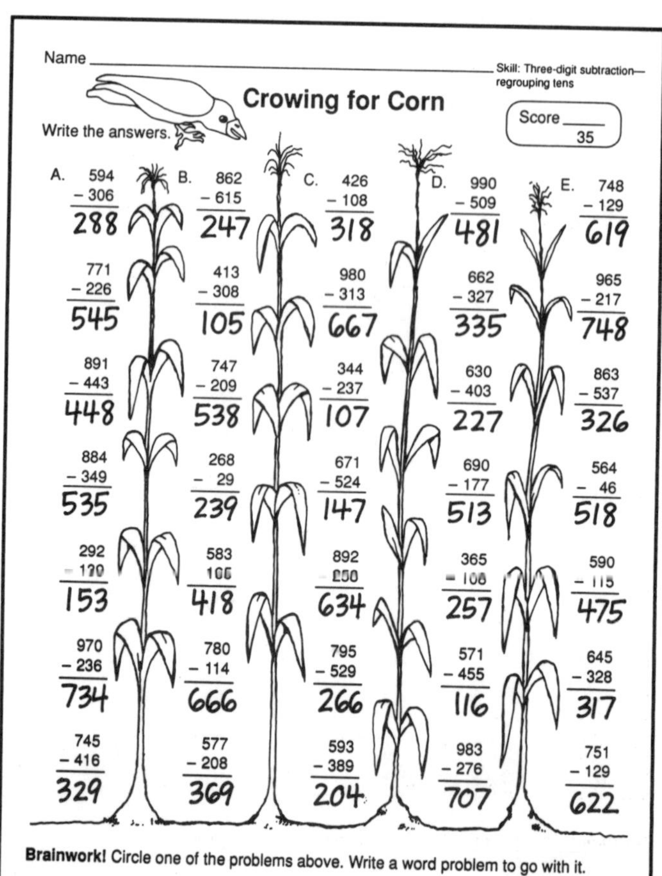

Name ______ Skill: Three-digit subtraction—regrouping tens

## Crowing for Corn

Score ___ 35

Write the answers.

| A. | B. | C. | D. | E. |
|---|---|---|---|---|
| 594 − 306 = 288 | 862 − 615 = 247 | 426 − 108 = 318 | 990 − 509 = 481 | 748 − 129 = 619 |
| 771 − 226 = 545 | 413 − 308 = 105 | 980 − 313 = 667 | 662 − 327 = 335 | 965 − 217 = 748 |
| 891 − 443 = 448 | 747 − 209 = 538 | 344 − 237 = 107 | 630 − 403 = 227 | 863 − 537 = 326 |
| 884 − 349 = 535 | 268 − 29 = 239 | 671 − 524 = 147 | 690 − 177 = 513 | 564 − 46 = 518 |
| 292 − 139 = 153 | 583 − 165 = 418 | 892 − 258 = 634 | 365 − 108 = 257 | 590 − 115 = 475 |
| 970 − 236 = 734 | 780 − 114 = 666 | 795 − 529 = 266 | 571 − 455 = 116 | 645 − 328 = 317 |
| 745 − 416 = 329 | 577 − 208 = 369 | 593 − 389 = 204 | 983 − 276 = 707 | 751 − 129 = 622 |

**Brainwork!** Circle one of the problems above. Write a word problem to go with it.

Page 56

# Answer Key

Name ______________________ Skill: Three-digit subtraction—regrouping hundreds

## Subtraction Balancing Act

Score ____ 35

Subtract and write the answers.

| | | | | | | |
|---|---|---|---|---|---|---|
| A. | 737 − 450 = 287 | 956 − 895 = 61 | 638 − 147 = 491 | 968 − 486 = 482 | 928 − 345 = 583 | 526 − 336 = 190 |
| B. | 627 − 282 = 345 | 919 − 622 = 297 | 958 − 262 = 696 | 959 − 571 = 388 | 829 − 179 = 650 | 419 − 350 = 69 |
| C. | 814 − 362 = 452 | 628 − 390 = 238 | 375 − 193 = 182 | 837 − 762 = 75 | 637 − 481 = 156 | 847 − 464 = 383 |
| D. | 946 − 794 = 152 | 748 − 273 = 475 | 849 − 254 = 595 | 727 − 465 = 262 | 768 − 674 = 94 | 829 − 558 = 271 |
| E. | 768 − 398 = 370 | 989 − 197 = 792 | 478 − 181 = 297 | 619 − 546 = 73 | 437 − 296 = 141 | 847 − 683 = 164 |
| F. | 437 − 77 = 360 | 759 − 585 = 174 | 672 − 280 = 392 | 549 − 183 = 366 | 876 − 283 = 593 | |

**Brainwork!** Write a subtraction word problem about a circus seal. Solve the problem.

**Page 57**

Name ______________________ Skill: Three-digit subtraction—regrouping tens and hundreds

## Funny Frog

Score ____ 25

First subtract and write the answers. Then use the key to write a letter below each problem. Read the riddle and its answer.

| 522 − 246 | 881 − 93 | 550 − 174 | 721 − 196 | | 943 − 278 | 842 − 186 |
|---|---|---|---|---|---|---|
| 276 | 788 | 376 | 525 | | 665 | 656 |
| W | H | A | T | | D | O |

| 851 − 587 | 617 − 259 | 955 − 299 | 488 − 199 | 782 − 296 |
|---|---|---|---|---|
| 264 | 358 | 656 | 289 | 486 |
| F | R | O | G | S |

| 933 − 268 | 610 − 252 | 630 − 176 | 666 − 478 | 797 − 198 | | 741 − 365 | 820 − 295 |
|---|---|---|---|---|---|---|---|
| 665 | 358 | 454 | 188 | 599 | | 376 | 525 |
| D | R | I | N | K | | A | T |

| 754 − 169 | 762 − 386 | 627 − 269 | 912 − 387 | 651 − 197 | 610 − 133 | 683 − 197 |
|---|---|---|---|---|---|---|
| 585 | 376 | 358 | 525 | 454 | 477 | 486 |
| P | A | R | T | I | E | S ? |

| Key | |
|---|---|
| 188 | = N |
| 264 | = F |
| 276 | = W |
| 289 | = G |
| 358 | = R |
| 376 | = A |
| 454 | = I |
| 477 | = E |
| 486 | = S |
| 525 | = T |
| 585 | = P |
| 599 | = K |
| 656 | = O |
| 665 | = D |
| 788 | = H |

**Answer:** CROAKA-COLA!

**Brainwork!** Write subtraction problems and a matching key to spell out a name for the frog. Have a friend solve your puzzle.

**Page 58**

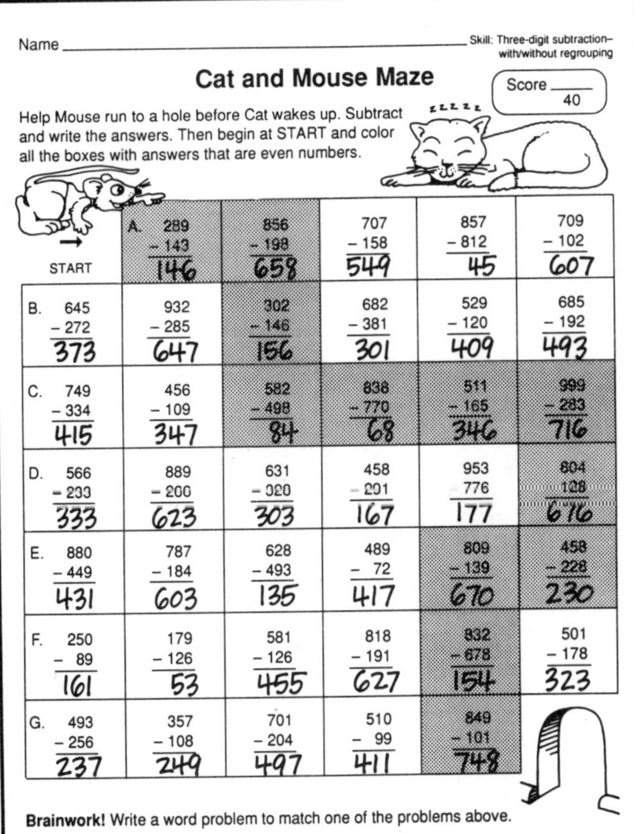

Name ______________________ Skill: Three-digit subtraction—with/without regrouping

## Cat and Mouse Maze

Score ____ 40

Help Mouse run to a hole before Cat wakes up. Subtract and write the answers. Then begin at START and color all the boxes with answers that are even numbers.

| | | | | | |
|---|---|---|---|---|---|
| START | A. 289 − 143 = 146 | 856 − 198 = 658 | 707 − 158 = 549 | 857 − 812 = 45 | 709 − 102 = 607 |
| B. 645 − 272 = 373 | 932 − 285 = 647 | 302 − 146 = 156 | 682 − 381 = 301 | 529 − 120 = 409 | 685 − 192 = 493 |
| C. 749 − 334 = 415 | 456 − 109 = 347 | 582 − 498 = 84 | 838 − 770 = 68 | 511 − 165 = 346 | 999 − 283 = 716 |
| D. 566 − 233 = 333 | 889 − 200 = 623 | 631 − 020 = 303 | 458 − 291 = 167 | 953 − 776 = 177 | 804 − 128 = 616 |
| E. 880 − 449 = 431 | 787 − 184 = 603 | 628 − 493 = 135 | 489 − 72 = 417 | 809 − 139 = 670 | 458 − 228 = 230 |
| F. 250 − 89 = 161 | 179 − 126 = 53 | 581 − 126 = 455 | 818 − 191 = 627 | 832 − 678 = 154 | 501 − 178 = 323 |
| G. 493 − 256 = 237 | 357 − 108 = 249 | 701 − 204 = 497 | 510 − 99 = 411 | 849 − 101 = 748 | |

**Brainwork!** Write a word problem to match one of the problems above.

**Page 59**

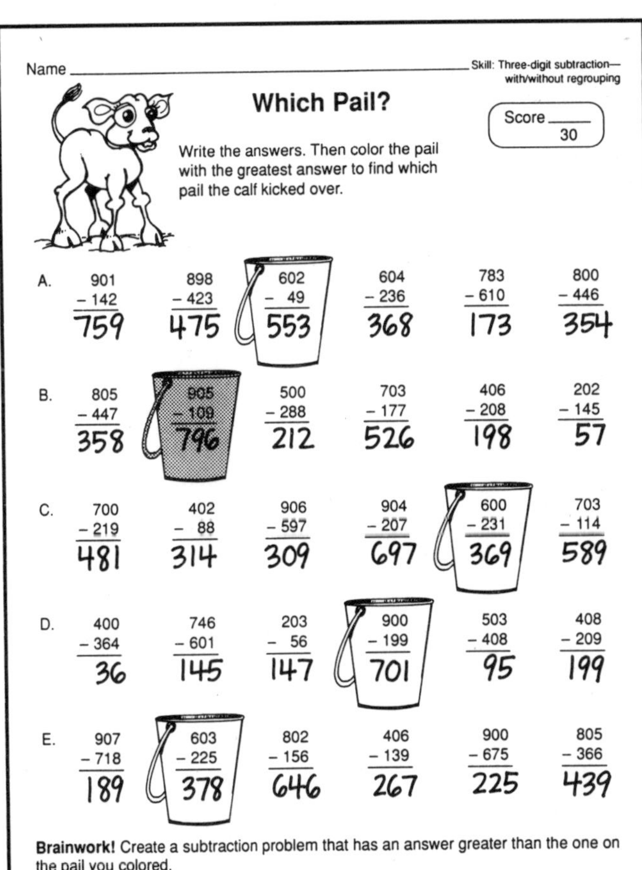

Name ______________________ Skill: Three-digit subtraction—with/without regrouping

## Which Pail?

Score ____ 30

Write the answers. Then color the pail with the greatest answer to find which pail the calf kicked over.

| | | | | | | |
|---|---|---|---|---|---|---|
| A. | 901 − 142 = 759 | 898 − 423 = 475 | 602 − 49 = 553 | 604 − 236 = 368 | 783 − 610 = 173 | 800 − 446 = 354 |
| B. | 805 − 447 = 358 | 905 − 109 = 796 | 500 − 288 = 212 | 703 − 177 = 526 | 406 − 208 = 198 | 202 − 145 = 57 |
| C. | 700 − 219 = 481 | 402 − 88 = 314 | 906 − 597 = 309 | 904 − 207 = 697 | 600 − 231 = 369 | 703 − 114 = 589 |
| D. | 400 − 364 = 36 | 746 − 601 = 145 | 203 − 56 = 147 | 900 − 199 = 701 | 503 − 408 = 95 | 408 − 209 = 199 |
| E. | 907 − 718 = 189 | 603 − 225 = 378 | 802 − 156 = 646 | 406 − 139 = 267 | 900 − 675 = 225 | 805 − 366 = 439 |

**Brainwork!** Create a subtraction problem that has an answer greater than the one on the pail you colored.

**Page 60**

# Answer Key

Name ______________________ Skill: Subtracting money—with/without regrouping

## Money Matters

Score ___ / 40

Write the answers. Remember to write the decimals and the dollar signs.

| | | | | | | |
|---|---|---|---|---|---|---|
| A. | $4.00 − 3.23 = $.77 | $4.25 − 2.07 = $2.18 | $5.43 − 2.72 = $2.71 | $3.59 − 1.26 = $2.33 | | |
| B. | $9.50 − 6.20 = $3.30 | $.95 − .42 = $.53 | $7.76 − 1.98 = $5.78 | $8.00 − 7.06 = $.94 | $10.00 − 5.50 = $4.50 | $6.40 − .39 = $6.01 |
| C. | $8.88 − 1.27 = $7.61 | $5.42 − 1.30 = $4.12 | $.88 − .16 = $.72 | $5.00 − 2.25 = $2.75 | $8.62 − 1.59 = $7.03 | $9.64 − 2.74 = $6.90 |
| D. | $.70 − .20 = $.50 | $.89 − .43 = $.46 | $5.00 − 3.00 = $2.00 | $2.53 − 1.99 = $.54 | $7.86 − 5.95 = $1.91 | $6.30 − 5.17 = $1.13 |
| E. | $7.51 − 2.41 = $5.10 | $1.40 − .70 = $.70 | $3.80 − .62 = $3.18 | $5.17 − 1.66 = $3.51 | $9.08 − .99 = $8.09 | $3.12 − .48 = $2.64 |
| F. | $8.73 − 1.65 = $7.08 | $.85 − .13 = $.72 | $8.25 − 2.64 = $5.61 | $18.00 − 9.00 = $9.00 | $7.00 − 2.77 = $4.23 | $9.44 − 6.66 = $2.78 |
| G. | $9.68 − 1.92 = $7.76 | $8.40 − 2.15 = $6.25 | $8.00 − 5.07 = $2.93 | $1.10 − .60 = $.50 | $8.20 − 3.33 = $4.87 | $12.00 − 7.00 = $5.00 |

**Brainwork!** Write a subtraction word problem about money. Solve it.

Page 61

Name ______________________ Skill: Four-digit subtraction—with/without regrouping

## Coiled for Math

Score ___ / 35

Subtract and write the answers.

| | | | | | | |
|---|---|---|---|---|---|---|
| A. | 8,283 − 4,145 = 4,138 | 6,660 − 4,190 = 2,470 | 3,382 − 1,179 = 2,203 | 7,252 − 1,718 = 5,534 | 8,619 − 2,315 = 6,304 | 4,782 − 1,732 = 3,050 |
| B. | 3,284 − 2,695 = 589 | 6,986 − 3,047 = 3,939 | 1,434 − 126 = 1,308 | 8,188 − 6,589 = 1,599 | 2,318 − 1,094 = 1,224 | 8,964 − 1,151 = 7,813 |
| C. | 6,494 − 3,077 = 3,417 | 8,545 − 3,180 = 5,365 | 8,701 − 8,034 = 667 | 7,040 − 1,190 = 5,850 | 7,365 − 5,278 = 2,087 | 7,782 − 1,053 = 6,729 |
| D. | 8,643 − 2,489 = 6,154 | 5,913 − 2,907 = 3,006 | 4,915 − 2,163 = 2,752 | 8,987 − 2,323 = 6,664 | 8,162 − 2,596 = 5,566 | 3,456 − 1,111 = 2,345 |
| E. | 4,303 − 1,884 = 2,419 | 5,421 − 2,187 = 3,234 | 9,682 − 3,335 = 6,347 | 9,481 − 9,003 = 478 | 9,949 − 2,336 = 7,613 | 4,652 − 1,572 = 3,080 |
| F. | 8,919 − 3,222 = 5,697 | 9,413 − 7,625 = 1,788 | 5,556 − 1,118 = 4,438 | 8,403 − 1,126 = 7,277 | 9,829 − 4,647 = 5,182 | |

**Brainwork!** Choose one of the four-digit numbers above that begin with 7, 8, or 9. Subtract this year's date from it.

Page 62

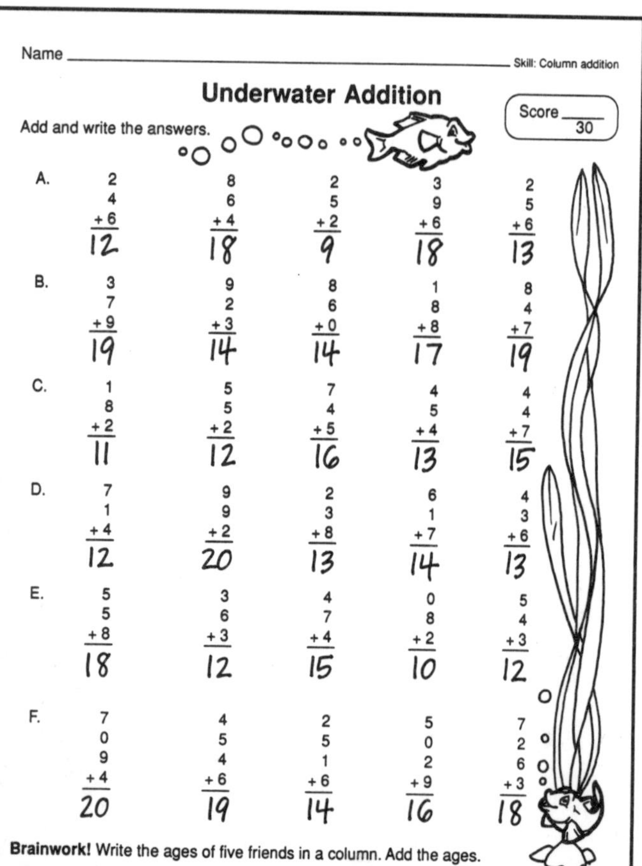

Name ______________________ Skill: Column addition

## Underwater Addition

Score ___ / 30

Add and write the answers.

| | | | | | |
|---|---|---|---|---|---|
| A. | 2 + 4 + 6 = 12 | 8 + 6 + 4 = 18 | 2 + 5 + 2 = 9 | 3 + 9 + 6 = 18 | 2 + 5 + 6 = 13 |
| B. | 3 + 7 + 9 = 19 | 9 + 2 + 3 = 14 | 8 + 6 + 0 = 14 | 1 + 8 + 8 = 17 | 8 + 4 + 7 = 19 |
| C. | 1 + 8 + 2 = 11 | 5 + 5 + 2 = 12 | 7 + 4 + 5 = 16 | 4 + 5 + 4 = 13 | 4 + 4 + 7 = 15 |
| D. | 7 + 1 + 4 = 12 | 9 + 9 + 2 = 20 | 2 + 3 + 8 = 13 | 6 + 1 + 7 = 14 | 4 + 3 + 6 = 13 |
| E. | 5 + 5 + 8 = 18 | 3 + 6 + 3 = 12 | 4 + 7 + 4 = 15 | 0 + 8 + 2 = 10 | 5 + 4 + 3 = 12 |
| F. | 7 + 0 + 9 + 4 = 20 | 4 + 5 + 4 + 6 = 19 | 2 + 5 + 1 + 6 = 14 | 5 + 0 + 2 + 9 = 16 | 7 + 2 + 6 + 3 = 18 |

**Brainwork!** Write the ages of five friends in a column. Add the ages.

Page 63

Name ______________________ Skill: Column addition—two- and three-digit numbers

## Chimp Challenge

Score ___ / 30

Write the answers.

| | | | | | | |
|---|---|---|---|---|---|---|
| A. | 74 + 213 + 112 = 399 | 324 + 210 + 707 = 1,241 | 316 + 550 + 22 = 888 | 760 + 432 + 24 = 1,216 | 49 + 72 + 116 = 237 | 601 + 126 + 50 = 777 |
| B. | 217 + 128 + 150 = 495 | 208 + 194 + 334 = 736 | 112 + 113 + 511 = 736 | 202 + 322 + 62 = 586 | 201 + 242 + 501 = 944 | 660 + 90 + 907 = 1,657 |
| C. | 522 + 127 + 227 = 876 | 26 + 448 + 121 = 595 | 51 + 153 + 45 = 249 | 666 + 121 + 401 = 1,188 | 140 + 220 + 101 = 461 | 55 + 346 + 123 = 524 |
| D. | 221 + 231 + 262 = 714 | 146 + 140 + 190 = 476 | 128 + 428 + 481 = 1,037 | 714 + 281 + 102 = 1,097 | 227 + 52 + 311 = 590 | 84 + 312 + 302 = 698 |
| E. | 22 + 622 + 132 = 776 | 837 + 262 + 231 = 1,330 | 242 + 285 + 51 = 578 | 454 + 14 + 404 = 872 | 102 + 102 + 141 = 345 | 346 + 12 + 491 = 849 |

**Brainwork!** Write three numbers whose sum is 1,000.

Page 64

# Answer Key

Name ______________________ Skill: Addition 11-18

Write the number sentence and answer.

| | |
|---|---|
| | 1. Bill rode to Bob's house and then to Jan's. How many miles did he ride in all?<br>8+6=14<br>Bill rode 14 miles. |
| 2. Jan went to Bill's house and then to Bob's. How many miles did she ride all together?<br>9+8=17<br>Jan rode 17 miles. | 3. If Bob rides to Jan's house and then to Bill's, how far will he go?<br>6+9=15<br>Bob would go 15 miles. |
| 4. How many miles will Bill go if he rides to Jan's house and back home again?<br>9+9=18<br>Bill will go 18 miles. | 5. How far is it for Bob to ride to Jan's house, go back home, and then ride to Bill's?<br>6+6+8=20<br>It is 20 miles. |

Page 65

Name ______________________ Skill: Subtraction 11-18

Write the number sentence and answer.

| | |
|---|---|
| 1. Tom had 14 balloons. Bill popped 5 of them. How many were left?<br>14-5=9<br>Tom had 9 balloons left. | |
| 2. Ann had 17 little cars. She gave 8 of them to Tom. How many did she have left?<br>17-8=9<br>Ann had 9 cars left. | 3. Mike had 16 play snakes. His mother threw 8 of them away. How many does he have now?<br>16-8=8<br>Mike has 8 snakes now. |
| 4. Nancy had 13 yo-yos. Her brother broke 6 of them. How many does she have?<br>13-6=7<br>Nancy has 7 yo-yos now. | 5. John had 11 marbles. He lost 9 of them. How many does he have now?<br>11-9=2<br>John has 2 marbles now. |

Page 66

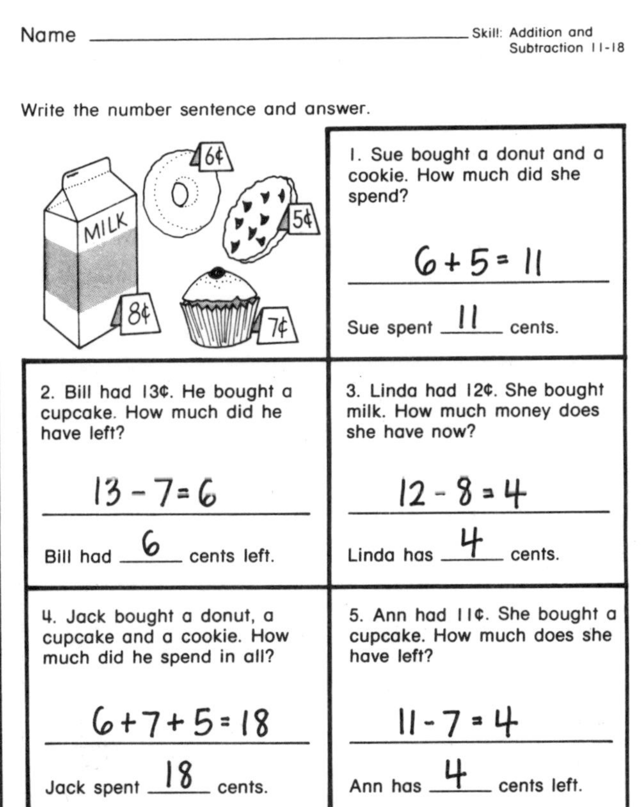

Name ______________________ Skill: Addition and Subtraction 11-18

Write the number sentence and answer.

| | |
|---|---|
| | 1. Sue bought a donut and a cookie. How much did she spend?<br>6+5=11<br>Sue spent 11 cents. |
| 2. Bill had 13¢. He bought a cupcake. How much did he have left?<br>13-7=6<br>Bill had 6 cents left. | 3. Linda had 12¢. She bought milk. How much money does she have now?<br>12-8=4<br>Linda has 4 cents. |
| 4. Jack bought a donut, a cupcake and a cookie. How much did he spend in all?<br>6+7+5=18<br>Jack spent 18 cents. | 5. Ann had 11¢. She bought a cupcake. How much does she have left?<br>11-7=4<br>Ann has 4 cents left. |

Page 67

Name ______________________ Skill: Comparisons 11-18

Write the number sentence and answer.

| | |
|---|---|
| 1. Ann is 11 years old. Her sister is 3. How much older is Ann than her sister?<br>11-3=8<br>8 years older. | 2. John is 16 years old. Bill is 7. How much older is John than Bill?<br>16-7=9<br>9 years older. |
| 3. Jim is 11 years old. Frank is 9. How much younger is Frank than Jim?<br>11-9=2<br>2 years younger. | 4. If Mike is 14 and Nancy is 9, how much older is Mike than Nancy?<br>14-9=5<br>5 years older. |
| 5. Jeff, who is 13 years old, has a brother who is 6. How much younger is Jeff's brother?<br>13-6=7<br>7 years younger. | |

Page 68

# Answer Key

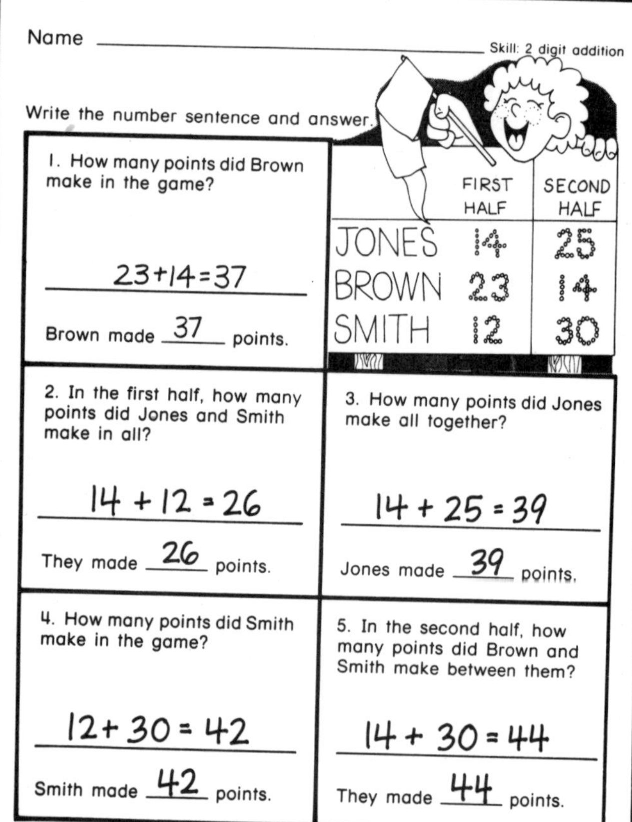

Name ______________________ Skill: 2 digit addition

Write the number sentence and answer.

| | FIRST HALF | SECOND HALF |
|---|---|---|
| JONES | 14 | 25 |
| BROWN | 23 | 14 |
| SMITH | 12 | 30 |

1. How many points did Brown make in the game?

23+14=37

Brown made 37 points.

2. In the first half, how many points did Jones and Smith make in all?

14 + 12 = 26

They made 26 points.

3. How many points did Jones make all together?

14 + 25 = 39

Jones made 39 points.

4. How many points did Smith make in the game?

12+ 30 = 42

Smith made 42 points.

5. In the second half, how many points did Brown and Smith make between them?

14 + 30 = 44

They made 44 points.

Page 69

Name ______________________ Skill: 2 digit subtraction

Write the number sentence and answer.

1. Mary had 26 goldfish. The cat ate 12. How many does Mary have now?

26-12=14

Mary has 14 goldfish.

2. John caught 38 lizards. 15 of them got away. How many lizards are left?

38 - 15 = 23

John has 23 lizards left.

3. Sue had 14 cats. She gave 12 of them to a friend. How many cats does Sue have now?

14 - 12 = 2

Sue has 2 cats now.

4. Jim had 29 baby hamsters. He gave 14 to a pet shop. How many does he have left?

29 - 14 = 15

Jim has 15 hamsters left.

5. Bill had 45 rabbits. He sold 25 of them. How many does he have now?

45 - 25 = 20

Bill has 20 rabbits now.

Page70

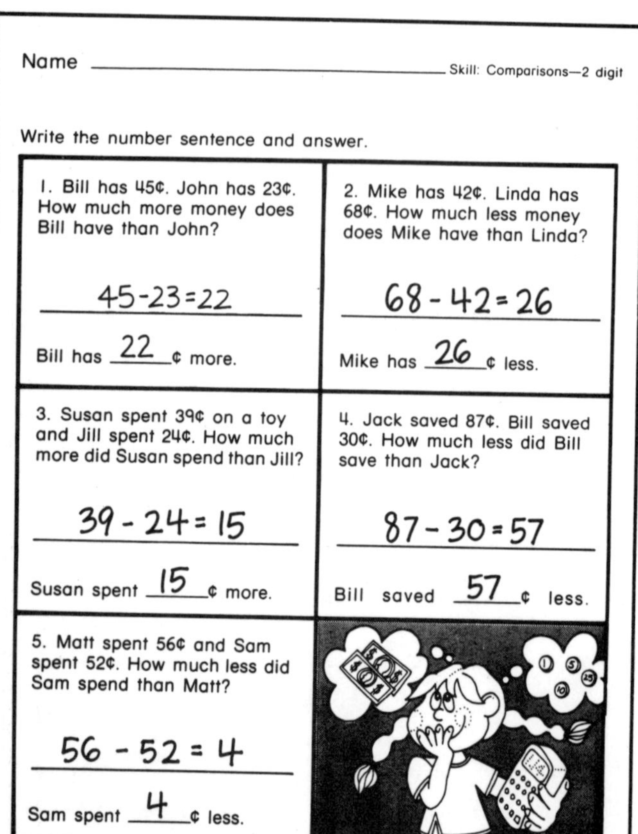

Name ______________________ Skill: Comparisons—2 digit

Write the number sentence and answer.

1. Bill has 45¢. John has 23¢. How much more money does Bill have than John?

45-23=22

Bill has 22 ¢ more.

2. Mike has 42¢. Linda has 68¢. How much less money does Mike have than Linda?

68 - 42 = 26

Mike has 26 ¢ less.

3. Susan spent 39¢ on a toy and Jill spent 24¢. How much more did Susan spend than Jill?

39 - 24 = 15

Susan spent 15 ¢ more.

4. Jack saved 87¢. Bill saved 30¢. How much less did Bill save than Jack?

87 - 30 = 57

Bill saved 57 ¢ less.

5. Matt spent 56¢ and Sam spent 52¢. How much less did Sam spend than Matt?

56 - 52 = 4

Sam spent 4 ¢ less.

Page 71

Name ______________________ Skill: 2 digit addition and subtraction

Write the number sentence and answer.

1. Nancy found 32 ants. John found 26. How many did they find in all?

32 + 26 = 58

They found 58 ants.

2. John caught 47 worms but 25 got away. How many worms were left?

47 - 25 = 22

John had 22 worms left.

3. Nancy caught 28 beetles. She gave 17 to John. How many does she have now?

28 - 17 = 11

Nancy has 11 beetles.

4. John put 12 snails in a box and Nancy put in 14. How many snails are there in all?

12 + 14 = 26

There are 26 snails.

5. The children had 58 pill bugs. They gave away 35. How many do they have now?

58 - 35 = 23

They have 23 pill bugs.

Page 72

# Answer Key

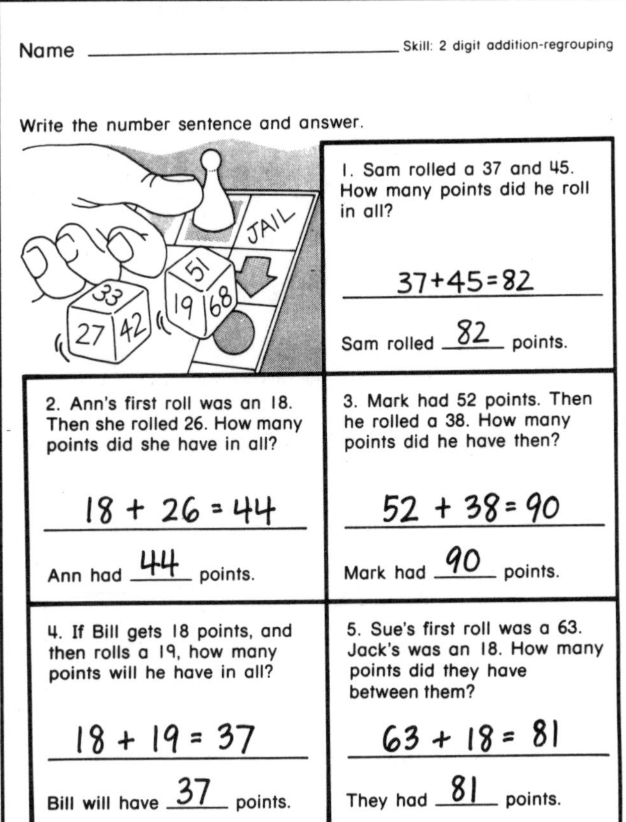

Name ____________ Skill: 2 digit addition-regrouping

Write the number sentence and answer.



1. Sam rolled a 37 and 45. How many points did he roll in all?

37+45=82

Sam rolled 82 points.

2. Ann's first roll was an 18. Then she rolled 26. How many points did she have in all?

18 + 26 = 44

Ann had 44 points.

3. Mark had 52 points. Then he rolled a 38. How many points did he have then?

52 + 38 = 90

Mark had 90 points.

4. If Bill gets 18 points, and then rolls a 19, how many points will he have in all?

18 + 19 = 37

Bill will have 37 points.

5. Sue's first roll was a 63. Jack's was an 18. How many points did they have between them?

63 + 18 = 81

They had 81 points.

Page 73

Name ____________ Skill: 2 digit subtraction-regrouping

Write the number sentence and answer.

1. Bill had 62¢ in his piggy bank. He spent 38¢. How much did he have left?

62-38=24

Bill had 24¢ left.

2. John saved 81¢. He gave 35¢ to his sister. How much does he have now?

81-35 = 46

John has 46¢ now.

3. Linda had 54¢. If she bought a toy for 19¢, how much did she have then?

54-19 = 35

Linda has 35¢.

4. Susan put 37¢ in her piggy bank. She took out 8¢. How much does she have left in the bank?

37-8 = 29

Susan has 29¢ left.

5. Mike made 40¢ working for his Dad. He put 26¢ in his bank. How much does he have left to spend?

40-26 = 14

Mike has 14¢ to spend.

Page 74

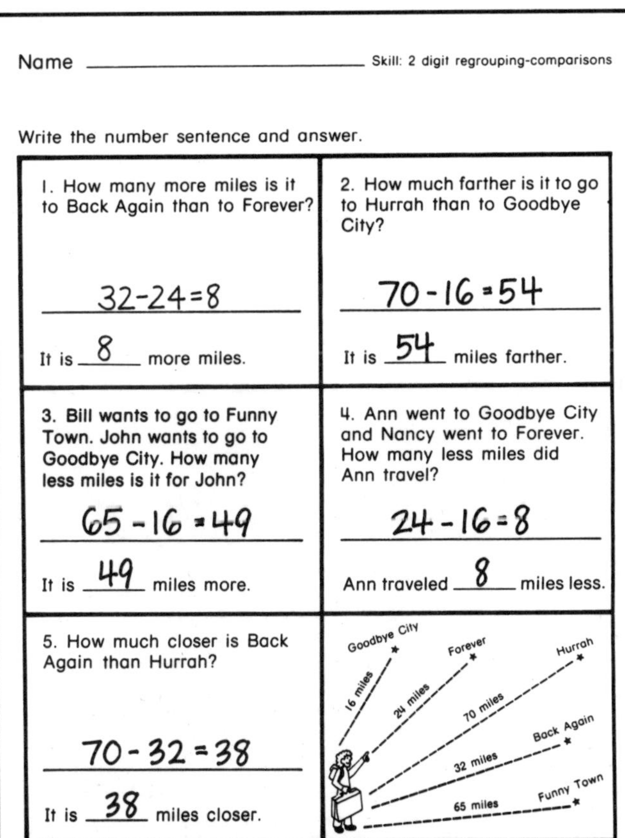

Name ____________ Skill: 2 digit regrouping-comparisons

Write the number sentence and answer.

1. How many more miles is it to Back Again than to Forever?

32-24=8

It is 8 more miles.

2. How much farther is it to go to Hurrah than to Goodbye City?

70-16 = 54

It is 54 miles farther.

3. Bill wants to go to Funny Town. John wants to go to Goodbye City. How many less miles is it for John?

65-16 = 49

It is 49 miles more.

4. Ann went to Goodbye City and Nancy went to Forever. How many less miles did Ann travel?

24-16 = 8

Ann traveled 8 miles less.

5. How much closer is Back Again than Hurrah?

70-32 = 38

It is 38 miles closer.



Page 75

Name ____________ Skill: 2 digit addition and subtraction-regrouping

Write the number sentence and answer.

1. Frank bought a hamburger and a glass of milk. How much did he spend?

54 + 19 = 73

Frank spent 73¢.

2. Jan wanted a hot dog and milk. How much money did she need?

48 + 19 = 67

Jan needed 67¢.

3. Bill had 52¢. He bought a piece of cake. How much did he have left?

52 - 25 = 27

Bill had 27¢ left.

4. John had 43¢. He bought a glass of milk. How much money did he have then?

43 - 19 = 24

John had 24¢ then.

5. If Sue buys cake and milk, how much will she pay?

25 + 19 = 44

Sue will pay 44¢.

Page 76

# Answer Key

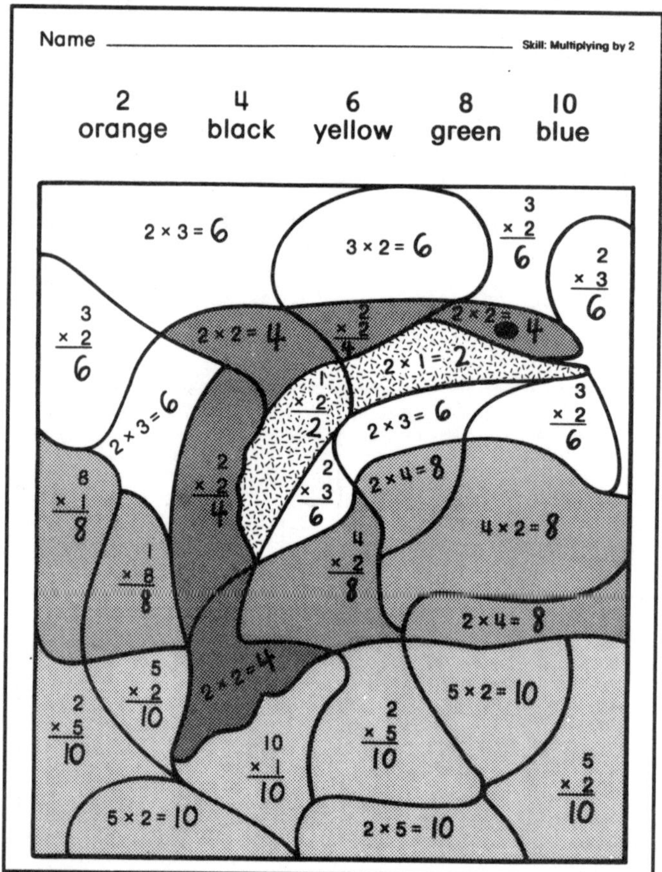

Page 77

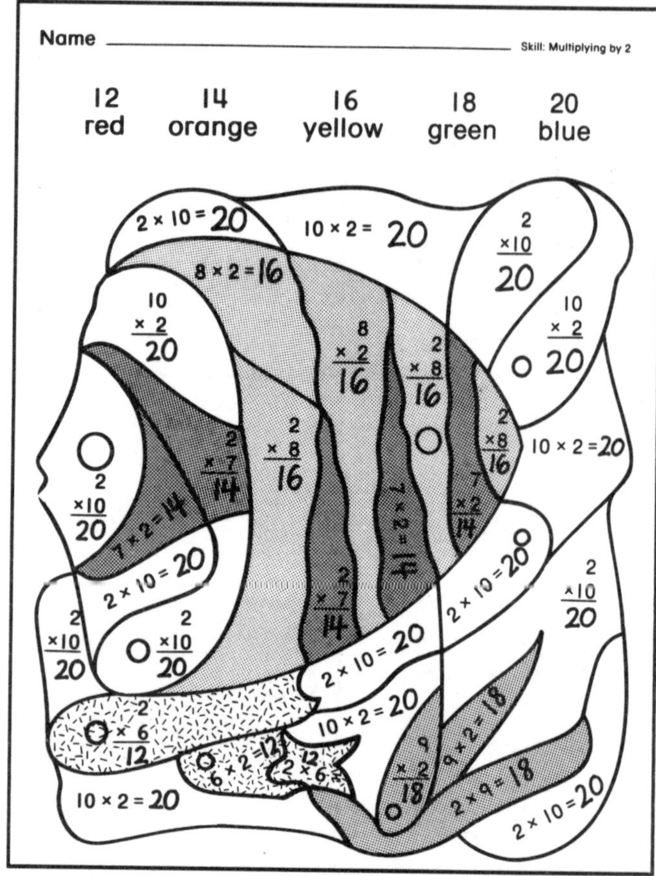

Page 78

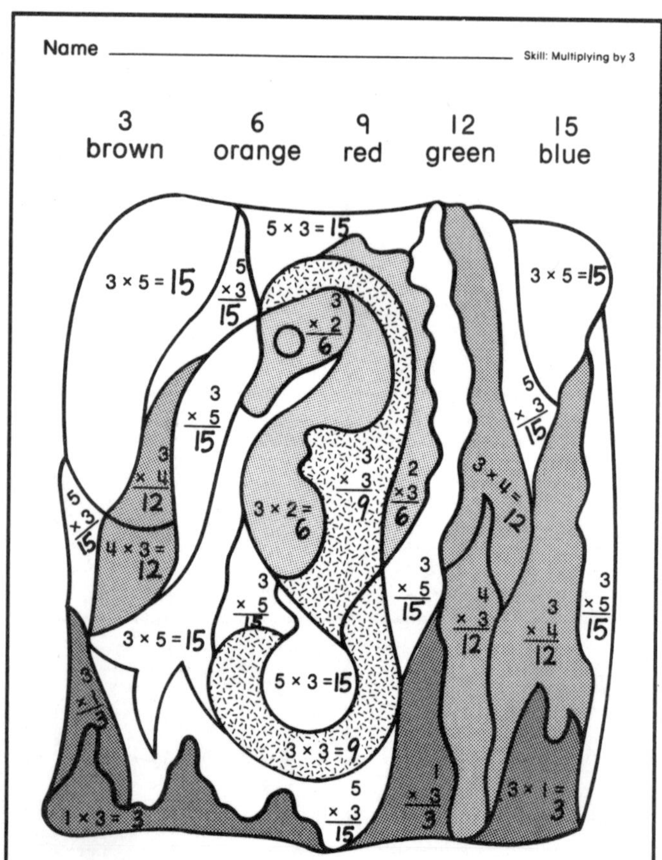

Page 79

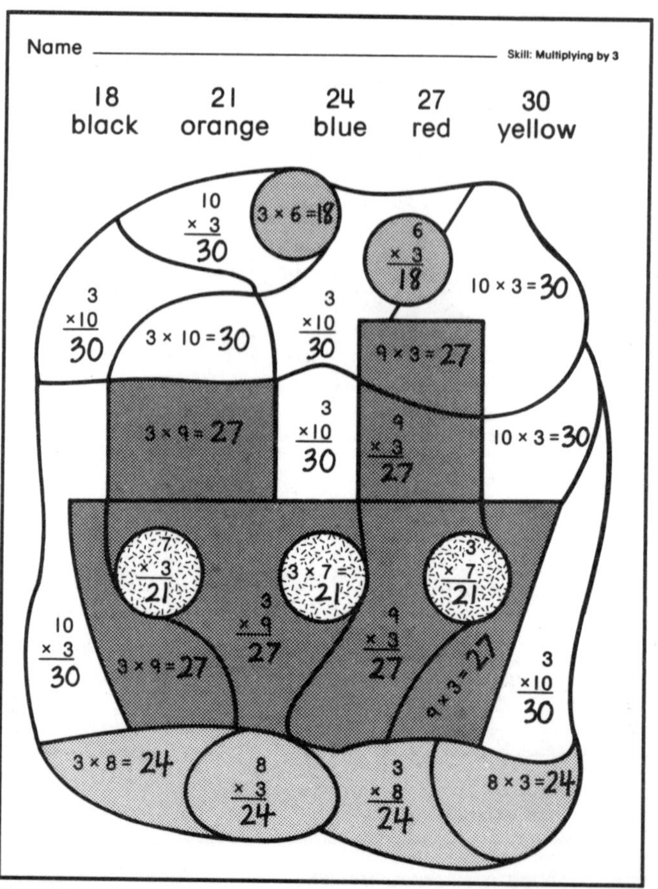

Page 80

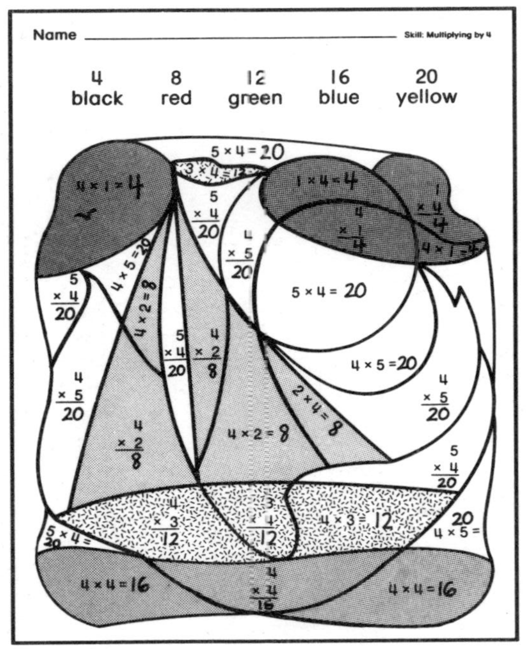


Page 81

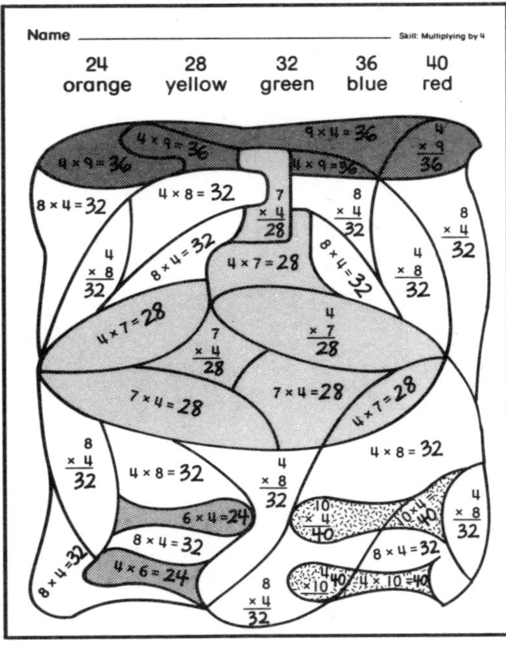


Page 82

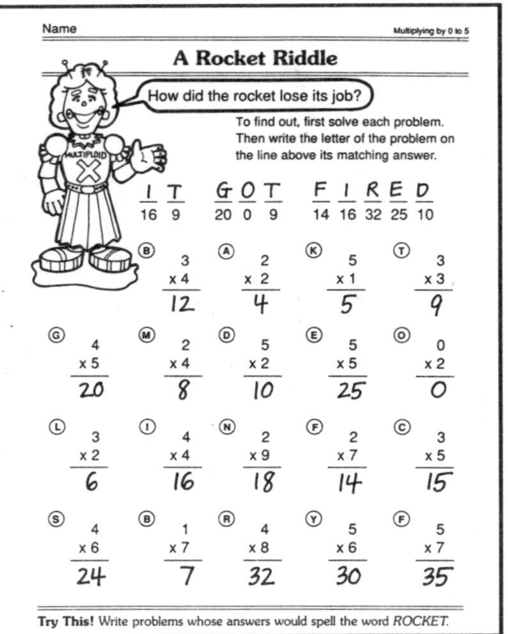
Name — Multiplying by 0 to 5

**A Rocket Riddle**

How did the rocket lose its job?

To find out, first solve each problem. Then write the letter of the problem on the line above its matching answer.

I T (16 9) G O T (20 0 9) F I R E D (14 16 32 25 10)

| | | | | |
|---|---|---|---|---|
| B: 3 × 4 = 12 | A: 2 × 2 = 4 | K: 5 × 1 = 5 | T: 3 × 3 = 9 | |
| G: 4 × 5 = 20 | M: 2 × 4 = 8 | D: 5 × 2 = 10 | E: 5 × 5 = 25 | O: 0 × 2 = 0 |
| L: 3 × 2 = 6 | I: 4 × 4 = 16 | N: 2 × 9 = 18 | F: 2 × 7 = 14 | C: 3 × 5 = 15 |
| S: 4 × 6 = 24 | B: 1 × 7 = 7 | R: 4 × 8 = 32 | Y: 5 × 6 = 30 | F: 5 × 7 = 35 |

**Try This!** Write problems whose answers would spell the word *ROCKET*.

Page 83

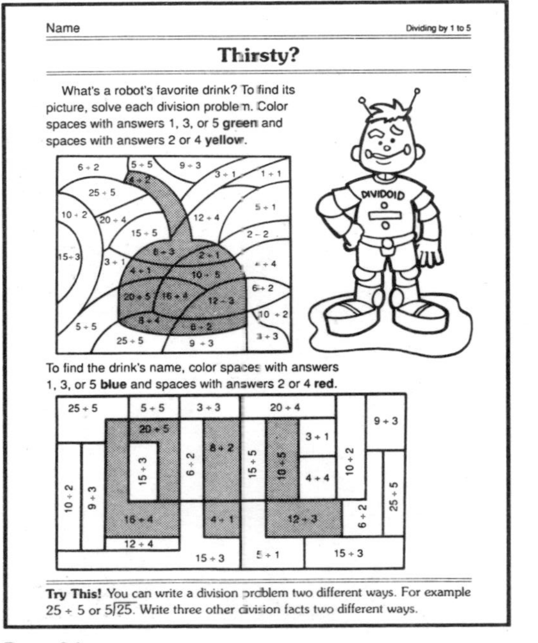
Name — Dividing by 1 to 5

**Thirsty?**

What's a robot's favorite drink? To find its picture, solve each division problem. Color spaces with answers 1, 3, or 5 **green** and spaces with answers 2 or 4 **yellow**.

To find the drink's name, color spaces with answers 1, 3, or 5 **blue** and spaces with answers 2 or 4 **red**.

**Try This!** You can write a division problem two different ways. For example 25 ÷ 5 or 5)25. Write three other division facts two different ways.

Page 84

Name — Addition facts to 18—timed drill

## Let's Add

| | | | | | | | |
|---|---|---|---|---|---|---|---|
| 1. 6 + 4 = 10 | 2. 2 + 3 = 5 | 3. 7 + 1 = 8 | 4. 9 + 2 = 11 | 5. 5 + 5 = 10 | 6. 2 + 6 = 8 | 7. 4 + 7 = 11 | 8. 5 + 8 = 13 |
| 9. 9 + 4 = 13 | 10. 5 + 1 = 6 | 11. 6 + 3 = 9 | 12. 8 + 8 = 16 | 13. 4 + 1 = 5 | 14. 7 + 5 = 12 | 15. 8 + 6 = 14 | 16. 3 + 3 = 6 |
| 17. 7 + 7 = 14 | 18. 2 + 8 = 10 | 19. 7 + 3 = 10 | 20. 6 + 5 = 11 | 21. 4 + 0 = 4 | 22. 1 + 8 = 9 | 23. 3 + 5 = 8 | 24. 9 + 8 = 17 |
| 25. 4 + 4 = 8 | 26. 3 + 6 = 9 | 27. 10 + 2 = 12 | 28. 5 + 9 = 14 | 29. 2 + 2 = 4 | 30. 8 + 7 = 15 | 31. 3 + 9 = 12 | 32. 3 + 8 = 11 |
| 33. 7 + 9 = 16 | 34. 9 + 9 = 18 | 35. 4 + 3 = 7 | 36. 6 + 7 = 13 | | | | |

I got ____ right out of 36 in ____ minutes.

Page 85

Name — Skill: Sums to 18

## Addition Facts Test

Score ___ / 100

Write the answers.

| | | | | | |
|---|---|---|---|---|---|
| A. | 8 + 2 = 10 | 9 + 4 = 13 | 3 + 8 = 11 | 6 + 6 = 12 | 1 + 4 = 5 |
| B. | 5 + 7 = 12 | 2 + 8 = 10 | 9 + 3 = 12 | 0 + 6 = 6 | 3 + 0 = 3 |
| C. | 1 + 0 = 1 | 6 + 7 = 13 | 0 + 5 = 5 | 6 + 3 = 9 | 4 + 1 = 5 |
| D. | 7 + 3 = 10 | 3 + 1 = 4 | 4 + 9 = 13 | 2 + 3 = 5 | 8 + 3 = 11 |
| E. | 5 + 0 = 5 | 8 + 9 = 17 | 4 + 0 = 4 | 1 + 6 = 7 | 2 + 0 = 2 |
| F. | 9 + 1 = 10 | 0 + 0 = 0 | 2 + 7 = 9 | 5 + 9 = 14 | 4 + 8 = 12 |
| G. | 2 + 2 = 4 | 6 + 4 = 10 | 5 + 1 = 6 | 9 + 3 = 12 | 9 + 6 = 15 |
| H. | 6 + 8 = 14 | 1 + 7 = 8 | 7 + 2 = 9 | 1 + 1 = 2 | 3 + 2 = 5 |
| I. | 9 + 0 = 9 | 3 + 9 = 12 | 1 + 5 = 6 | 5 + 6 = 11 | 0 + 2 = 2 |
| J. | 2 + 4 = 6 | 8 + 7 = 15 | 6 + 2 = 8 | 5 + 8 = 13 | 7 + 5 = 12 |
| K. | 8 + 0 = 8 | 0 + 9 = 9 | 3 + 3 = 6 | 4 + 2 = 6 | 9 + 2 = 11 |
| L. | 6 + 1 = 7 | 8 + 1 = 9 | 0 + 7 = 7 | 7 + 9 = 16 | 3 + 7 = 10 |
| M. | 7 + 8 = 15 | 3 + 4 = 7 | 6 + 0 = 6 | 5 + 2 = 7 | 1 + 9 = 10 |
| N. | 2 + 1 = 3 | 7 + 1 = 8 | 1 + 2 = 3 | 0 + 1 = 1 | 4 + 7 = 11 |
| O. | 6 + 5 = 11 | 4 + 3 = 7 | 8 + 4 = 12 | 4 + 6 = 10 | 0 + 8 = 8 |
| P. | 3 + 5 = 8 | 9 + 7 = 16 | 9 + 8 = 17 | 1 + 3 = 4 | 7 + 0 = 7 |
| Q. | 7 + 7 = 14 | 0 + 3 = 3 | 5 + 4 = 9 | 3 + 6 = 9 | 6 + 9 = 15 |
| R. | 2 + 9 = 11 | 8 + 8 = 16 | 2 + 5 = 7 | 4 + 4 = 8 | 2 + 6 = 8 |
| S. | 8 + 6 = 14 | 5 + 3 = 8 | 7 + 4 = 11 | 1 + 8 = 9 | 8 + 5 = 13 |
| T. | 0 + 4 = 4 | 9 + 9 = 18 | 5 + 5 = 10 | 7 + 6 = 13 | 4 + 5 = 9 |

Page 86

# Answer Key

Name ____ Subtraction facts to 18—timed drill

## Let's Subtract

| | | | | | | | |
|---|---|---|---|---|---|---|---|
| 1. 12 − 3 = 9 | 2. 8 − 2 = 6 | 3. 14 − 5 = 9 | 4. 9 − 4 = 5 | 5. 10 − 2 = 8 | 6. 7 − 5 = 2 | 7. 13 − 4 = 9 | 8. 9 − 3 = 6 |
| 9. 3 − 2 = 1 | 10. 16 − 7 = 9 | 11. 8 − 5 = 3 | 12. 15 − 7 = 8 | 13. 6 − 3 = 3 | 14. 17 − 8 = 9 | 15. 13 − 6 = 7 | 16. 5 − 3 = 2 |
| 17. 5 − 1 = 4 | 18. 11 − 2 = 9 | 19. 12 − 6 = 6 | 20. 18 − 9 = 9 | 21. 13 − 5 = 8 | 22. 7 − 2 = 5 | 23. 8 − 4 = 4 | 24. 12 − 5 = 7 |
| 25. 11 − 6 = 5 | 26. 12 − 4 = 8 | 27. 10 − 3 = 7 | 28. 9 − 1 = 8 | 29. 11 − 7 = 4 | 30. 15 − 6 = 9 | 31. 9 − 5 = 4 | 32. 12 − 7 = 5 |
| 33. 7 − 4 = 3 | 34. 16 − 8 = 8 | 35. 6 − 2 = 4 | 36. 14 − 6 = 8 | | | | |

I got ____ right out of 36 in ____ minutes.

Page 87

Name ____ Skill: Subtracting from 18 or less

## Subtraction Facts Test

Score ____/100

Write the answers.

| | | | | | |
|---|---|---|---|---|---|
| A. | 6 − 0 = 6 | 12 − 6 = 6 | 13 − 7 = 6 | 10 − 0 = 10 | 9 − 0 = 9 |
| B. | 5 − 5 = 0 | 10 − 7 = 3 | 8 − 5 = 3 | 11 − 6 = 5 | 2 − 2 = 0 |
| C. | 2 − 0 = 2 | 8 − 0 = 8 | 11 − 9 = 2 | 3 − 0 = 3 | 15 − 8 = 7 |
| D. | 1 − 0 = 1 | 16 − 9 = 7 | 9 − 8 = 1 | 8 − 3 = 5 | 5 − 4 = 1 |
| E. | 14 − 9 = 5 | 8 − 4 = 4 | 13 − 5 = 8 | 10 − 1 = 9 | 8 − 2 = 6 |
| F. | 3 − 1 = 2 | 12 − 8 = 4 | 10 − 9 = 1 | 13 − 6 = 7 | 11 − 2 = 9 |
| G. | 10 − 6 = 4 | 8 − 1 = 7 | 9 − 1 = 8 | 8 − 6 = 2 | 16 − 7 = 9 |
| H. | 1 − 1 = 0 | 14 − 5 = 9 | 10 − 2 = 8 | 7 − 5 = 2 | 7 − 2 = 5 |
| I. | 12 − 9 = 3 | 9 − 7 = 2 | 15 − 7 = 8 | 7 − 1 = 6 | 9 − 9 = 0 |
| J. | 6 − 3 = 3 | 7 − 7 = 0 | 12 − 3 = 9 | 11 − 8 = 3 | 7 − 6 = 1 |
| K. | 5 − 3 = 2 | 10 − 3 = 7 | 7 − 4 = 3 | 18 − 9 = 9 | 10 − 5 = 5 |
| L. | 15 − 6 = 9 | 17 − 9 = 8 | 9 − 2 = 7 | 10 − 8 = 2 | 13 − 9 = 4 |
| M. | 6 − 2 = 4 | 11 − 3 = 8 | 12 − 5 = 7 | 6 − 4 = 2 | 7 − 3 = 4 |
| N. | 11 − 7 = 4 | 6 − 5 = 1 | 8 − 7 = 1 | 9 − 3 = 6 | 17 − 8 = 9 |
| O. | 4 − 3 = 1 | 14 − 7 = 7 | 9 − 4 = 5 | 13 − 8 = 5 | 6 − 1 = 5 |
| P. | 10 − 4 = 6 | 3 − 2 = 1 | 11 − 4 = 7 | 12 − 4 = 8 | 14 − 6 = 8 |
| Q. | 16 − 8 = 8 | 11 − 5 = 6 | 4 − 4 = 0 | 5 − 0 = 5 | 7 − 0 = 7 |
| R. | 3 − 3 = 0 | 5 − 1 = 4 | 6 − 6 = 0 | 9 − 6 = 3 | 15 − 9 = 6 |
| S. | 4 − 0 = 4 | 13 − 4 = 9 | 4 − 2 = 2 | 2 − 1 = 1 | 5 − 2 = 3 |
| T. | 8 − 8 = 0 | 4 − 1 = 3 | 9 − 5 = 4 | 12 − 7 = 5 | 14 − 8 = 6 |

Page 88

Name ____ Addition/subtraction facts through 10

## Let's Review the Facts

Write the sums . . .
or differences.

A. 2 + 8 = 10; 9 − 5 = 4; 4 + 4 = 8

B. 3 + 6 = 9; 10 − 3 = 7; 2 + 5 = 7; 8 − 5 = 3; 1 + 9 = 10

C. 7 + 3 = 10; 5 − 3 = 2; 6 + 2 = 8; 4 − 1 = 3; 5 + 4 = 9

| | | | |
|---|---|---|---|
| D. | 7 − 3 = 4 | 3 + 4 = 7 | 3 − 1 = 2 |
| E. | 1 + 2 = 3 | 8 − 2 = 6 | 0 + 8 = 8 |
| F. | 10 − 8 = 2 | 5 + 5 = 10 | 9 − 3 = 6 |
| G. | 4 + 6 = 10 | 6 − 4 = 2 | 2 + 4 = 6 |
| H. | 9 − 6 = 3 | 7 + 2 = 9 | 2 − 2 = 0 |

**Try This!** Do you find it easier to add or subtract? Write to explain why.

Page 89

Name ____ Mixed facts to 10—timed drill

## Add and Subtract to 10

| | | | | | | | |
|---|---|---|---|---|---|---|---|
| 1. 7 − 5 = 2 | 2. 4 + 6 = 10 | 3. 3 + 3 = 6 | 4. 10 − 3 = 7 | 5. 7 − 6 = 1 | 6. 0 + 9 = 9 | 7. 7 + 2 = 9 | 8. 9 − 4 = 5 |
| 9. 5 + 3 = 8 | 10. 4 − 2 = 2 | 11. 5 + 5 = 10 | 12. 2 + 6 = 8 | 13. 9 − 7 = 2 | 14. 8 − 0 = 8 | 15. 5 + 4 = 9 | 16. 6 − 4 = 2 |
| 17. 10 − 8 = 2 | 18. 4 + 4 = 8 | 19. 8 − 5 = 3 | 20. 3 + 6 = 9 | 21. 2 + 8 = 10 | 22. 5 − 3 = 2 | 23. 10 − 6 = 4 | 24. 1 + 5 = 6 |
| 25. 4 + 2 = 6 | 26. 9 − 3 = 6 | 27. 5 + 2 = 7 | 28. 8 − 6 = 2 | 29. 7 + 1 = 8 | 30. 8 − 2 = 6 | 31. 3 + 4 = 7 | 32. 10 − 5 = 5 |
| 33. 9 − 2 = 7 | 34. 4 + 4 = 8 | 35. 7 − 4 = 3 | 36. 3 + 2 = 5 | | | | |

I got ____ right out of 36 in ____ minutes.

Page 90

Name ____ Mixed facts to 18—timed drill

## Add and Subtract to 18

| | | | | | | | |
|---|---|---|---|---|---|---|---|
| 1. 7 − 5 = 2 | 2. 2 + 9 = 11 | 3. 13 − 8 = 5 | 4. 6 + 6 = 12 | 5. 9 − 5 = 4 | 6. 5 + 2 = 7 | 7. 11 − 9 = 2 | 8. 8 + 8 = 16 |
| 9. 12 − 4 = 8 | 10. 3 + 4 = 7 | 11. 17 − 8 = 9 | 12. 0 + 6 = 6 | 13. 8 − 3 = 5 | 14. 10 + 4 = 14 | 15. 3 + 5 = 8 | 16. 16 − 7 = 9 |
| 17. 10 − 7 = 3 | 18. 6 + 7 = 13 | 19. 8 + 3 = 11 | 20. 3 − 1 = 2 | 21. 18 − 9 = 9 | 22. 7 − 5 = 2 | 23. 9 + 6 = 15 | 24. 4 − 3 = 1 |
| 25. 3 + 7 = 10 | 26. 15 − 9 = 6 | 27. 4 + 8 = 12 | 28. 7 + 9 = 16 | 29. 6 − 4 = 2 | 30. 8 + 5 = 13 | 31. 12 − 3 = 9 | 32. 7 + 8 = 15 |
| 33. 13 − 7 = 6 | 34. 6 + 3 = 9 | 35. 5 − 3 = 2 | 36. 1 + 8 = 9 | | | | |

I got ____ right out of 36 in ____ minutes.

Page 91

Name ____ Skill: Two-digit addition review

## Turtle Sums

Score ____/40

Add.

A. 43 + 17 = 60; 24 + 34 = 58; 6 + 67 = 73; 28 + 51 = 79

B. 25 + 33 = 58; 44 + 32 = 76; 80 + 17 = 97; 64 + 27 = 91

C. 38 + 33 = 71; 17 + 42 = 59; 51 + 19 = 70; 47 + 17 = 64; 83 + 10 = 93

D. 18 + 37 = 55; 22 + 19 = 41; 31 + 36 = 67; 20 + 20 = 40

E. 28 + 45 = 73; 28 + 68 = 96; 55 + 6 = 61; 49 + 49 = 98; 24 + 13 = 37

F. 29 + 26 = 55; 45 + 32 = 77; 36 + 38 = 74; 24 + 14 = 38

G. 47 + 40 = 87; 18 + 39 = 57; 33 + 16 = 49; 45 + 17 = 62; 61 + 18 = 79

H. 28 + 49 = 77; 23 + 34 = 57; 39 + 4 = 43; 66 + 21 = 87

I. 25 + 23 = 48; 75 + 15 = 90; 78 + 17 = 95; 59 + 37 = 96; 49 + 35 = 84

Page 92

# Answer Key

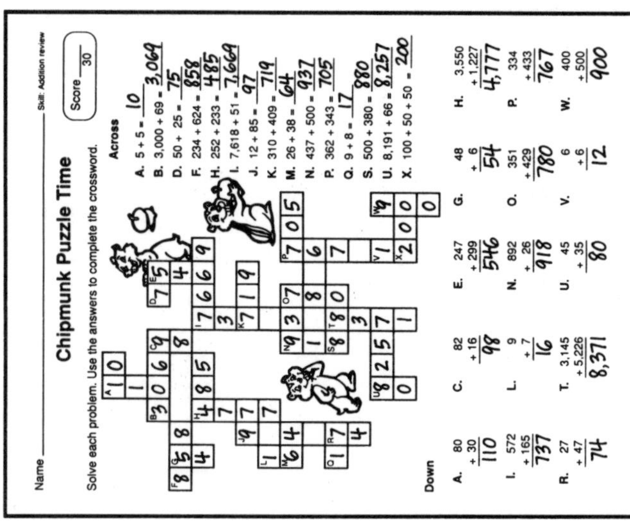

Chipmunk Puzzle Time

Page 95

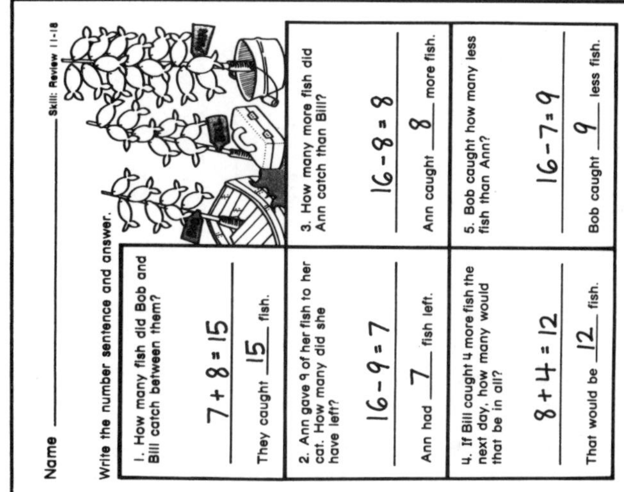

Page 98

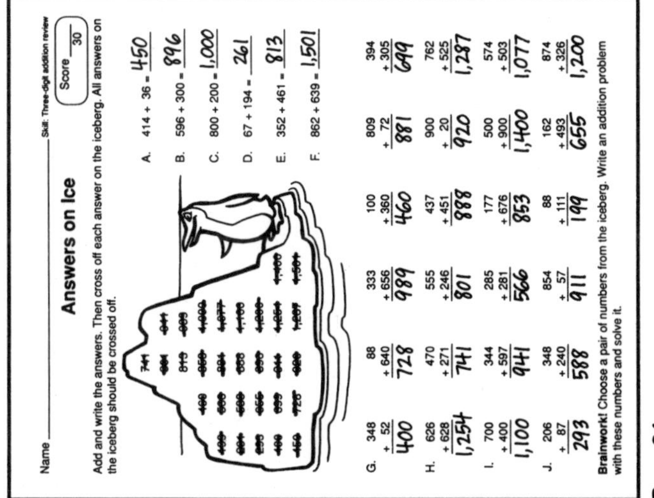

Answers on Ice

Page 94

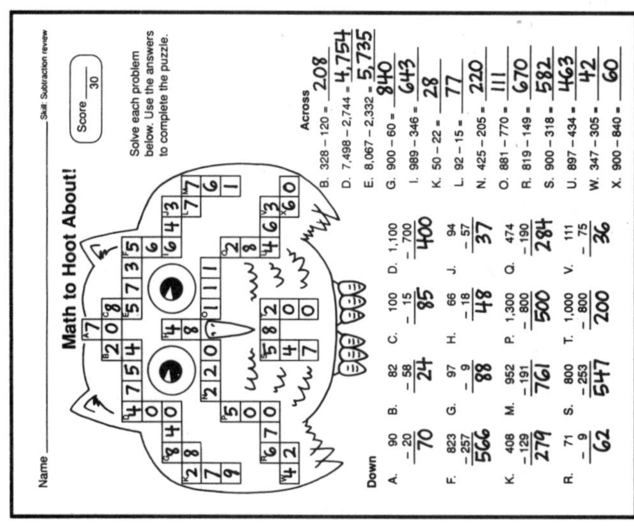

Math to Hoot About!

Page 97

Prizewinning Pig

Page 93

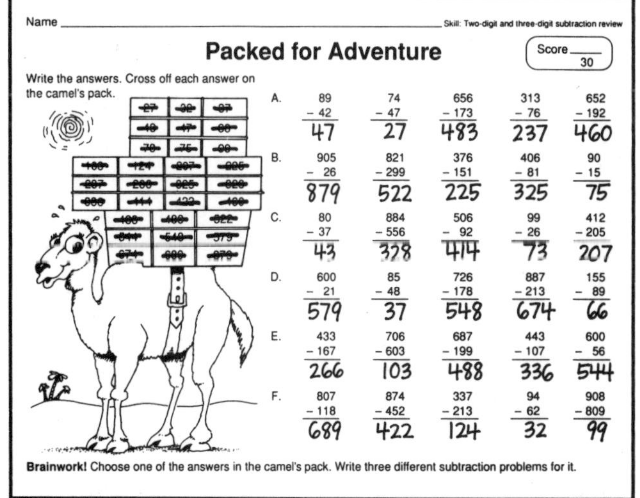

Name ______ Skill: Two-digit and three-digit subtraction review

## Packed for Adventure

Score ___ 30

Write the answers. Cross off each answer on the camel's pack.

| | | | | | |
|---|---|---|---|---|---|
| A. | 89 − 42 = 47 | 74 − 47 = 27 | 656 − 173 = 483 | 313 − 76 = 237 | 652 − 192 = 460 |
| B. | 905 − 26 = 879 | 821 − 299 = 522 | 376 − 151 = 225 | 406 − 81 = 325 | 90 − 15 = 75 |
| C. | 80 − 37 = 43 | 884 − 556 = 328 | 506 − 92 = 414 | 99 − 26 = 73 | 412 − 205 = 207 |
| D. | 600 − 21 = 579 | 85 − 48 = 37 | 726 − 178 = 548 | 887 − 213 = 674 | 155 − 89 = 66 |
| E. | 433 − 167 = 266 | 706 − 603 = 103 | 687 − 199 = 488 | 443 − 107 = 336 | 600 − 56 = 544 |
| F. | 807 − 118 = 689 | 874 − 452 = 422 | 337 − 213 = 124 | 94 − 62 = 32 | 908 − 809 = 99 |

**Brainwork!** Choose one of the answers in the camel's pack. Write three different subtraction problems for it.

Page 96

# Answer Key

## Page 99

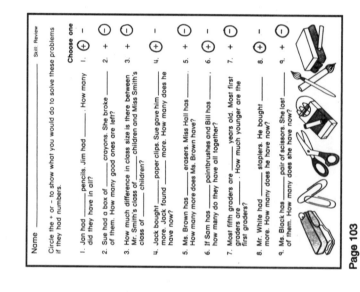

Name ______________ Skill: Review—2 digits

Write the number sentence and answer.

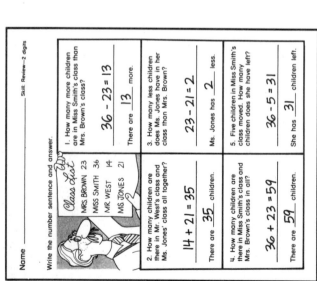

Class List
MRS. BROWN 23
MISS SMITH 36
MR. WEST 14
MS. JONES 21

1. How many more children are in Miss Smith's class than Mrs. Brown's class?
36 - 23 = 13
There are 13 more.

2. How many children are there in Mr. West's class and Ms. Jones' class all together?
14 + 21 = 35
There are 35 children.

3. How many less children does Ms. Jones have in her class than Mrs. Brown?
23 - 21 = 2
Ms. Jones has 2 less.

4. How many children are there in Miss Smith's class and Mrs. Brown's class in all?
36 + 23 = 59
There are 59 children.

5. Five children in Miss Smith's class moved. How many children does she have left?
36 - 5 = 31
She has 31 children left.

## Page 100

Name ______________ Skill: 2 digit regrouping-review

Write the number sentence and answer.

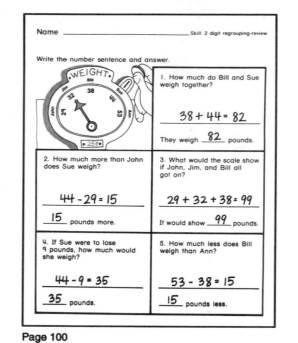

WEIGHT
John 29, Jim 32, Bill 38, Sue 44, Ann 53
25¢

1. How much do Bill and Sue weigh together?
38 + 44 = 82
They weigh 82 pounds.

2. How much more than John does Sue weigh?
44 - 29 = 15
15 pounds more.

3. What would the scale show if John, Jim, and Bill all got on?
29 + 32 + 38 = 99
It would show 99 pounds.

4. If Sue were to lose 9 pounds, how much would she weigh?
44 - 9 = 35
35 pounds.

5. How much less does Bill weigh than Ann?
53 - 38 = 15
15 pounds less.

## Page 101

Name ______________ Skill: Review

Write the number sentence and answer.

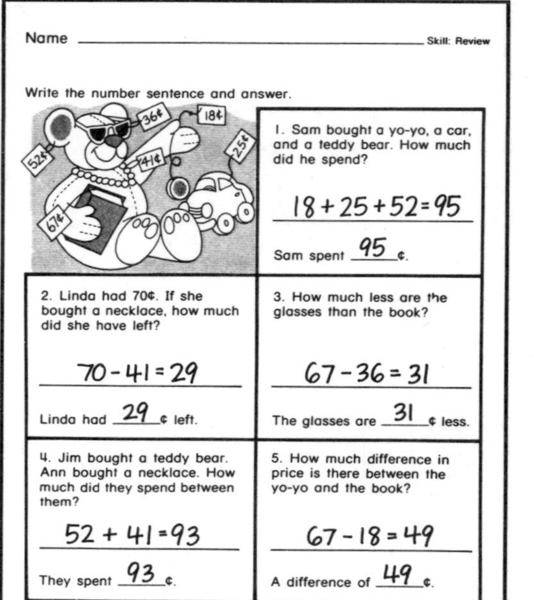


1. Sam bought a yo-yo, a car, and a teddy bear. How much did he spend?
18 + 25 + 52 = 95
Sam spent 95 ¢.

2. Linda had 70¢. If she bought a necklace, how much did she have left?
70 - 41 = 29
Linda had 29 ¢ left.

3. How much less are the glasses than the book?
67 - 36 = 31
The glasses are 31 ¢ less.

4. Jim bought a teddy bear. Ann bought a necklace. How much did they spend between them?
52 + 41 = 93
They spent 93 ¢.

5. How much difference in price is there between the yo-yo and the book?
67 - 18 = 49
A difference of 49 ¢.

## Page 102

Name ______________ Skill: Review

Circle the letter of the correct number sentence. Fill in **all** answers.

1. The school library has 26 old books about cats and 38 new ones. How many cat books does the library have?
   a. 38−26= 12 books
   (b) 26+38= 64 books
   c. 38+26= 64 bananas

2. The library has 52 books about dinosaurs. If 13 are checked out, how many are left?
   a. 52−13= 39 apples
   b. 42−23= 19 dinosaurs
   (c) 52−13= 39 books

3. Mrs. Smith gave 17 new books to the library, Mr. Brown gave 24, and Ms. Jones gave 38. How many new books were given in all?
   (a) 17+24+38= 79 books
   b. 38+17+24= 79 trees
   c. 38−24= 14 books

4. Mrs. Black brings her class of 32 students to the library. Mr. Black brings 28. How much difference in class size is there?
   a. 32+28= 60 books
   (b) 32−28= 4 students
   c. 32−28= 4 books

5. There were 82 books on the top shelf. 14 of them fell off. How many were on the shelf then?
   a. 82−14= 68 children
   b. 82+14= 96 books
   (c) 82−14= 68 books

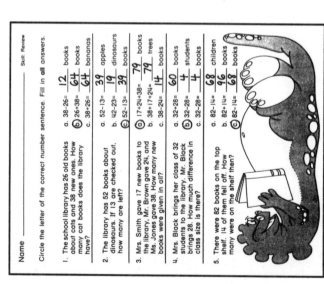

## Page 103

Name ______________ Skill: Review

Circle the + or − to show what you would do to solve these problems if they had numbers.

Choose one

1. Jan had ______ pencils. Jim had ______. How many did they have in all? — 1. (+) −
2. Sue had a box of ______ crayons. She broke ______ of them. How many good ones are left? — 2. + (−)
3. How much difference in class size is there between Mr. Smith's class of ______ children and Miss Smith's class of ______ children? — 3. + (−)
4. Jack bought ______ paper clips. Sue gave him ______ more. Jack found ______ more. How many does he have now? — 4. (+) −
5. Ms. Brown has ______ erasers. Miss Hall has ______. How many more does Ms. Brown have? — 5. + (−)
6. If Sam has ______ paintbrushes and Bill has ______, how many do they have all together? — 6. (+) −
7. Most fifth graders are ______ years old. Most first graders are ______. How much younger are the first graders? — 7. + (−)
8. Mr. White had ______ staplers. He bought ______ more. How many does he have now? — 8. (+) −
9. Ms. Black has ______ pair of scissors. She lost ______ of them. How many does she have now? — 9. + (−)

## Page 104

Name ______________ Skill: Pre/Post Test

Write the number sentence and answer.

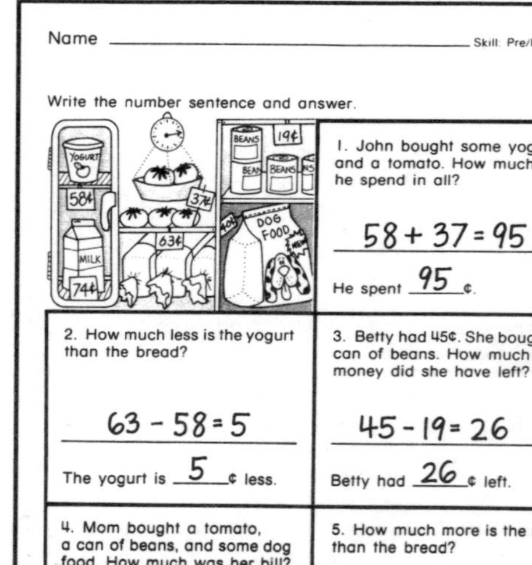


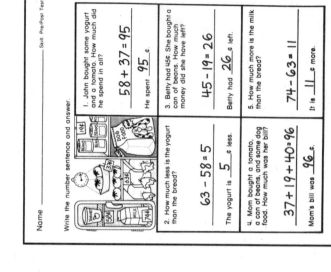

1. John bought some yogurt and a tomato. How much did he spend in all?
58 + 37 = 95
He spent 95 ¢.

2. How much less is the yogurt than the bread?
63 - 58 = 5
The yogurt is 5 ¢ less.

3. Betty had 45¢. She bought a can of beans. How much money did she have left?
45 - 19 = 26
Betty had 26 ¢ left.

4. Mom bought a tomato, a can of beans, and some dog food. How much was her bill?
37 + 19 + 40 = 96
Mom's bill was 96 ¢.

5. How much more is the milk than the bread?
74 - 63 = 11
It is 11 ¢ more.